The American Histoɪ

WITHDRAWN

Donald R. Wright
STATE UNIVERSITY OF NEW YORK—CORTLAND, EMERITUS

African Americans in the Colonial Era: From African Origins through the American Revolution

Third Edition

HARLAN DAVIDSON, INC.
WHEELING, ILLINOIS 60090-6000

Except as permitted under United States copyright law, no part of
this publication may be reproduced or distributed in any form or by
any means, or stored in a database or any retrieval system, without
prior written permission of the publisher. Address inquiries to Harlan
Davidson, Inc., 773 Glenn Avenue, Wheeling, Illinois 60090-6000.

Library of Congress Cataloging-in-Publication Data

Wright, Donald R.
 African Americans in the Colonial era : from African origins through
the American Revolution / Donald R. Wright. — 3rd ed.
    p. cm. — (The American history series)
 Includes bibliographical references and index.
 ISBN 978-0-88295-274-1
 1. African Americans—History—To 1863. 2. Slavery—United
States—History. 3. United States—History—Colonial period, ca.
1600–1775. I. Title.
 E185.W94 2010
 973'.0496073—dc22

                                        2009036333

Cover illustration: Bringing tobacco to market in early Virginia.
Woodcut. *Copyright © North Wind Picture Archives — All rights
reserved, Image # AGRI3A-00131*

Manufactured in the United States of America
04 03 02 01 00 1 2 3 4 5 MG

In memory of David K. Wright
1943–2008

CONTENTS

PREFACE TO THE
THIRD EDITION
AND ACKNOWLEDGMENTS

> *The history of early American slavery*
> *sometimes seems long on generalization*
> *and short on personality.*
>
> —T. H. BREEN

After writing the first edition of this book, I returned to my original interest in history, Africa, and wrote *The World and a Very Small Place in Africa* (1997, 2004, forthcoming 2010), describing how for half a millennium events in an ever-widening world affected people living along the Gambia River in West Africa. Thereafter I and four other historians collaborated to write the first survey of Atlantic history, Egerton et al., *The Atlantc World: A History, 1400–1888* (2007). My work on these books convinced me all the more how one must view the history of mainland North America during the colonial era as part of a larger Atlantic history that comprised Africans, Europeans, and Native Americans, mixing and melding their thoughts and ways. I contend that one cannot understand the history of early America or the historical experience of any subgroup in it without placing that understanding in the larger Atlantic context and without knowing something of whence each group came and what each one brought to the milieu. More so than its predecessors, this edition of *African Americans in the Colonial Era* reflects that judgment.

An exceptional group of historians performed the careful investigation, lived with the primary sources, and wrote the studies over the last half century that made this synthesis possible. It would be a mistake for one to read this book without looking carefully at the Bibliographical Essay and noticing the wealth of outstanding historical study upon which it is based. As in the first two editions, my biggest debt, by far, is to the authors of these books and articles.

I dedicate this book to the memory of my brother David, whom everyone referred to as "the writer in the family," implying, I always believed, "the *good* writer in the family." His early death, on top of the deaths of other family members and friends (including both of the original editors of this series) reinforces my awareness of the reality of human suffering, making it possible to realize on a deeper level how all the writing about enslavement and the middle passage and "seasoning" and punishment and human misery and death through cold statistics and chilly generalizations masks what in every case was the most painful, individual, human experience. Recognition of this fact can bring some of us in the present to try to do something—in this case, study and think and write—to attend to the pain associated with the African-American past. The further into the future we go, the more we recognize the common humanity of all. It seems increasingly important in 2010 that we look back and pay proper attention to the periods, not long ago, when we lacked that recognition.

I am grateful to living persons as well. Douglas R. Egerton permitted me to read his excellent *Death or Liberty* prior to its publication. He and Alison Games continue to inspire me with wit, wisdom, and the occasional haiku. Doris Wright and Andrew Davidson devoted themselves to ferreting out my clunky sentences and reworking discussions of ideas that Doris (who is allowed wider latitude in expressing her sentiments) says, or at least implies, "no one besides you is going to understand." Knowing Doris has made me a better person as well as a better writer. Knowing Andrew and Linda Gaio-Davidson, both devoted fans of the Chicago Cubs, has provided insight into ways to keep my hopes high in the face of regular, continuing, even predictable disappointment.

An advertisement of a cargo of slaves aboard the Bance-Island, *anchored off Charleston (Charles Town until 1783), during a plague of smallpox.* Library of Congress, Prints & Photographs Division, LC-USZ62-10293.

INTRODUCTION

*The Atlantic world was a zone of
multiple interactions, where Europeans
and Africans sometimes behaved in ways that
an oversimplified view simply cannot explain.*

—RANDY SPARKS

When I began writing the first edition of this book, at the end of
the 1980s, the study of the lives of African Americans in slavery
was out of temporal and geographical balance. Chattel slavery
existed as a legal institution in this country for about two hundred
years, roughly from the middle of the seventeenth century to the
middle of the nineteenth century. Most of that time—about two-
thirds of it—was the colonial period of American history. From
before 1650 to after 1790, slavery was a viable American institution mainly on the plantations and smaller farms around the Chesapeake Bay in Virginia and Maryland; throughout the coastal Low
Country of South Carolina and Georgia; along the lower Mississippi River; and in cities and some rural areas of New England,
New York, New Jersey, Delaware, and Pennsylvania. In only the
last fifty years of its existence in this country did slavery move
into the lands of the Deep South and undergo a switch from use
predominately in tobacco and rice production to that of cotton, as
the institution disappeared, mostly gradually, north of the Penn-
sylvania-Maryland border and the Ohio River. Yet the focus of the

study of American slavery—and indeed of the history of all African Americans before the Civil War, back to the time of Ulrich B. Phillips's *American Negro Slavery* (1918)—had been on the institution as it operated in the Cotton South between 1830 and 1860. As late as the 1980s, the best-known books on slavery or slave society in America were such classics as Kenneth Stampp's *The Peculiar Institution: Slavery in the Antebellum South* (1956), John Blassingame's *The Slave Community: Plantation Life in the Antebellum South* (1972), and Eugene Genovese's *Roll, Jordan, Roll: The World the Slaves Made* (1972), each one an examination of antebellum slavery with its center in the Deep South.

Naturally, this skewed the presentation of American slavery in high school and college textbooks and, consequently, the image of slavery that most Americans held. It all lacked perspective of time and place. When considering slavery in the country's history, most Americans thought of enormous plantations in Alabama or Mississippi; of black men, women, and children living in quarters resembling small villages; of slaves working in gangs picking cotton; and of their efforts to escape toward the free states in the North. All of these were concepts pertinent to the situation in the middle of the nineteenth century, but they did not reflect the lives of African Americans during the two hundred years before the Cotton Kingdom. Thus, the first edition of this book was an effort to right this imbalance by examining the experience of African Americans throughout the colonial era in all of England's mainland North American colonies.

Ten years later, when the second edition of this book came out, the situation had changed. By the late 1990s, thanks largely to a group of historians who came out of a respected tradition going back to the work of Benjamin Quarles, Winthrop Jordan, and Peter Wood, the imbalance was no longer so great. Not only in textbooks, which had come a long way over a short period, but in such elaborate television productions as the five-part *Africans in America,* which millions of Americans watched on PBS in 1998, the experience of persons of African descent in America's earliest centuries began to get its due. (One sign of the maturation of the subject was that two of the most highly regarded historical studies published in this country in 1998 were about African Americans during colonial times: Ira Berlin's *Many Thousands Gone: The First Two Centuries of Slavery in North America* and Philip D. Morgan's *Slave Counterpoint: Black Culture in the Eighteenth-Century Chesapeake and Low Country*.) This allowed the second edition of this book to have less of a corrective tone than the first and, following the best of the new scholarship of the time, to emphasize how slavery differed regionally and temporally over the colonial period and to offer greater detail on the lives of the Africans and African Americans, in and out of bondage, who lived through the period.

The second edition also appeared at a time when historians generally were beginning to examine the past with a wider lens. For early American history, this meant placing experiences in Great Britain's American colonies in the context of a wider, Atlantic-centered world. (One trusts these historians recognized their intellectual debt to W. E. B. Du Bois and Marcus Garvey as well as to such early world historians as Philip D. Curtin and William H. McNeill.) Graduate students working on colonial American topics in the 1990s and into the first decade of the new millennium were encouraged to cast their eyes to the whole Atlantic rather than, say, to one discrete North American mainland colony and its "mother country" for its major influences. The result has been a maturing of the Atlantic-centered trend, which has resulted in seeing United States history not so much as something exceptional going on in a world of less-telling events and more as something fitting broader patterns of thought and action. The value of this for all who study United States history has been enormous.

In following this scholarship, this third edition emphasizes the experience of African Americans in the British North American mainland colonies more as their contemporaries recognized them: as elements of a vast, vibrant, complex Atlantic world where people from four continents interacted over a period of 180 years to create an economy that fit into the grander patterns of Atlantic commerce, a society that reflected the mix of Atlantic cultures, and eventually a polity that used current European ideas to support creation of the best situation possible for those who emerged with the greatest benefits from their colonial circumstances. Those who came from Africa and their descendants, while adding greatly to the economic and cultural viability of these colonies, ended up in 1789 with the least possibility of benefit from the nation they helped bring into existence. It is telling that this same circumstance existed then and long afterward in most of the lands bordering the Atlantic.

As with the prior editions, the heart of this book involves the integration into the narrative of fresh ideas and new perspectives from recent scholarship. Of the books and articles referred to in this book's Bibliographical Essay—which, by necessity, is more selective than its earlier versions—119 (plus one on-line database) have been published just since 1999. These publications make up the body of work that has done the most to broaden our notion of the African-American experience in Colonial America, which was not in most ways exceptional, but which fit with the experiences of Africans and persons of African descent living up and down the African and American sides of the Atlantic.

The newer scholarship upon which this book is based does not necessitate altering its original, organizational framework. If anything, it reinforces the story's beginning in Africa, for the African heritage continues as one of the most important factors in shaping the lives of African Americans. The first chapter examines the variety of living conditions and social relationships in Atlantic Africa that formed the basis for African-American culture. Then it addresses the institution that brought Africans to America, the Atlantic slave trade. Throughout the twentieth century this topic received too little attention in works of American history, partly because of a lack of usable evidence. To remedy this, under sponsorship of Harvard University's W. E. B. Du Bois Institute, a group of historians and statisticians in the late 1980s began compiling data on trans-Atlantic slaving voyages, a project that after one decade furnished a data set on CD-ROM and after a second made available, on-line, information on more than 80 percent of all such voyages taken between 1519 and 1867. The historian Bernard Bailyn likens the effect of this data set on historians' knowledge of the Atlantic Diaspora to that of the Hubble Space Telescope on scientists' knowledge of cosmic phenomena. Access to such a body of evidence has allowed historians fresh, informed insight into many aspects of the Atlantic trade. Chapter One of this book includes information from their studies.

The book then examines the lives of African Americans primarily in the English colonies of mainland North America, but also in the Spanish and French colonies of Florida and the lower Mississippi, from their first arrival to the last decade of the eighteenth century, when the infant United States was getting on its feet and black chattel slavery was further entrenched in the country's legal system. In its coverage of roughly one and two-thirds centuries, the study asks the fundamental question of how race-based slavery could come to exist in a land that simultaneously developed ideas about personal liberty. The answer is different for the different regions of the North American mainland: the Chesapeake Bay, the Carolina and Georgia Low Country, the Lower Mississippi valley, and New England and the Middle Colonies. Some degree of racism existed in America before the first Africans were sold into colonial Virginia, but the fact of having persons of African descent and no one else in the legally defined, debased position of slavery broadened and strengthened the existing racial prejudice.

A second topic is the beginning and early manifestations of African-American culture, treated in Chapter Three. The process of culture formation varied, too, according to time and place. Blacks in America first had to have extensive social contacts with other blacks—they had to exist in black communities—before they could develop group values, ways, and beliefs. And because of demographic configurations and living and working conditions, it took a long time for black communities to exist in the mainland colonies, and their nature differed from place to place. Once formed, black communities were perpetuated by the African-American family, the integral conduit for passing down and preserving manifestations of black culture. The chapter treats recent arguments about African and African-American identity and about how "African" was early African-American culture.

The third topic, dealt with in Chapter Four, is the considerable changes African Americans experienced during the tumultuous quarter century of the Revolutionary era. The American Revolution raised basic questions over the morality of slavery largely because the Founding Fathers justified their break with England on the self-evident truth that all men are created equal. The Revolutionary era led to the ending of slavery in states north of Maryland and considerable manumission in the Upper South and Lower Mississippi, while making slavery more strongly entrenched and the lives of all blacks more restricted in the states where slavery remained. The Revolutionary era also brought new strength to the racist justification for slavery and a second-class citizenship for all African Americans, slave and free, that would plague them and their descendants for more than two centuries after the conflict had run its course. For this, historians now tend to agree, the country's founders bear considerable responsibility.

Beyond this, several ideas form the foundation of, or emerge from, this newer study of African Americans in the colonial era. One is simply that a wide variety of experiences characterized the lives of blacks between the time of their existence in Africa and their living as African Americans in the United States near the end of the eighteenth century—experiences that, again, differed considerably over time and across space. Where possible, this study emphasizes their temporal and geographical variety. Still more than before, it directs attention to the fact that it was a broader Atlantic context, rather than only a mainland North-American one, in which colonial African-American history took shape.

Another basic idea of this study—no longer so new but still useful to point out—is that blacks in West Africa through the slave trade years and blacks in America through colonial times were different sorts of people than older, racist or romantic portrayals led people to believe. These African and African-American men and women were neither perpetual candidates for the objective case, always being done unto and never doing, nor all a bunch of wily calculators, constantly thinking, whether out of necessity or revenge, of ways to dupe their masters. They were normal human beings with varying personal qualities who made rational decisions under varied and difficult circumstances. Simply recognizing this enables one to appreciate that blacks had a hand in many of the good things, and some of the bad things, that happened to them and to others throughout their history. Certainly, at this time of the election of an African American to the presidency of the United States, it is more appropriate than ever to step away from stereotypes, exaggerations, and oversights so we can emphasize black humanity and agency, and to turn away from efforts to make either whites or blacks into heroes or villains so we can work toward developing a clearer picture of the human interaction, albeit in unequal circumstances, that forged and shaped American life and society, as it existed then and as it exists today.

Two more somewhat-related ideas come from recent scholarship. One is that both the character of individual black men and women and the nature of African-American culture in its various forms around the North American mainland were far more complex than previously recognized. The other is that race was an important determinant for the experience of blacks in Colonial America, but only one of many. The more we consider these matters, the more it becomes apparent that an overriding focus on race was more characteristic of the thinking of wealthy white men than it was of common folk, of whatever physical makeup, and women. That we have emphasized the importance of race in colonial African-American history may speak more about American society today than American society over two centuries ago.

A final idea in this book is that through the long period of the evolution of slavery and black society in the colonial period, the course for much of the subsequent history of African Americans had been set. By 1790 the basic American institutions and attitudes concerning slavery and racism were established, and by that time forces were in motion that would lead to the expansion of slavery, the struggle that would fuel sectionalism and help bring on the Civil War, and the rapid move toward second-class citizenship for African Americans following the legal demise of slavery in 1865. Also, by 1790 the most important elements of African-American culture—family, religion, a spirit of resistance, and a host of truly distinctive ways of living—already underlay a stable black community. From this base, African-American community and culture would evolve through the next two centuries, over which time they would provide black Americans a group identity and help them cope with a hostile world. Thus, in the broadest sense, the colonial era encompassed the truly formative years of the African-American experience.

CHAPTER ONE

Atlantic Origins

> *In retrospect, it appears that
> the entire New World enterprise
> depended on the enormous and expandable
> flow of slave labor from Africa.*
>
> —David Brion Davis

On July 17, 1727, an English barque, the *John and Betty,* sailed up Chesapeake Bay and into the mouth of the Rappahannock River with 140 African slaves on board. The vessel had left Liverpool, England, the previous January 13 laden with cloth, iron, beads, crystal, cutlasses—the items then in greatest demand on Africa's Atlantic coast. The captain and crew had then exchanged the goods at several ports between the Senegal River in the north and the Gold Coast in the south for 175 captive men, women, and children, thirty-five of whom had not survived the ocean crossing.

Once in the calm waters of the Rappahannock, the ship's master, William Denton, brought the vessel to anchor off the main wharf of Robert "King" Carter's enormous plantation, where Carter had amassed a fortune managing slave production of sweet-scented Oronoco tobacco. Denton called on Carter, and the planter agreed to manage the sale of the slaves. For three weeks running, Carter rowed daily to the barque, where he held forth with fellow planters, dealing for the slaves. The human cargo was smaller than many straight from Africa; still, it was in the middle of the four-month window of intensified tobacco production, meaning demand for labor was high. So on typical days Carter sold half a dozen slaves, often in pairs, at from £12 to £20 each. When he finished he was wealthier from his percentage of each transaction and convinced that he had performed a service for his peers, the white planters who dominated the export economy of tidewater Virginia.

Less noticeable than the Carters in the historical record, the 140 Africans, who ended up scattered about the area, proceeded to learn their work and seek keys to getting by in their new situation. They now were part of the labor force of the eighteenth-century British colonies on the North American mainland. If they survived long under the difficult conditions of this new environment, they would begin the lengthy process of acculturation that would lead to their descendants being African Americans.

What occurred on the Rappahannock in 1727 took place in varied fashion over three and a half centuries along the Atlantic side of the New World, from the British colonies of mainland North America down to the Spanish, Portuguese, and French colonies of the Caribbean, Central America, and mainland South America. All of the colonies were part of an enormous economic system that linked the four continents bordering the Atlantic Ocean. The system relied on European management, capital, and shipping for New World production of staple goods, mostly sugar, for European consumption. By the seventeenth century those in control of the system preferred African slaves as the colonial labor force.

The idea of importing labor from some distance for intensive work on export crops was an old one. Romans had done this on a grand scale two centuries before the Christian era, when slaves made up perhaps 40 percent of the population of the Italian Peninsula and large gangs of enslaved men and women worked the estates of the Roman grandees. Although slavery declined gradually as a European economic institution following the Roman Empire's collapse, populations around the Mediterranean heart of the old empire and in much of continental Europe continued to accept the Roman legal status of slaves, which considered such humans as chattel, the property of another. Much later this would help provide a legal basis for Crusaders to enslave their captive enemies—as Muslims had been doing to Christians for some time, using their own rationale—and to sell such captives off to the rural agricultural enterprises that were popping up in the eastern Mediterranean after the eleventh century.

By the end of the thirteenth century a plantation system had come into being, one centered on the island of Cyprus and geared to providing sugar to a European market. Like the plantations across the Atlantic of half a millennium later, these Mediterranean concerns relied on European capital, management, and shipping. Some who worked in the cane fields were free and some were serfs, but increasingly sugar production came to be identified with slave labor. Mediterranean shippers brought in workers from the Balkans and southern Russia (people who spoke Slavic languages; thus the word "slave," from "Slav") along with others from Asia Minor and North Africa. Some of the men and women purchased in North Africa had been marched across the Sahara Desert from their original homes in the Western Sudan. For over two centuries the Mediterranean plantations made profits and the institution of slavery spread, first to Crete and Sicily and then to coastal Spain and Portugal. By 1450, on the eve of European expansion into the South Atlantic, slave-based sugar plantations existed in the western Mediterranean and even on nearby Atlantic islands.

Many of the men who ventured away from their European homelands after the middle of the fifteenth century and established outposts or acquired vast lands on both sides of the Atlantic had motives less selfless than spreading Christianity or increasing geographical knowledge. European rulers sponsored many such enterprises to garner wealth for the state, and most individuals involved had an eye out for personal gain as well. Some state-sponsored enterprises found wealth in the parts of Africa or America that held gold or silver, but most of the lands bordering the Atlantic did not possess such obvious riches. So in the coastal and insular areas the newcomers turned to export agriculture, with sugar as the focus. A model for doing so already existed. Thus developed, at a slow but regular pace, an agricultural economy along the tropical Atlantic rim, first on islands off West Africa, with São Tomé becoming the leading sugar producer by the beginning of the sixteenth century, and then, by the end of that century, in northeastern Brazil. By 1640 a staple-export economy had spread to the great sugar islands of the Lesser Antilles in the Caribbean and, on a smaller scale and outside the tropics, to English tobacco-growing colonies on the North American mainland. As the Atlantic economy expanded, the plantation model, on a larger scale than ever before, became the accepted way of making profits from the great expanses of land.

But establishing plantations in distant territories had a hitch. Although sugar remained in great demand, the land was productive, the weather appropriate, and the technology to process sugar cane existed and steadily improved, finding adequate numbers of workers to grow this most labor-intensive of crops became difficult. Those native to America, the so-called Indians, never worked out as field workers in the way European landowners had hoped they would. Once in captivity or even in close proximity to Europeans, Native Americans died rapidly from the diseases long endemic to the Eurasian and African landmasses—mainly smallpox, mumps, and measles—that the newcomers had brought with them. Those Indians who did not perish after having been enslaved proved remarkably able to resist pressures to adapt to strict work regimes, partly because they could run away relatively easily—their homes and extended families being close by and their knowledge of the surroundings often superior to that of their captors.

But what about Europeans? Even with labor needs in the Americas rising sharply, Europeans were unwilling to enslave other Europeans in the same way they enslaved people they encountered off the Continent. "Bonded" persons—most often criminals sentenced to periods of labor or men who willingly agreed (in an indented document called an indenture) to a period of labor in exchange for passage to America and, they hoped, subsequent opportunity—were not a great deal better at performing regimented work across the Atlantic than the Indians. White laborers fell victim to a different host of diseases, among them the tropical scourges malaria and yellow fever. And should they run away, white servants might pass themselves off as members of the ruling society. Just as important, rising opportunities for poor Europeans at home, either with armies during the almost continual continental warfare of the era or in jobs paying wages that rose steadily over the seventeenth and eighteenth centuries, limited the number of those willing to make the arduous ocean passage for the rigorous labor that awaited them, with only a sketchy promise of economic or social gain.

Africans, however, performed effectively—at least relatively speaking—as plantation workers under the regimented conditions in the Americas, and European planters soon recognized this even if they did not understand why it was so. The African homelands of black slaves were places where Afro-Eurasian and tropical diseases were endemic. Africans who survived into adolescence had already acquired some immunity to smallpox, mumps, and measles as well as to malaria and yellow fever. So in the fresh mix of diseases up and down the Atlantic rim of the Americas, even under the harsh conditions of the plantation environment, Africans lived longer—three to five times longer than their white counterparts. This alone made them more productive workers and, hence, better investments. Finally, Africans could not run home or be mistaken for a member of the white society of planters.

None of this, of course, would have made any difference had African laborers been in short supply or too expensive for American planters to purchase. But through most of the years of the Atlantic trade, prices for Africans remained favorable in relation to the price of the crops they produced. For example, an English planter on the Caribbean island of Jamaica in 1690 had to pay £20 for a "prime" male African, direct from Guinea. That laborer could produce about 500 pounds of sugar in a year, which the planter could sell for £20, and thus in a year recover the original cost of the slave. In short, African laborers turned out to be the best deal in economic terms, which were the only terms of real interest to the landowners, shippers, financiers, and merchants involved in the plantation system.

Atlantic Africa

Slaves came to the British mainland colonies of North America over one of two general routes. One was from the West Indies and normally involved shippers of general merchandise, who topped off their cargoes with slaves as opportunities offered. A good number of ships came to the colonies so laden, especially in the earlier years of slave trading, but they brought relatively few slaves to the area that would become the United States before the abolition of the importation of slaves there in 1808. The overwhelming number of slave imports, close to nine out of ten of the men, women, and children, arrived directly from Africa or a West-Indian island after only a brief stop for recuperation from the trans-Atlantic passage. With notable exceptions, especially in the early years of settlement, these newcomers were unacculturated, raw, frightened—Chesapeake planters characterized them as "outlandish"—persons not long away from their homes in Africa.

Nearly all slaves brought to English North America came from the coast and interior of West and West Central Africa. Traders from England or one of the English North-American-mainland colonies acquired and carried 97 percent of the nearly 300,000 slaves arriving in the mainland colonies through the colonial period, and these slavers never developed close, long-standing links with merchants of just one or two specific African regions. Instead, they purchased captives at different markets along about 3,500 miles of African coastline, from Senegal in the north to Angola in the south. Certain regions supplied more captives at some times than at others, depending on such factors as population density, level of warfare, religious conflict, and environmental conditions. Conflicts in Europe that spilled onto the high seas affected when and where slavers sought cargoes. The particular market a captain visited might depend on long-standing trade relationships forged with a local merchant community, but it might depend as well on intelligence of good trading circumstances at a given port.

Over 27 percent of slave imports to the mainland colonies came from Senegambia, the coastal region beginning north of the Senegal River and ending 500 miles south of there, in today's Guinea, and including the Cape Verde Islands. Cyclical drought, fairly constant warfare across a broad hinterland, and late-eighteenth-century conflict associated with the spread of Islam lay behind this region's steady supply of slaves. Europeans identified men and women purchased from this region as Mandingo (Mandinka), Fula (Fulbe), Wolof, Serer, Floop (Jola), Bambara, Balanta, or Papel.[1] Another 21 percent came from West Central Africa, which includes all of Africa's Atlantic coast south of Cape Lopez, 450 miles north of the Congo River. Ecological crises played a big role in this region's having a large supply of slaves. Portuguese merchants dominated the southern part of this trade and carried most of their slaves to Brazil, but English slavers frequented the ports north of the Congo and brought many persons whom they identified as Kongo, Tio, and Matamba. As the eighteenth century progressed, more slaves came to North America from the Portuguese ports of Luanda and Benguela and were identified as Ovimbundu and Kwanza.

The Bight of Biafra, today's coastal southeastern Nigeria (where the Ibo, or Igbo, and Ibibio languages are spoken), Cameroon, Equatorial Guinea, and northern Gabon, was the supplier of another 20 percent. Here, a higher population density as compared to other regions and broadening commercial relationships between English shippers and local suppliers were the reasons for the volume of slave exports to English America. Other regions of supply for the mainland market included the Gold Coast (roughly today's coastal Ghana), 14 percent (Ashanti, Fanti); Sierra Leone, the coastal region including most of today's Guinea and all of Sierra Leone, 7 percent (Susu, Mandinka, Jalonka, Temne, Mende); and the Windward Coast (on both sides of Cape Palmas, between Sierra Leone and the Gold Coast), 6 percent (Vai, Gouru, Kpelle, Kru). Three and 2 percent, respectively, came from the Bight of Benin, between the Gold Coast and the Bight of Biafra, and South-East Africa, the lands around the Cape of Good Hope and up the eastern side of the African continent.

The lands of West and West Central Africa's Atlantic zone are among the continent's most livable. The population of these lands

---

[1] Regions of Africa's Atlantic coast designated here are those used in *The Transatlantic Slave Trade: An Enhanced and On-line Database,* viewable at http://www.slavevoyages.org. Each of the regions has a significant hinterland. When referring to groupings of African people, it is important to recognize that the designations are Europeans' notions of who Africans were rather than necessarily the Africans' sense of it. It is not certain that Africans held the same idea of their identity as European did.

was light by comparison to recent times, but it seems generally to have been substantial back through the centuries. At the heart of the region are the rain forests of the Guinea Coast and Congo River basin. Here proximity to the equator keeps the land under the influence of tropical convergence zones that generate regular and often bountiful rainfall. Vegetation is lush in spite of the region's compact soils. Palms and hardwoods abound, overshadowing smaller plants that compete for sunlight filtering through the canopy of leaves and branches. As one moves away from the equator, rainfall diminishes, as does plant life. North of the Guinea Coast, forests give way gradually to wooded savanna, the ground cover becoming less dense the farther north one travels. Across the central belt of West Africa stretch the enormous sky and seemingly endless horizons that make up the broad reaches of the Western Sudan. This is the land that played with the minds of British colonials, inspiring them to write home about "miles and miles of bloody Africa." Most of the population here sustains itself through a combination of farming and herding. Farther north still, rolling grasslands peppered with trees become drier until vegetation grows sparse. North African Arabs called this dry zone the *Sahel,* the southern "shore" of the Sahara Desert. It holds a small population of herders who move their animals with the rainfall, sometimes over considerable distances.

Similarly, to the south the Congo forests blend gradually into the southern savannas, and even into desert below Angola. Rains come to both savanna areas seasonally, through their respective summer months, when vegetation takes on new life and crops thrive. Human life is not so healthy during the rains, however, for disease-spreading mosquitoes come out in profusion, using standing ponds and puddles for breeding grounds. Back through time it was in the dry season, when crops were in and lands dried out, that the savannas saw more travel, long-distance trade, and, no doubt, warfare.

Any broad discussion of the lives of Africans prior to their enslavement and shipment to America has to misrepresent the way things were. Individual and localized African societies differed greatly to begin with, and they changed over time. More

Africa in the Era of Atlantic Trade,
Seventeenth and Eighteenth Centuries

and more, too, we are finding out how the centuries-long procurement of captives for the Atlantic trade fundamentally altered the way people lived across vast regions inland from the ocean. The peoples of West and West Central Africa spoke several hundred mutually unintelligible languages (or dialects thereof) and practiced social customs that, in some extremes, were as different from one another as they were from those of Europeans. Furthermore, the English colonies of North America imported Africans for nearly 200 years, and African societies changed as much over this time as did the American society the slaves entered—or perhaps, because of all of the slave capturing, even more. Life in, say, Angola in 1600 was different in many ways from life in Senegal at the same time, just as it was different from life in Angola in 1800. So the task of describing the "African background" of African Americans seems even more difficult than describing life in America from 1607 to 1790.

Still, in a broad sense, black Africans from the slave-trading area exhibited some elements of cultural homogeneity through the seventeenth and eighteenth centuries, as they did before and after. Most identified primarily with family and descent groups. An extended family occupying a section of a village was a group that lived and worked together. West Africans, with the exception of the Akan of the Gold Coast, traced descent through the male side of the family while West Central and Central Africans followed matrilineal descent. Most practiced polygyny, men exhibiting their wealth and status with the number of their wives and the size of their families. Security lay in numbers of kinsmen, sometimes distant, upon whom one's family could rely in times of need, and in stores of food or animals on the hoof. Although larger centers for trade existed, particularly in some of the interior river towns, small villages were common throughout the whole region. Villagers worked out a sense of community and cooperation that enabled them to gain the most security and pleasure from their varied situations.

The vast majority of these African men and women also relied on one of two basic modes of subsistence: pastoralism or agriculture. Herdsmen kept cattle, sheep, or goats on the northern and southern extremes of the Atlantic's slave-gathering area, where rainfall was not sufficient for growing crops. Farmers of the savannas north or south of the equatorial forests grew rice, millet, sorghum, or maize—the latter introduced from the Americas by the Portuguese before 1540. Those of the more heavily wooded areas nearer the equator grew yams and manioc (another import from across the Atlantic) or harvested bananas, plantains, or palm products. Some of these distinctions are not so important when one considers that Senegalese millet farmers, Nigerian yam farmers, and Angolan maize farmers used similar methods of cultivation, mostly variations of slash-and-burn with hand tools, or that herders of the savannas often lived in close, symbiotic relationships with grain farmers, exchanging products from their animals (including dung for fuel and fertilizer) for foodstuffs for themselves and their livestock.

Students of African-American history have been among those pointing out some of the cultural principles and assumptions that most West and West-Central Africans shared. Mechal Sobel in *The World They Made Together: Black and White Values in Eighteenth-Century Virginia* (1987) calls attention to common African concepts of space, time, home, and the afterlife; Philip D. Morgan in *Slave Counterpoint: Black Culture in the Eighteenth-Century Chesapeake and Lowcountry* (1998) mentions shared assumptions of work, personal interaction, and aesthetic expression, among others. These authors note the commonalities in the broad range of African cultures to show the basis for the African-American subculture that would come into existence in America—and Sobel argues there is much from these African thoughts and ways that entered into American culture generally.

Still, it is important to note that in many parts of Atlantic Africa local identity and different local or regional languages tempered any broad sense of unity. Maps that show large language families spanning great stretches of the savannas and forests fail to give a complete picture of black Africa's linguistic diversity, and there were even greater political than linguistic differences, a fact that the existence of large conquest states or "empires" of earlier or later times often masks. In no sense did black Africans identify themselves as members of a "tribe" and thus take their place in a large sociopolitical realm of "tribal Africa." Colonial officials, early anthropologists, museum curators, and others inclined to use European taxonomies to bring understanding to the wealth of new people they encountered—and thus give cartographers the kind of information they needed to construct "tribal" maps—created that false sense, and it is one that dies hard.

Individual allegiances were normally to the extended family and the village. Sometimes they carried more broadly, and nebulously, to a descent group or clan. In places there also was strong identification with, and attachment to, a social class, as with the vaunted *ceddo* warriors in Senegambia. When in need of protection from enemies or when conquered and forced, families, villages, and clans developed identities with a larger political unit—a state or even an empire. Indeed, increased raiding that accompanied the quest for slaves to meet the growing Atlantic demand brought persons in some areas to seek protection through greater political organization. Certainly relations existed among and across political and language boundaries. Long-distance traders moved among people, religions and secret societies spread and provided a commonality in larger areas, and momentous historical events united Africans at various times. But most frequently blacks from West and West Central Africa had a restricted definition of their own group. In general, outlooks were local. "We" included the people of the lineage, the village, the small political unit. "They" included everyone else.

Among many of the pastoral and agrarian societies of West and West Central Africa, slavery had long been an established social and economic institution. There is no longer any real doubt concerning slavery's importance in much of precolonial Africa: in some regions of West Africa in the nineteenth century slaves, or persons subservient to and dependent on others, made up from two-thirds to three-quarters of the population. Why this was the case and what slavery in precolonial African societies was like are questions that have perplexed outside observers for a long time.

John Thornton discusses slavery's existence in Africa's Atlantic zone in *Africa and Africans in the Making of the Atlantic World, 1400–1800* (2nd ed., 1998). "Slavery was widespread in Atlantic Africa," he writes, "because slaves were the only form of private, revenue-producing property recognized in African law." Land was owned communally and parceled out to families for their use according to need; need was based on the number of laborers the family could marshal to work the land. So to increase production, certain groups needed to obtain additional laborers outside their lineage. On the one hand, they could do this by paying the brideprice—the exchange of wealth that was part of most African marital relationships, symbolic of mutual obligations and integral to the maintenance of the extended kinship network that held together society—for having sons marry and then waiting for the offspring of the marriage to mature. This explains at least partly the widespread African proclivity to have large numbers of children. But this investment might never pay off because of high infant and childhood mortality, and it took years to rear productive offspring, even in the best of circumstances. On the other hand, they could invest in a slave, one who could be put to work almost immediately in productive ways to help the family and thus bring a rapid return on the investment. Women slaves also could bear children, who eventually would further augment the size of the labor force.

Who owned or sought to acquire slaves? Simply put, all in the appropriate classes with sufficient means and desire to preserve or increase their wealth, status, and power. Farming families obtained slaves to step up crop production; herding families used slaves to help manage and tend to the livestock. Rulers and others with the means to do so owned slaves to perform their routine work, guard their courts or homesteads, grow their crops, tend their animals, weave cloth, mine ores, and more. When societies became more militaristic and required larger armies for protection or to launch offensive raids, rulers obtained slaves to make them soldiers of the state. Traders used slaves to provide foodstuffs for them and their families, freeing them to indulge in commerce and in some places to raid for slaves. Persons specializing in religious work kept slaves to produce food while they and their offspring conducted religious training or performed any of a variety of supernatural activities for their clientele. Although slavery in Africa differed from the chattel slavery that existed in the Americas, it is difficult to point out the generalized differences between the two systems because slavery in Atlantic Africa was different from one place or circumstance to another.

One thing that seems to have varied less than others was the role prescribed for women. Indeed, women made up the majority of slaves in some regions of West and West Central Africa, and sometimes they brought a higher price, especially if headed for the trans-Sahara market, than did men. This stemmed from the obvious reasons that women could produce useful offspring and were coveted by men who had concubines or large harems, but also from the fact that in many ways women proved to be the main producers in African societies. Women also were more easily assimilated into a new society and less likely to escape from it.

Slaves associated with a family often performed the same variety of tasks as did other family members, though sometimes individuals specialized in a single craft, such as weaving. Over several generations, and increasingly with marriage and childbirth, slaves might become recognized members of the household, no longer liable for sale and forced relocation. Slaves of royal lineage might serve in offices of state, as soldiers or administrators, and become important personages. The key difference was that slaves and their descendants always remained outsiders, making them perpetually vulnerable to exploitation by the insiders, the original family members, when the latter deemed such action in their interest. Although slaves' fortunes rose with the wealth and position of the family, they never entirely lost their status as persons other than kin.

As in most places where slavery existed, in African societies slaves were most often obtained initially by more or less violent means. Warfare—including formal engagements between opposing forces and less-formal raids, banditry, and kidnapping—was the most common method. ("It is inaccurate to think that Africans enslaved their brothers," writes Paul E. Lovejoy in *Transformations in Slavery: A History of Slavery in Africa*, 2nd ed. (2000). "Rather, Africans enslaved their enemies.") The Bambara wars along the upper Niger in the first half of the eighteenth century supplied prisoners for the holds of European vessels visiting Senegambia ports at the time, for example, just as wars related to the expansion of Islam did in the same ports and in Sierra Leone for the half-century that followed. But in Old Calabar, in the Bight of Biafra, "The great Bulk of [slaves]," according to English sailor William James, were not taken as prisoners in formal warfare, but "in piratical Excursions, or by Treachery and Surprise." Even wars not fought explicitly to garner slaves often bore such results, for prisoners of war were usually enslaved and sold or put to work locally to help defray the costs of waging the war. If ransom was out of the question, there were other considerations. Young boys could be trained as future soldiers; girls and women could be made concubines; and slaves of either sex could be given as gifts to elders in charge of religious shrines. But generally captives were not of greatest value, in any capacity, near their place of capture. Those close to home were likely to escape. Wise captors, therefore, moved prisoners rapidly and sold them away quickly when no pressing needs existed for their labor. And even if the local need for labor was strong, it was often better to sell off local captives and buy slaves from some distance away. For these reasons African armies often had a following of merchants eager to buy prisoners at low prices and then march them to distant markets where they would bring a better price.

Less violent methods of enslaving people involved condemnation through judicial or religious proceedings for civil crimes or supposed religious wrongdoing. West Africans did not put people in jail for long periods; instead they relied on physical punishment or enslavement. As Atlantic slaving grew heavy, slavery probably became a more common punishment for an increasing number of offenses—for adultery, kidnapping, witchcraft, and theft. Even enslavement for indebtedness seems to have occurred more frequently as time went on. And, finally, there is evidence of individuals voluntarily enslaving their offspring, or even themselves, because they could not feed or otherwise take care of their families. The Scottish surgeon and explorer Mungo Park encountered a Mandinka ruler west of the Niger River in 1796, who had purchased a woman's son. "Observe that boy," said the man as he pointed to a five-year-old child. "[H]is mother has sold him to me for forty days' provision for herself and the rest of her family. I have bought another boy in the same manner."

African societies that regularly acquired slaves were also accustomed to trading them. In fact, export of slaves from black Africa had roots far deeper than the earliest individuals exported via the Atlantic. Various groups across West Africa sold slaves into the trade that led to and across the Sahara to North Africa, around the Mediterranean, and even beyond. The trans-Sahara slave trade out of black Africa lasted longer than the Atlantic trade, from before A.D. 700 to the eve of the twentieth century; over this time it was the means of exporting between 8 and 10 million people. The volume of the Atlantic slave trade did not surpass that of the trans-Sahara routes until the seventeenth century. For about the same length of time, Central Africans sold captives eastward toward the Indian Ocean for transportation north and east across that body of water to Arabia and Persia. All of this, in combination with the Atlantic trade, is what historians recognize as the African Diaspora—the movement of peoples from their sub-Saharan African homes to permanent locations in lands covering half the world.

So the onset of the Atlantic slave trade did not signal something altogether new for the men, women, and children living in West and West Central Africa. Once foreign demand for slave labor appeared along the Atlantic coast, Africans already had social and economic institutions in place to provide slaves in exchange for commodities they wished to obtain. Little was different about trading slaves coastward instead of inland beyond the eventual buyers and their destination. Europeans via the Atlantic even brought most of the same products that African traders had long received in exchange for slaves: cloth, decorative items, metalware, horses, weapons, and more. What eventually proved to be novel about the Atlantic trade, however, was its scale. No other exporting of slaves, at any time or place before or since, came close to the massive, involuntary movement of people out of West and West Central Africa to the Americas over the three and one-half centuries following 1500.

The Atlantic Trade

The enterprise that brought African men and women to the Western Hemisphere, and after 1619 specifically to the areas of the North American mainland under English control, was what we now call the Atlantic slave trade. It was an undertaking of massive proportions in terms of duration, area, and numbers of people involved. In its fullest sense, it began shortly before 1450 with the export of African slaves to continental Europe and sugar plantations on the Atlantic islands off Africa, and lasted until after the middle of the nineteenth century. Over the course of more than four centuries it caused the greatest intercontinental migration in world history to that time—more Africans arrived in the Americas than Europeans prior to the late nineteenth century—and it affected people and the destiny of their offspring on all lands bordering the Atlantic.

For many years, historians' estimates of the number of Africans transported across the Atlantic varied widely. All agreed it was hard to determine. Records were sparse, in several languages, and difficult to come by. "The short answer is that nobody knows or ever will know," wrote Basil Davidson in *Black Mother* (1961). "[E]ither the necessary records are missing or they were never made. The best one can do is to construct an estimate from confused and incomplete data." Davidson's estimate was 15 million. But in 1969 Philip D. Curtin, a historian familiar with shipping records in the Atlantic trade, produced a monumental work, *The Atlantic Slave Trade: A Census,* which began by showing the shoddy chains of evidence for previous estimates and then attempted to determine the volume of the trade based on existing records. He offered a total of 9,216,100 slaves imported into the Americas, which meant that, based on an average mortality rate during the Atlantic crossing of 15 percent (and figuring in a small number of slaves taken to continental Europe or Atlantic Islands), approximately 11 million captive men, women, and children were taken from Africa over all the years of Atlantic slaving. Debate generated by Curtin's lowering of the most accepted estimates lasted for several decades, producing a slight upward revision of his figures.

This was the background for a project, launched in the late 1980s, to bring together data on slaving voyages gathered by a dozen or so researchers into one grand dataset that could provide the most complete understanding of Atlantic slaving. When it was first published in 1999, *The Transatlantic Slave Trade, 1562–1867: A Database CD-ROM,* contained information of 27,233 slave voyages, or about 70 percent of all those undertaken. Then, between 2001 and 2005, more data were included covering underrepresented voyages to Latin America, and in 2006 Emory University received funding to provide public access, though a Web site, to the continually expanding dataset, which at last count contained records of 34,941 vessels that left Africa bound for the Americas with slaves, an estimated 81 percent of all such voyages that occurred between 1514 and 1866.

So we now state with confidence that 12.5 million captive men, women, and children embarked on slave ships from sub-Saharan Africa and that 10.7 million of these arrived at a port in the Americas. Annual averages of slaves crossing the Atlantic grew from 3,000 in the last quarter of the sixteenth century to 72,000 over the last quarter of the eighteenth century. No enterprise of such proportion could have existed through casual contact or chance capture. The Atlantic slave trade was carefully planned and organized, big business.

Study of the Atlantic slave trade sometimes involves more numbers and percentages than one might wish, but the numbers and percentages have their role. They are important for putting segments of the trade in temporal and spatial perspective. Only a small portion of the Atlantic trade brought captives to the English North American mainland. Of all the Africans who crossed the Atlantic as part of the slave trade, slightly over 4 percent of the total (over 100,000 fewer than entered the 166-square-mile Caribbean island of Barbados) came to the mainland colonies. A recent study, which factors in more transshipments from other colonies, puts the figure for mainland slave imports between 1619 and 1807 at 453,000. However, in such decades as the 1730s, when slave trading to the North American mainland was especially heavy, it accounted for over 12 percent of the total, and it was a much greater portion, more than one-fourth, of the slave trading conducted by the English at the time. In fact, through several decades on either side of 1750 the British mainland colonies vied with Barbados for second place, always behind Jamaica, as England's leading slave market.

From 1650 to after 1800, demand for slaves varied at ports all along America's Atlantic and Gulf seaboard, from Salem in the Massachusetts Bay Colony down through Savannah in Georgia and around the northern Gulf of Mexico to New Orleans. The two largest and steadiest markets were the Chesapeake Bay, which touched the coasts of Virginia and Maryland, and coastal South Carolina and Georgia. The Chesapeake was the earliest big market. More than 160 slaves, on average, entered there each year of the 1660s, a number that jumped to 500 per year by the 1690s and then to nearly 1,600 each year between 1701 and 1770. South Carolina did not begin importing persons directly from Africa in any number until after 1700, but once it began to do so it quickly became the mainland colonies' largest importer—at that time and eventually for all time. By the 1730s South Carolina was importing, on average, more than 2,500 slaves each year. Demand for workers in neighboring Georgia appeared after 1755, when planters opened new lands, but Georgia relied strictly on the re-export trade from the West Indies for its slaves until 1766, when the first vessel arrived in Savannah from the African coast. Thereafter, direct and much larger shipments became the norm.

The other two mainland market areas were the northern port cities—Philadelphia, New York, Providence, Boston, and Salem—and the northern Gulf of Mexico, primarily New Orleans. The northern cities provided a steadier market: between 1730 and 1770 nearly 22,000 slaves entered Pennsylvania, New York, or one of the New England colonies from Africa, which was almost one-third as many as entered the Chesapeake. The northern Gulf market was more sporadic. Most of its 11,000 slave imports before 1790 arrived either in the 1720s (6,400) or 1780s (2,250), with most in the later period, when Spain ruled Louisiana, coming from one or another Caribbean island.

The first persons of African descent to set foot on land that would become the United States did so long before the English so much as thought of establishing American colonies. Ira Berlin in *Many Thousands Gone: The First Two Centuries of Slavery in North America* (1998) identifies "Atlantic creoles," persons of mixed African, European, and eventually American ancestry, as products of the intercultural experience that occurred with the waxing Atlantic commerce. Atlantic creoles emerged first around European outposts along Africa's west coast, but they soon gravitated to Iberian ports and then accompanied the earliest European explorers and settlers of the Americas. "Familiar with the commerce of the Atlantic," Berlin writes, "fluent in its new languages, and intimate with its trade and cultures, they were cosmopolitan in its fullest sense."

Blacks accompanied such noted Spanish explorers as Ponce de León and Hernando de Soto, serving as everything from cultural broker to soldier to scout; one African, the celebrated Estévan, survived Pánfilo de Narváez's ill-fated 1528 expedition in Florida and with the other survivors embarked on an eight-year trek across the continent to the Pacific Coast, picking up native languages and negotiating for his small party along the way. By this time, African slaves were being taken to Spanish possessions in the Caribbean and South America. Once Spain established a military outpost at St. Augustine in Florida in 1565, blacks worked on fortifications and participated continuously in garrisoning the fort.

Atlantic creoles arrived soon after the English settled Jamestown, too. A Dutch ship brought the first Africans to the English North American mainland in 1619. In January 1620 Jamestown tobacco planter John Rolfe described the event in a letter to Sir Edwin Sandys: "About the latter end of August, a Dutch man of Warr of the burden of a 160 tunnes arrived at Point-Comfort. . . . He brought not any thing but 20 and odd Negroes, wch the Governor and Cape Marchant bought for victualle. . . ."

Dutch merchants never played a significant role in the mainland slave trade, however. English-owned and operated vessels carried the lion's share of slaves to British North America. Bristol, Liverpool, and London were the major English ports where ship owners outfitted their vessels for the trans-Atlantic venture, with Liverpool, for a variety of reasons, gaining ascendancy over the others after 1740. Also entering into the trafficking of slaves, especially after the middle of the eighteenth century, were colonial merchants. At various times, Boston, Newport, New York, and Charleston were chief ports for outfitting slavers. Over the quarter century before the American Revolution, 10 percent of slaves sold into the British mainland arrived in vessels that had departed from a mainland port.

Historians once believed that many, perhaps even most, of the captives imported into British mainland North America were "seasoned" slaves—that is, men and women coming from one of the islands in the Caribbean, where they already had made it through the difficult adjustment to a new environment and learned enough English and enough of what was required of them to get by and serve their owners efficiently. We now know that this was not so. Such importation of Caribbean slaves that occurred—mostly before 1700, and not topping 15 percent of the total—was not so much the result of the preference of the mainland planters for seasoned workers as it was a function of the mainland market being insufficiently strong to draw vessels with larger numbers of captives directly from Africa. In fact, buyers in Virginia, Maryland, and South Carolina soon realized that the only reason island planters wanted to sell slaves who had adapted to the environment and plantation routine was that the captive workers had proved to be recalcitrant or rebellious, sent away "for their Roguery." Experienced mainland buyers much preferred persons straight from Africa. Thus, certainly for the eighteenth century, nearly all of the slaves imported into Virginia and Maryland, the Carolinas, and Georgia arrived on a ship directly from Africa. Almost none of the men and women arriving from Africa in the eighteenth century were Atlantic creoles, as were the first Africans imported into the mainland colonies a century earlier.

In addition to English and colonial merchants, French entrepreneurs brought a smaller number of slaves to the North American mainland. Employees of the *Compagnie des Indies* imported 612 Africans into the French colony of Louisiana in the summer of 1719, and over the following decade brought in over 7,000 more, nearly all of them directly from Africa. The importation of slaves into Louisiana practically ceased from 1731 through the years of the American Revolution.

The magnitude of the whole African trade into the Atlantic world, or even that of the trade to mainland North America, makes it impossible to describe the way it operated in simple generalities. Trading differed considerably along the African and American coasts. Operations often were different a few hundred miles apart. Ease of procuring captives or methods of doing so could change from one year to the next, let alone over periods of half a century or more, and various African and American ports matured as slave markets at different times. In *The Diligent: A Voyage Through the Worlds of the Slave Trade* (2002), Robert Harms takes the reader on a single slaving voyage in 1731–32 and shows how, at various ports of call on Africa's Atlantic coast, the vessel and its crew passed in and out of different "worlds," each affected by local and international political and economic circumstances. Yet, through the centuries and across the boundaries of cultural areas, certain broad modes of operation persisted from shortly after the opening of the trade through the eighteenth century.

Trading slaves into the Atlantic world was always part of a larger body of exchange. Persons in Europe fitting out vessels for Atlantic trading did so with economic gain in mind and did not limit their considerations of profit to human cargo. Thus, slaves were but one African export commodity among a variety of trade goods. For the first two centuries of Atlantic commerce, until after 1650, Europeans exported from Africa a combination of other commodities in greater amounts (by value) than slaves, including gold especially. Around 1700, slaves became the principal African export into the Atlantic, however, and remained so until after 1850.

From the beginning, Europeans realized they were not seeking slaves from a vast, undeveloped wilderness where savages spent days in idleness and nights in levity. That white traders believed such misinformation is a notion that arose long after the fact—during the wave of pseudoscientific racism of the late nineteenth century. The western coast of Africa was the outward edge of a commercial network of considerable size and scope that had thrived in one or another form since long before Europe nipping at the waterside with commodities to exchange. Long-distance trading was an occupational specialty that West and West Central Africans held in high regard. The Atlantic hinterland of black Africa contained a grid of trade routes dotted with commercial settlements. These formed a network that permitted traders to travel widely among communities where they could employ local associates as their aids and agents. Taxes and tolls, plus access to valued goods, kept village and clan heads or rulers of states amenable to the enterprise. For hundreds of years before the coastwise trade in slaves, itinerant merchants had funneled gold, kola nuts, and slaves to the port cities of the Sahel for transport across the great Sahara. In return they had carried goods from North Africa, including salt, metalware and glassware, figs and dates, back from the desert's southern edge to locales across the western savannas and into the coastal forests. Central Africans had traded copper, hides, and ivory toward the west coast for palm cloth, palm oil, and salt. Once demand for slaves and other products—some of which, such as foodstuffs, were ancillary to the slave trade—became evident along the coastal periphery of the commercial network, it did not take long for the traders to extend operations to the sailing ships and then the newly sprouting European outposts at the mouths of rivers and on Atlantic beaches and islands. Thus, fairly rapidly, a commercial system was in place to supply products Europeans wanted and to distribute goods Africans desired in exchange.

Great temporal and regional variance characterized African products in European demand. At different times Europeans sought gold, gum, hides, ivory, and beeswax from Senegambia; gold and peppers from Sierra Leone; gold from the Gold Coast; palm products from the Niger Delta; copper, ivory, and dyewoods from the Congo basin. In addition, throughout the length of Africa's Atlantic coast Europeans obtained African products, kola nuts or palm cloth, for instance, to exchange elsewhere on the coast for other locally produced commodities. But all along the 3,500-mile coastline slaves were in fairly constant and growing demand after 1650. In some areas, Angola for example, slaves were almost always the principal item the Europeans wanted.

Africans were no less careful in designating the products they wanted in exchange.[2] Meeting their varied and changing demands was a necessity for the ship captain who wanted to obtain slaves at a good price. The ships that sailed down the Guinea Coast thus had to serve as something akin to floating hardware, drygoods, and fashion stores with spirits in the cellar, and fitting out these ships with the proper variety of goods, often imported from distant parts of the globe, was the largest expense of the total voyage, averaging more than the costs of the ship and its crew. Items of apparel and personal decoration made up almost half of all imports, with preferences shifting from beads to cloth and sometimes including semiprecious stones. As nearly everywhere today, dress and personal decoration were important ways Africans displayed their wealth or indicated their social status. In addition, cloth was an important element in payment of brideprice, and European traders needed to keep current on preferred types and styles. Africans in many locales also wanted metals and metalware—these constituted another third of all imports. Spirits, normally in the form of brandy or rum, also were in demand. (Following a visit to the Gambia River in 1764, the French scholar Abbé Demanet wrote, "Without iron and alcohol one cannot live there, much less trade.") Horses (which, because of sleeping sickness, bred with difficulty in areas infested with the tsetse fly) for cavalry use, cutlery, firearms, and gunpowder were also in greater or lesser demand, depending on local supplies and, in some areas, regional hostilities. But variety remained the key: an inventory by Dutch traders in 1728 revealed

---

[2] It remains necessary to expose what one-third of a century ago Philip D. Curtin referred to, in *Economic Change in Precolonial Africa: Senegambia in the Era of the Slave Trade* (1975), as "the gewgaw myth": "that Africans foolishly bought articles of adornment or luxuries that served no basic human need, and in return for a basic resource—human beings." Stanley B. Alpern points out, in "What Africans Got for Their Slaves: A Master List of European Trade Goods" in *History in Africa: A Journal of Method,* 22 (1995), that ideas about Africa being "a dumping ground for European rubbish . . . ignore the business acumen of African merchants who . . . knew good commodities from bad, and how to play off one European trader against another to their own profit." Along the West African coast during the years of the Atlantic trade, writes Alpern, "it was, indeed, a seller's market."

218 types of merchandise stored at Elmina Castle, a fort on the Gold Coast, for use in the acquisition of slaves.

Whether exporting or importing, it was the mesh of the organized commercial networks that made the magnitude of the exchange possible. It is obvious that without European shipping and demand for labor on the plantations of the New World the Atlantic slave trade could not have taken place. It is less obvious, mostly because of old and incorrect notions of African incapacity or the related lack of knowledge of Africa and its history, that without the existing commercial operations in the hinterland of Africa's Atlantic coast and without sufficient African demand for European products, the supply of slaves could never have reached the massive proportions that it did.

The first Europeans to sail down the northwest coast of Africa were the Portuguese. They were the vanguard of what would be, in African eyes, a long line of men with sharp noses, straight hair, and light skin who wedded a capitalist economic system (with special desire to invest in long-distance trade) to advanced maritime technology, and it was they who dominated foreign trade with black Africa for the first two centuries of European contact. The earliest encounters the Portuguese had with coastal-dwelling Africans below the Sahara taught them lessons about cross-cultural trading they would not forget for centuries. In the 1440s, Portuguese "adventurers" along the Atlantic coasts of Morocco and Mauritania began going ashore and capturing locals, taking them by surprise and sending them back to Lisbon. Below the Sahara, where populations were larger, surprise was harder to effect. In 1446 Nuno Tristão sailed into the Gambia River in search of "prisoners" for the pleasure of his patron, Dom Henrique (the often-noted "Henry the Navigator"). With twenty-two armed men in two boats, Tristão was closing in on a populated settlement along the riverbank when eighty Africans in many more, much larger vessels gave chase and rained poisoned arrows on the intruders. Tristão lost three-quarters of his crew, and the survivors were fortunate to make it back to Lisbon to tell their story.

Such misfortune did not have to recur often before Europeans in their ships, far from home and few in number, realized what should have been obvious from the beginning: that Africans were not going to wait passively until the next vessel full of marauders arrived to fall upon their dwindling numbers; that Africans were not different from others in their interest in and willingness to exchange commodities, including human beings (for the most part strangers), for products they needed or wanted; and that Atlantic sailors could, therefore, more easily and safely acquire slaves by trade than by capture. (Only nine years after Tristão's voyage, Portuguese merchants were coming peacefully to the Gambia and trading. In the words of a Portuguese court chronicler, "deeds in those parts [after the mid-fifteenth century] involved trade and mercantile dealings more than fortitude and exercise of arms.") Eventually it would become still more apparent to most European traders that African groups were powerful and did not want Europeans raiding or doing much else on land in their vicinities without their permission. "No European nation can feel safe on the Coast," wrote a Dutch factor on the Gold Coast in 1702, "unless the surrounding Natives are on its side." In addition, it soon became clear (though not accurately understood that the agents of death were diseases endemic to the tropics) that Europeans could not live long enough in tropical Africa, generally speaking, to be able to maintain an effective raiding force over the long term. These latter issues did not, however, bear on the initial decision to acquire slaves through exchange of goods. Thus, within a few decades of Portuguese contact with black Africa, a broad pattern of European-African trade came into being that, with minor changes, would be the standard way of obtaining slaves from north of the Senegal River to south of Angola until the last years of the Atlantic trade.

With rare exceptions, the Europeans stopped at or stayed close to the waterside, leaving to the Africans the conduct of their own political and military affairs. The Europeans had little choice. Africans were insistent on remaining as middlemen in the trade to the interior. Any white person who marched inland or went far upriver usually paid dearly for that temerity. But Europeans had their hands full just manning their coastal outposts because of the overwhelming loss of life in these places to disease. Death rates varied, but before the use of quinine to temper malaria (after about

1850), European mortality rates in tropical Africa ranged from 250 to 750 per thousand per year. In some locales over certain years it was worse. "The stench of decay and death was everywhere," writes Joseph C. Miller of the eighteenth-century trading port of Luanda, Angola, in *Way of Death: Merchant Capitalism and the Angolan Slave Trade, 1730–1830* (1988). "Only the fortunate left alive."

Following the model of the successful Dutch and English East India companies, European governments sought initially to conduct slaving through the granting of monopolies to private, joint-stock companies. In the ideal, a single company would carry out its nation's African trade, using its inordinately large profits from the monopoly to offset the high startup costs of the trade and those of maintaining fortified outposts on the coast. England attempted two such ventures, first with the Company of Royal Adventurers for nine years after 1663, and then with the better known and somewhat more successful Royal African Company from 1672 through the end of the century. But by early in the eighteenth century it was clear that the state-sanctioned monopolies could not hold their own. There were too many "interlopers" trading with anyone out of gunshot of company forts, too many Africans willing to exchange merchandise without regard to nationality, and too many planters across the Atlantic wanting to pay bottom prices for workers, regardless of seller. The Royal African Company's loss of political backing at home hurried its end, but it came at a time when exclusive trade for any nation's carriers was becoming outdated. After 1700, independent shippers carried the bulk of the trade, and the competition grew fierce with the rising demand for slaves in the New World.

The end of monopolies did not mean the end of European outposts or "factories" on West Africa's small islands, riverbanks, or ocean beaches, however. Masters of vessels straight from Europe needed persons on the spot with knowledge of local conditions and customs, and residents of the outposts, sometimes having marital and social ties to important African families in the region, sold their services as cross-cultural brokers. It was the original intention also of several European nations to have places along the coast where products, gold especially, could be obtained from African sellers and then protected from local raiders or pirates until a vessel from its nation arrived to convey the commodity wherever necessary. Once slave trading eclipsed the trade of other commodities, the forts' focus was reoriented to the human traffic. Many believed it would be in the ship captain's interest (thus prompting him to pay a hefty markup) to be able to show up, purchase slaves on hand, obtain food, water, and firewood, and be off within a short time for American markets. This was based on the correct notion that waiting to load slaves not yet arrived from the interior or coasting along from market to market in search of a cargo was profitless downtime for the slavers—while crew and captives still had to be fed at the owner's expense. It was based, too, on the knowledge that time spent on the coast meant time spent in the tropical disease environment where crew and human cargo were liable to sicken and die. In an extreme situation in the mid-eighteenth century, a ship slaving in Loango Bay north of the Congo River needed nine months in port to acquire 348 slaves. By the time the vessel was ready to sail, 83 of the Africans on board had died.

But not all, or even most, of the coastal forts and factories held many slaves for shipment, largely because of the impracticality and expense of doing so.[3] Rare was the outpost that produced its own food; most purchased grain, fish, and meat from neighboring Africans. This meant there was little work for slaves to engage in while awaiting shipment, and holding slaves on hand meant increased demand for food and water, which might prompt local suppliers of both to raise prices, and create the need for a body of auxilia-

---

[3] On the H-Africa discussion network (http://www.h-net.org/~africa/: search Gorée) one can read arguments about the French outpost on Gorée Island off Cape Verde. As most European outposts, the one on Gorée never held—or bulked, or even trans-shipped—nearly as many slaves as some contend. The "House of Slaves" on the island in particular, now a UNESCO World Heritage site, built originally in the mid-1770s, was not as portrayed to visitors (including a pope and a United States president). Over the last third of the twentieth century, a story of its former importance in the slave trade has grown—some would say "has been manufactured"—and it has become a symbol of that horrible traffic. The site's caretaker has claimed that between 20 million and 40 million slaves passed through the House of Slaves and exited its "Door of No Return"—with 5 million of them ending up in the United States.

ries to keep an eye on and tend to the captives. African merchants and rulers usually had ways to put slaves to work, in agricultural production if it was the right time of year, until slavers arrived. Sometimes they held slaves until enough slaving vessels arrived to provide competition and drive up prices. Thus, it is largely myth that the European forts on Africa's Atlantic islands and beaches housed vast numbers of slaves in dungeon-like enclosures before their loading aboard vessels for the voyage to the Americas. Only the largest forts on the Gold Coast did so, and then in greater or lesser quantity at different periods.

From Saint Louis, at the mouth of the Senegal River, to Benguela on the Angola Coast, whether under English, French, Dutch, Danish, Swedish, or Portuguese flags, the outposts were similar in operation if not in form. They might be large, walled castles like the English Royal African Company's center for operations at Cape Coast on the Gold Coast; they might be smaller stone forts like James Fort on a little island twenty-five miles up the Gambia River; or they might be thatched-roof dwellings along a high-surfed Guinea beach. Most were fortified to protect against attacks from pirates or national enemies by sea and from African enemies or thieves by land. The typical fort housed a small number of agents, a larger force of garrisoned soldiers, and typically in greatest number, a body of African auxiliaries. Referred to as "castle slaves" or *gromettos*, from a Portuguese word for a sailor's slave, these last were normally captives from somewhere else along the coast, so less inclined to run home, who accomplished most of the grueling manual labor: gathering firewood, fetching water, cleaning, and rowing boats. The compound also contained a warehouse for trade goods and a store for food and water. Residents of the forts usually had to pay Africans for occupancy of their territory as well as for food, water, and firewood. Once the outposts were established and manned, African merchants from the near and more distant interior brought slaves and other commodities for exchange. Sometimes, in West Central Africa especially, caravans left a particular outpost for the interior laden with trade goods obtained on credit, charged specifically to return with slaves. In all locations the residents of European outposts worked hard at keeping good relations with Africans, regularly giving gifts to and entertaining visiting merchants and local potentates. Their job was to grease the wheels of trade and tap into the commercial and political intelligence of the hinterland.

Around the European outposts developed small but important commercial communities. Their influence usually spread up rivers as far as fair-sized vessels could navigate, along neighboring Atlantic beaches, and to smaller outposts of their own short distances away from the major points of cross-cultural contact. In these communities were groups of people, sometimes whole families and sometimes larger groups that included aids of chiefs and rulers, who served as intermediaries—cultural as well as commercial brokers—between European shippers and African sellers. A number of these intermediaries were the offspring of more or less formal unions between European men (who normally came to the coast, fathered a child or children, and died or returned to Europe) and African women. With attachment to each cultural milieu, these Afro-Europeans were in some places the key links in the chain of production, transportation, and acquisition of slaves on the coast. In a few areas where Portuguese influence was considerable—south of the Gambia River in Upper Guinea, for instance, or south of the Congo in Angola—Afro-Portuguese communities of long duration controlled much of the trade and used their commercial positions to influence local politics. Individual members of this culturally hybrid group spread around the Atlantic rim of all four continents and helped facilitate trade and cultural interaction.

Not all slavers chose to sail to government-subsidized or company-affiliated outposts, where the most thoroughly integrated commercial communities existed. Some visited reputed slaving locations along the coast and carried on less formal dealings shipboard. The appearance of a vessel anchored off the coast might bring out one or several traders in longboats to talk with captains about slaving prospects or to deal for slaves on hand. These traders were sometimes Europeans, sometimes Africans, and sometimes Afro-Europeans, individuals or small groups who had struck out on their own to make a profit in the thriving commerce. Some of these traders were dirt poor, barely scratching out an existence, without capital, trade goods, or credit worthy of note. Others were heads of businesses that dated back several generations and were the masters or mistresses of organized "trading houses" who had connections, often through marriage, with important African political and commercial leaders and traders from the established ports in Europe, had their own store of goods and foodstuffs, secured credit from European shipboard traders, and in turn advanced credit to Africans and other Afro-European traders.

Along the coast of Sierra Leone in the middle of the eighteenth century, one could encounter persons at both extremes of prosperity. Near the Sherbro region was Irishman Nicholas Owen, who ventured to Africa to recover his family's lost fortune. Of his operation, Owen admitted, ". . . if any of the blacks comes I buy their commodities at as cheap a rate as I can, which enables me to trade aboard the ships once or twice a month, which just keeps me from sinking in the principle stock." But from Owen's location a slaver did not have to sail far to encounter one of his rivals, the mulatto Henry Tucker, a man who had traveled in Europe and lived "in the English manner." Tucker had six wives and many children who participated in his operations. He even maintained his own fields with slave labor to grow provisions for slave ships. Owen writes enviously of his wealthy competitor:

His strength consists of his own slaves and their children, who have built a town about him and serve as his gremetos upon all occasions. This man bears the character of a fair trader among the Europeans, but to the contrary among the blacks. His riches set him above the kings and his numerous people above being surprised by war; almost all the blacks owe him money, which brings a dread of being stopt upon that account, so that he is esteemed and feared by all who have the misfortune to be in his power.

Meshing with the European system in the vicinity of the outposts and ports was an African economic network of equal complexity. Throughout the hinterland of sub-Saharan Africa's Atlantic coast there developed, over time, slave-gathering, delivery, and marketing systems that were organized, systematic, efficient, and competitive. These systems were integrated with the movement of other goods to the coast and with the dispersal of European wares brought in exchange. If no two systems were alike, they fell within general patterns of operation according to region and time of trade.

Across the western savannas, from Senegambia to Lake Chad and as far south as the central Gold Coast, slave caravans tended to be under the control of specialized Muslim African merchants. These politically neutral international traders, themselves slave owners and users, relied on personal connections and a broad sense of occupational solidarity throughout the dispersed communities of the trading network to ease the movement of their caravans and get the most from their trade. When Englishman Richard Jobson was trading some distance up the Gambia River in 1620, he dealt with such an African trader, who appealed to Jobson's feeling for fellow merchants. "In our time of trading together," Jobson writes,

if it were his owne goods he bartered for, he would tell us, this is for my self, and you must deale better with me, than either with the Kings of the Country or any others, because I am as you are, a Julietto, which signifies a Merchant, that goes from place to place, neither do I, as the Kings of our Country do which is to eate, and drinke, and lye still at home among their women, but I seeke abroad as you doe.

Caravans of hundreds of persons and scores of pack animals trekked across great distances of West Africa's savannas. Islamic religious wars along the upper Senegal River and in the Futa Jalon highlands to the south, and secular warfare among the Bambara of the upper Niger provided captives for such caravans at different times in the eighteenth century. Terry Alford in *Prince Among Slaves,* 30th anniversary ed., (2007) provides a rare glimpse of the experience of one such captive, Abd al-Rahman Ibrahima, son of the ruler of Timbo in Futa Jalon (in today's Guinea). Early in 1788, at age twenty-six, Ibrahima mistakenly led his father's cavalry into an ambush and was captured and sold to slave traders. "They made me go barefoot one hundred miles," Ibrahima later remembered, eventually to the middle Gambia River, where the caravan leader sold Ibrahima and his other captives to the master of a London brig.

The caravan leader was responsible for the arrangements—the dispensation of credit especially, but also supplies of food and water, protection, and local trading. Agents in towns along the way lent assistance. Such aid was vital to the success of a large caravan, in which problems of provisioning might rival those of a small army and which encountered local officials charging variable tariffs and tolls. When known agents were not available, caravan leaders relied on West Africa's centuries-old, institutional custom of hospitality and reciprocity, the "landlord-stranger relationship." Under such tacit agreements a villager of means saw to arranging for providing the caravan's needs, and in return the caravan leader, on departing, would give gifts commensurate with the services rendered.

When large caravans neared the coast, leaders exercised options on how and where to proceed with the sale of slaves. Prices offered, goods available, and local political circumstances affected decisions concerning routes to take or markets to seek. Through most years of the trade, slaves from the Muslim network were marched all the way to the Atlantic ports in Senegambia, as was Ibrahima, and they began reaching coastal markets between Guinea and Ivory Coast directly, without sales through middlemen, after 1720.

In the early years Muslim merchants also brought slaves to the Gold Coast and the Bight of Benin. After the mid-seventeenth century, however, strong African states gained control of trade between the Gold Coast and the Niger Delta, and another pattern of slave marketing arose there. Early slaving in this region brought new military technology—firearms to the Gold Coast and horses to the savanna hinterland of the Bight of Benin—and that technology enabled states to arise. Asante and Oyo were the most powerful and thus are best known, but other states existed at various times and became tributary to or incorporated into the larger entities. These states had the military power to prevent Muslim traders from penetrating their northern limits and to contain Europeans in their coastal outposts. In between, they controlled slave procurement and marketing, favoring their own government traders and restricting foreign and local merchants. For a time one of these states, Dahomey, even limited exchange on its coast to a single state agent, the Yovogon at Wydah.

Throughout the interior of the Bight of Benin, inland marketing centers existed where merchants met with representatives of outlying chiefs who had acquired slaves in a variety of ways— purchase, capture, tribute payment, or gift. After making sure their own labor supplies were adequate, chiefs exchanged slaves for luxury goods or military equipment, especially horses, that might help them capture more slaves. In larger markets special brokers fed slaves and provided them shelter before sale. Once the merchants acquired slaves, some marched them directly to the coast, using them as porters to carry leather goods, textiles, foodstuffs, or other items to exchange in local or regional trade. Others moved only a short way before selling their slaves, who then underwent passage through a chain of traders with smaller caravans generally heading coastward. On the edge of communities lining major routes of slave movement were *zangos,* resting places where merchants and their slaves and pack animals could get food, water, and shelter. Once on the coast, merchants exchanged slaves and other trade items for goods to take back into the interior. The traders sometimes retained some slaves to use as porters on the return trip.

Farther east and south, inland of the Bight of Biafra where the Ijaw, Ibo, and Ibibio lived, a private system of marketing control prevailed. Absence of centralized states here did not lessen the ability of African traders to produce slaves for export. A few decades into the eighteenth century, captains sailing out of Liverpool and Bristol began focusing on several Biafran ports that, lacking resident Europeans, depended on ship-based trade and the building of commercial relations with the Africans. At this last activity, Liverpool merchants became especially adept. What developed in response to the growing demand were clan-based commercial associations that competed to acquire slaves from the interior and for markets at such infamous ports as Bonny and Old Calabar. These associations often were tied to Ibo, Ijaw, Igala, and Aro religious shrines. Over time the Aro won almost complete control of slave procurement and delivery. By the mid-eighteenth century regular Aro markets operated across a web of trading routes in the interior. In some places Aro associations organized mercenary forces to conduct slave raids northward toward the Benue River valley.

Elaborate, institutionalized, social, and commercial relationships between English and African merchants made possible the efficient slaving operations. When European captains came to the Biafran coast they visited port towns near the mouths of rivers and extended credit in trade goods to one of the local, English- or Creole-speaking "trading houses." These families sent armed parties in enormous canoes up the rivers to the Aro markets, where they exchanged the goods the English merchants had advanced them for slaves; then they returned with the men and women captives to the coastal towns. Guaranteeing a return on the advanced goods were either human pawns, relatives of the trading families whom the English captains detained until the families repaid the debts in slaves, or long-standing relationships of trust between known shippers and local political-commercial authorities. In Old Calabar, the local male secret society, the *Ekpe*, became an agency of local government to regulate commerce and collect debts.[4]

Below the Bight of Biafra, along the Atlantic coast from roughly the equator to the Cape of Good Hope (but in practical terms to about the northern border of today's Namibia), an area

---

[4] An episode involving African brothers trading in Old Calabar, discussed in Randy L. Sparks's *The Two Princes of Calabar: An Eighteenth-Century Atlantic Odyssey* (2004), shows how commercial operations and human relationships around the Atlantic rim were far more complex than most have imagined. As part of a dispute between African merchants from two towns in 1767, the master of an English ship (in concert with five other English captains in the port) captured Little Ephraim Robin John and Ancona Robin Robin John, brothers of the "grandee" of one of the towns, took them with 334 other captives across the Atlantic, and sold them on the Caribbean island of Dominica. From that point, their command of the English language and knowledge of English ways helped them to get to England (after running away twice, via Virginia), where they argued effectively in English courts to gain their freedom. Taken to Bristol by an experienced slave trader who had known their family in Old Calabar, the brothers attended school, received religious instruction, and were baptized Methodists by Charles Wesley, brother of the religion's founder. Eventually, in late 1774, after expressing "kindest love" to the Wesleys, they returned to Old Calabar aboard a vessel going there to acquire slaves. Once there, the brothers were responsible for bringing the first Christian missionaries to the town. However, Little Ephraim apparently also returned to trading slaves. "[H]e had little choice," writes Sparks, "given the economic importance of the trade to Old Calabar and his position in the family."

referred to for convenience as West Central Africa, indigenous states on the one hand and the Portuguese centered in Luanda on the other tried mightily to control trade, but competition from private African traders made long-term monopoly impossible. Thus prices remained low. Within this structure developed a network of perhaps unequaled efficiency that in the eighteenth century was able to deliver for export nearly 2.4 million captives, 400,000 of them to English or North American shippers.

North of the Congo River were three major harbors, Loango Bay, Malomba, and Cabinda, where, particularly after 1680, masters of English, Dutch, and French ships met with representatives of the Vili kingdom to acquire slaves. Ship captains had to obtain licenses to trade and construct temporary shelters for the Africans they would acquire. Royal Vili officials negotiated customs fees and supervised brokers who helped sellers and buyers agree on prices. From these ports to the interior was a Vili trade diaspora. Rulers organized guarded caravans that ventured to markets several hundred miles away bearing salt, palm oil, and cloth. Merchants from farther inland brought slaves and ivory to these markets for exchange.

In contrast to Vili control of the coast north of the Congo, Portuguese crown officials, almost all Afro-Portuguese, dominated slave acquisition and marketing for several hundred miles into the interior to the south of the great river. For half a century after 1650, governors and *capitães mores* (captain-majors) based in Luanda exploited and abused the nearby populations. These officials provided recognition to African chiefs and then charged them tribute payments in slaves; they raided more distant African settlements for slaves, hiring their own soldiers for such work in violation of orders from Lisbon; and they granted sanction to private raiding parties organized by Afro-Portuguese entrepreneurs. Around the beginning of the eighteenth century, government-organized slave raiding diminished and private Portuguese, Afro-Portuguese, and African merchants took over. As happened farther up the coast, these traders left Luanda or Benguela with trade goods advanced them by commercial firms on the coast and headed for one of several major interior trading centers. There they exchanged their goods for captives and brought them back to the port for holding.

As demand on the coast increased, slaving markets developed in the near and far interior, the system of the coastal region reproducing itself in stages toward the interior, bringing African states to send their own agents farther inland to markets and fairs that drew slaves from their own hinterlands. By the end of the eighteenth century, slaves were coming to the Angola coast from beyond the upper Kasai River, seven hundred miles into the interior.

The variety of marketing systems that existed between Senegambia and Angola affected how European merchants acquired slaves but meant little to the men, women, and children who were the products of the systems. The hardships Africans encountered from the time of enslavement to the point of sale are frequently overlooked because of the absence of evidence and the traditional, if understandable, emphasis on the horrors of slaves' shipboard experience between Africa and America. In fact, the voyages to the New World averaged one to two months, whereas six months to a year elapsed between the time a slave was captured in Africa and the time he or she boarded a European slaving vessel for the Atlantic crossing. Even eighteenth-century British abolitionists, who focused their attack on the evils of the ocean passage to America, argued that over two-thirds of all human mortality associated with the slave trade occurred in Africa. Returning from explorations on the Niger River toward the Senegambian Atlantic coast in 1797, Mungo Park fell in with a slave caravan. Some of the slaves had been taken in raids and held for three years before their sale. Once on the march, Park writes, the slaves

are commonly secured, by putting the right leg of one, and the left of another, into the same pair of fetters. By supporting the fetters with a string, they can walk, very slowly. Every four slaves are likewise fastened together by the necks, with a strong rope of twisted thongs; and in the night, an additional pair of fetters is put on their hands, and sometimes a light iron chain passed round their necks.

Shelter for slaves was normally like that provided pack animals—a stockaded area of bare ground. The men and women on the march ate cheaply of the local fare. Maize, millet, or yams were staples, depending on location. Any cooked food the slaves consumed they prepared themselves. The caravans were largely self-contained, the slaves forced to carry items to meet the caravan's needs. On the march to the coast following his capture near his home in Guinea, six-year-old Broteer Furro had to carry on his head a twenty-five-pound stone for grinding the caravan's grain. Most slaves were forced to enhance the traders' profits by carrying trade goods as well, men sometimes having to tote over 50 pounds of goods and women over 30.

Another difficult time for slaves was the period of waiting in port, which averaged three months. Food was scarce in some seasons. Caravan leaders, buyers, sellers, and ship captains were all eager to skimp on supplies to reduce overhead. Where possible, merchants rented slaves to local people for work, especially during planting or harvesting season.

Overlooked for many years were the epidemiological difficulties slaves experienced when marched from one African disease environment to another. Men and women living in the savannas contracted sleeping sickness in the forests; those reared in drier or higher areas caught malaria or yellow fever in the wetter lowlands; and different strains of influenza and other diseases often lurked in regions even closer to their original homes. Death rates varied across the slave-trading area and through time; they are impossible to estimate with accuracy. It is clear, however, that the African man, woman, or child presented for sale to a ship captain for conveyance to the New World was already a survivor.

The Slaving Voyage

By the time English planters began importing slaves directly from Africa into mainland North America in good-sized numbers, the Atlantic trade had been in operation longer than two centuries. Enough word had passed through the shipyards and docks of Liverpool and London from experienced traders to make English captains wise to the business. Within broad parameters they knew where to go along the African coast, what types of trade goods to take, and how to get by under usual conditions. Although they always hoped for good winds and rapid transactions, they knew it would take three or four months to reach the farthest slave marts in Angola with necessary stops to take on fresh water and supplies; they knew loading was unpredictable but that having to linger at one or more ports over several months to procure slaves in small bunches, as well as to secure provisions for them, was likely; and with decent winds they figured on another ten weeks in the Atlantic crossing to North America, though less if departing from Senegambia and more if leaving from below the equator. They were also aware of other factors. The healthiest time of year for Europeans to sail close to Africa's tropical shores north of the equator was during the English winter months, vice versa for lands south of the line. They knew how disease could decimate a ship's crew and its human cargo. Finally they knew that the market for slaves in Virginia or South Carolina was greatest, and prices highest, during the cropping season of late April into early November, when it would also be easiest to obtain a return cargo of colonial produce. All of this required plans, which always were open to disruption from the vagaries of slave supply, the availability of food and water, adequate winds, and more. Nonetheless, records show just how good their plans were: less than 1 percent of all slave ships entering the Chesapeake in the first three quarters of the eighteenth century arrived between November and April, and only 9 percent of all slavers entering South Carolina did so over those same months.

In *The Slave Ship: A Human History* (2007), Markus Rediker calls the slave ship "a strange and potent combination of war machine, mobile prison, and factory," the last because it "produced" human laborers whose market value more than doubled with the ocean's crossing. The vessels the English used for slaving came in all sizes and shapes. To show the extremes, Rediker contrasts a small, eleven-ton sloop, fitting out in Bristol in 1787 for a voyage to take on 30 slaves, with a massive, 566-ton ship built in Liverpool in 1797 to carry 700 captives. In the heaviest slaving times of the eighteenth century, the typical vessel landing captives onto the North American mainland was one of "middling size," in the neighborhood of 200 tons, with a carrying capacity of over 300 slaves. Over time the tendency was to have larger and faster ships. Slaving vessels differed from most others in having more decks, some of them temporary platforms that carpenters built for the specific purpose of carrying people in the prone position, as well as side ports, grated bulkheads, and lattice hatches, all fashioned to direct fresh air into the lower decks. Most "slavers" also had a high barricade across the middle of the main deck, used to keep the captive women and children separated from the men and to serve as a fortification behind which the crew could defend themselves in the event of a slave insurrection. In addition to equipment particular to the slaving voyage—shackling irons and ropes mainly, but also nets to prevent escape overboard when near land—the slaver had to carry an inordinately large number of casks for food and potable water. One ship with 404 slaves and a crew of 47 left Africa with 6.5 tons of food, and the English slaver *Brookes* on a late-eighteenth-century voyage carrying 600 Africans and 45 sailors carried 34,000 gallons of water. More space still had to be allotted for vast iron or copper kettles and firewood for cooking.

Crews aboard slave ships were larger than normal, usually one member for every seven to ten slaves, because feeding and controlling the captives posed special tasks and risks not associated with inanimate cargo. It followed that for sailors African duty was more dangerous and, consequently, less popular than any other. Paid little and often crimped or taken from jail for service, the crew members of a slaver were generally hard men, victims themselves of the economic system that employed them. Exceptions were the captain, often the son of a man with a commercial background and often possessing for himself a stake in the slaving venture; the ship's surgeon, present as much to assure the purchase of healthy men and women in Africa as to maintain their health aboard ship; and various artisans: carpenters to build and maintain the extra decks, coopers to maintain water barrels, iron workers to keep the cuffs and restraints in working order. It is wrong to think of these crews as Europeans only. African men, and sometimes women, joined ships at different spots around the Atlantic.

Captains usually stuck to one of two modes of trade along the African Coast: on ship or on shore. Depending on the necessities of the location, however, most traded both ways. Good harbors, roadsteads, or river estuaries that appeared relatively free of disease brought buyers to shore. Rough surf, seasonal unhealthiness, or merchants willing to come to the ships led to shipboard transactions.

Shippers coming south from Europe found they had to deal, sometimes extensively, with local African political authorities. Those who wanted to take advantage of established outposts and the enterprise of the surrounding communities had to satisfy local African officials with payments of custom before trading could begin. Custom sometimes proved onerous in cost and time. In the Gambia River, slavers coughed up goods simply for the right to trade and lost time in what today one might call "red tape." Captain Charles Heatly, master of an English slaver in the 1660s, described the procedure:

When a ship arrives in the River Gambia she comes to an anchor at Gillofree Port, in the Kingdom of Barra, opposite James Fort on James' Island. . . . You send your boat on shore to acquaint the Alkaide or Mayor of the town of your arrival; he in common returns with the boat, and receives from you an anchorage-money. Ten gallons of liquor for the king, value 30s., and two iron bars for himself, value 7s., and perhaps presents, a few bottles of wine, beer, cyder, etc. He immediately despatches messengers with the liquor as above to the king, informing him that such vessel is arrived, and only wants to pay his Customs, intending to proceed up the river. The king consults his councillors for a proper day to receive the same, and sends word to the alkaide accordingly. After a detention of four, five, six and seven days, he sends his people to receive his Custom, 140 bars in merchandise, amount sterling on an average £16.

If slaves were on hand or not far away, the slaver could procure them and then decide whether to wait there for more or sail to another location. Most frequently, masters waited. This was not always a huge gamble, intelligence of such activity being good, and at big markets caravans arrived with regularity. News of the approach of large numbers of slaves traveled fast. Commanders at outposts or captains themselves could send word inland of desirable trade goods on board or the immediate demand for slaves on the coast in hopes of luring African traders to the factories or ships. Caravan leaders were usually aware of relative demand and competitive prices. At ports where captains advanced goods and held pawns, they waited for the return on their business dealing.

At times during the trade's heyday, from the 1740s through the rest of the century, competition at slaving markets on the coast grew exceptionally keen. A vessel that sailed to the Loango Coast north of the Congo in 1742 found fourteen European vessels there, and it took four months to purchase a cargo of 362 slaves. Many ships simply failed to get a full load and crossed the Atlantic with a partial cargo. On the ship Harms writes about, three months of trading at Jakin, on the Slave Coast, filled the *Diligent*'s hold with 256 captive men, women, and children.

Despite everything from the cost of trade goods and transportation to customs duties, broker fees, food costs, and markups by middlemen, slaves remained a good value for European buyers. Average prices rose steadily from the early years of the trade. In the 1680s one healthy adult slave cost a buyer in the Gambia River £5.47, £9.43 in the 1720s, £10.05 in the 1740s, £14.10 in the 1760s, and £20.95 in the 1780s. Profit is evident in prices paid for slaves in the American market. A healthy adult slave in Virginia in 1690 brought £15, in 1760, £45.

At the point of sale the buyer, usually in the company of a surgeon or an experienced hand, examined the available slaves. Parties typically figured the value of the captive humanity in a standard unit of labor, "one good slave," which was originally one young male slave between eighteen and twenty-five years old and in good health. Slaves below this standard in terms of gender, age, or health counted as a fraction. With the assistance of a multilingual broker, foreign buyer and African seller bargained until they agreed on a price for the lot of the people for sale. Bargaining was usually in a fictitious currency: they dickered in "bars" (from the original iron bars imported into West Africa) from Senegambia to the Ivory Coast, in "trade ounces" (based on an ounce of gold dust) on the Gold Coast, and in "manilas" (bracelet-like pieces of brass), cowry shells, and cloth currency elsewhere. The currencies fluctuated and separate rates of exchange existed for different exports, usually depending on the deal struck by the individuals. But the bargaining was not as simple as the buyer agreeing to provide so much cloth, for example, for so many slaves. African merchants were interested in an assortment of goods they could resell, and the shipper having the proper mix of imports saw the value of each rise accordingly. No English merchant with just a few commodities to exchange could expect a good deal on slaves. A typical assortment of goods exchanged for 180 Africans in the Gambia River in 1740–41 included 1,178 silver coins, 164 guns, 119 gallons of rum, 1,140 lbs. of gunpowder, 150 pieces of linen, 430 iron bars, 92 cutlasses, 450 gunflints, 66 lbs. of carnelian beads, 2,556 lbs. of salt, 63 pieces of Indian textile, 4,391 lbs. of glass beads, 219 yards of woolen cloth, 35 lbs. of lead balls, 288 lbs. of crystal, 102 brass pans, 662 lbs. of pewterware, 71 pairs of pistols, 37 lbs. of cowry shells, 30 pieces of Manchester textiles, 398 lbs. of fringe, 47 reams of paper, and 2 copper rods.

The meeting of African captive with European shipper was fraught with trauma for the slave. Notwithstanding the deep shock of initial enslavement, forced removal to the coast, and holding (and perhaps working) on the spot for several months, the person now confronted frightening new forces: an alien group occupying the strange construction of a sailing ship, afloat on the saltwater expanse of the unfamiliar Atlantic Ocean. Miller in *Way of Death* describes the experience at port towns along the Angola coast:

All the slaves trembled in terror at meeting the white cannibals of the cities, the first Europeans whom many of the slaves would have seen. They feared the whites' intention of converting Africans' brains into cheese or rending the fat of African bodies into cooking oil, as well as burning their bones into gunpowder. They clearly regarded the towns as places of certain death, as indeed they became for many, if not for the reasons slaves feared.

It is difficult to assess the psychological effect of the entire experience on the captive because of the lack of evidence, but some witnesses described what one might assume—a continued state of depression was the norm for Africans through much of the time following their enslavement. Surgeons on board slaving vessels noted "a gloomy pensiveness" on the visages of Africans. Such mental states likely had adverse effects on the captives' abilities to ward off illness, and in a number of cases their situations prompted men and women to commit suicide.

Not all slaves boarded a vessel at once. A person sent aboard just prior to departure for the Americas might be joining captives, some possibly obtained in another port, who had been on the ship for weeks. The treatment the Africans received at initial boarding did not lessen their sense of trauma. Some masters had crews wash and shave slaves, ostensibly for reasons of health. Shackles were common for all slaves while close to shore and for adult men even longer. When a vessel was in sight of land, an experienced captain would gird it with nets to prevent escapes overboard.

As with most topics relating to the Atlantic slave trade, assessing the voyage from the African coast to ports in America, the so-called middle passage, is difficult to do in a fair, accurate way. No more than a handful of the African men and women who experienced the trip left records, and those who did were atypical. Some voiced or wrote their accounts in an effort to end the slave trade. Englishmen who left written accounts of their experiences as masters or crewmen on slavers, or who testified before parliamentary committees investigating the traffic, usually did so with an end in mind: some wanted to justify slaving, so they likely underplayed the horrors of life on board ship; others wanted to have Parliament outlaw the trade, so they emphasized the worst parts of the slaving voyage. When considering the raw inhumanity of the whole episode, it is not easy to examine the middle passage and weigh its effects dispassionately. The most recent studies, able to focus on the statistical evaluation of thousands of voyages, aid one in doing so. These show that efforts toward more or less humane treatment of the captives mattered little in the way the uprooted Africans coped with the voyage. Random influences, or at least factors largely beyond the control of even the most experienced captains, had the greatest effect on slave health and mortality between Africa and the Americas.

In demographic terms, two times as many African males as females crossed the Atlantic from Africa to the North American mainland during the colonial period; one in five was a child; few approached middle age. Students of the trade long thought the larger number of adult men was a result solely of planter preferences in the Americas, but recent studies show it as a much more complicated matter that involved both supply and demand. "Much of the recent literature has suggested that African and European demand dovetailed in the sense that Africans wished to retain females (for labor and procreation) and Europeans desired males for plantation work," writes David Eltis in *The Rise of African Slavery in the Americas* (2000), but adding, "If this was the case, the fit was not smooth." Fairly early in the period of American plantation growth, planters broke from European custom and worked African (though not European) women alongside men in gangs, thus enhancing women's economic value while not always altering buyers' preferences. Africans in some regions—Senegambia and Angola, for example—simply offered more men for sale than women, while in such others as the Bight of Biafra and the Gold Coast, there were many more women for sale. Young children and older adults were simply less economical for Africans to sell: they cost as much to enslave and transport, yet they brought lower prices because of their inability to work as productively as young adults. But when ships on Africa's coast had trouble filling their holds with the prescribed number of "prime-age" men and women, and children or older adults were available, captains acquired what they could. In the end, Eltis writes, as with so much in the cross-cultural, slave-trading process, "the actual ratio of men, women, and children traded was a compromise."

Once at sea, the slave ship was a place where the horrors of the captives' experience were confined and concentrated. Africans simply had little room—between five and seven square feet of deck space per person. This was less than half the space accorded contemporary European shipboard convicts (like those who made the voyage to Australia, for example), emigrants (like those indentured servants settling the same colonies), or soldiers (like those the English hauled over to fight in the American Revolution). Slave decks were usually four or five feet high, but sometimes lower, and the space was confining. One person sold off a slave ship in Charleston remembered, "It was more than a week after I left the ship before I could straighten my limbs." Captains allowed the

Africans to remain topside through much of the day as weather permitted. It was better for them, cooler with fresher air and more room to move, and it enabled crews to go below and swab out. Most men remained connected to one another with leg irons that were fastened to chains running along the deck. In spite of such fettering, slaves were encouraged to be active. On occasion, captains forced adult men to perform the least popular tasks needed to keep the ship afloat and on the move. "Coerced by threats and kicks, if occasionally enticed with the promise of more food and momentary release from irons," writes W. Jeffrey Bolster in *Black Jacks: African American Seamen in the Age of Sail* (1997), "Africans aboard ship hauled halyards and manned windlasses. They pumped eternally, the most onerous of sailors' tasks."

However counterintuitive it may be, on some English Royal African Company ships in the late-seventeenth and early-eighteenth centuries, selected Africans also served as guardians to help control, and even discipline, their fellow captives. "We have some 30 or 40 gold coast negroes," wrote Captain Thomas Phillips of the slaver *Hannibal* in 1694, "which we buy, and are procur'd there by our factors, to make guardians and overseers of the *Whidaw* negroes, and sleep among them to keep them from quarrelling; and in order, as well as to give us notice, if they can discover any caballing or plotting among them, which trust they will discharge with great diligence." This was a cost-cutting measure, since roughly one-fifth of the cost of the middle passage for shippers went for measures to protect against revolt. Women, as well as men, took on this guardian role. In return for their services, the guardians benefited from better treatment—absence of shackles and freedom of movement aboard ship, for instance—and more food and water than the captives they supervised.

Ideas of hygiene on shipboard were primitive. Captains made an effort to guard food and water from contamination and to isolate the sickest slaves, but sanitary facilities were inadequate under the best of conditions, and bilges quickly grew foul. The worst times were when bad weather forced people below for long periods. In tropical and subtropical waters the temperature could become stifling, augmented, as it was, by the heat and sweat given off by the confined humanity. Grates and canvas airfoils admitted some fresh air, but below decks it could get downright fetid. Alexander Falconbridge, who served as surgeon on slave ships, tells of one such occasion:

Some wet and blowing weather having occasioned port-holes to be shut and the grating to be covered, fluxes and fevers among the negroes ensued. While they were in this situation, I frequently went down among them till at length their rooms became so extremely hot as to be only bearable for a very short time. But the excessive heat was not the only thing that rendered their situation intolerable. The deck, that is, the floor of their rooms, was so covered with the blood and mucus which had proceeded from them in consequence of the flux, that it resembled a slaughter-house.

Whether one could actually smell a slaver before sighting it, as was said, depended on wind speed and direction, but the idea suggests the unpleasant and unhealthy conditions for the persons on board. Dr. Alexander Garden, the Charleston port physician, who was often the first person to come on board a slaver upon its arrival from the Atlantic crossing, encountered the "Filth, putrid Air, putrid Dysenteries" and remarked, "it is a wonder any escaped with Life."

Captains normally brought along food from Europe—beans, biscuits, and barley being the most accepted and easily stored—and they purchased food for the crossing on the African coast. What the slaves ate depended in part on where they left Africa. Millet and rice were staples for vessels leaving the less-forested coasts of Senegambia and Angola. Maize was standard fare for Gold-Coast departures, and it was yams from the Niger Delta to the Congo River. Because rice was stored more easily than yams, however, and was plentiful between the Gambia River and Sierra Leone, argues Edda Fields-Black in *Deep Roots: Rice Farmers in West Africa and the African Diaspora* (2008), English masters increasingly stopped off along the "Rice Coast"—which she defines broadly as the coast between the Senegal River and Liberia—to fill up with provisions before sailing to the Gold Coast, the Bight of Biafra, or beyond. All of these items, sometimes in combination, often got cooked with peppers, palm oil, or bits of salted meat or fish. "Three meals a day" is a modern convention that concerned slavers little. Slaves normally ate twice, morning and evening, in small groups out of communal tubs. Captive women often were commandeered for help with food preparation. Whatever was fixed usually turned out to be a soup or stew-like concoction without much variety. Each African on board consumed daily, on average, about 2,000 calories.

Daily intake of water was more immediately important. Each person received about a pint of water with a meal, which, even augmented by the food's liquid, was not enough to meet normal bodily needs, let alone the enhanced requirements of persons confined in the heat and humidity below decks and likely suffering from diarrhea. Dehydration was thus an enormous problem for the men and women on board. It produced the condition that the British termed "fixed melancholy" and the Portuguese knew as *banzo*—the sunken eyes, weakness, emaciation, apathy, inability to eat, and delirium that accompanied water and electrolyte loss and the ensuing fall of blood pressure—that slaves often exhibited before their death.

Old ideas about the density of slaves on board—"tight packing" or "loose packing"—and the length of time of the trans-Atlantic voyage having great effect on mortality, however logical they still appear, are simply inaccurate. Figures from the new trans-Atlantic slave-trade database show that mortality rates did not increase with the number of slaves on board or the number of days in transit. The primary variable associated with middle-passage mortality was the ship's point of departure from Africa's coast. Vessels that departed from the Bight of Biafra had the highest mortality rate; those from the Loango Coast, south of Biafra, among the lowest. Why this was the case is puzzling, but the individual's health at embarkation seems to have been keenly important. Such uncontrollable factors as the length of the march to the port; regional epidemics, drought, or famine; or strength of demand on the coast (prompting Africans to sell weaker persons when prices were higher) affected health and, consequently, mortality on the voyage.

Mortality rates on the middle passage between Africa and the North American mainland in the eighteenth century were higher than for the rest of trans-Atlantic slaving voyages at the same time:

17.6 percent versus 13.4 percent. A factor behind this difference is that ships from Great Britain and Britain's North American mainland colonies (the United States of America after 1783) carried nearly 97 percent of the slaves disembarked onto the mainland between 1700 and 1801, and these ships had higher mortality rates on their voyages than such other big participants as Portugal and the Netherlands. In any event, these are astronomical figures given that slaves on Atlantic vessels were almost all of prime age—older adolescents and young adults—and thus not at all likely to die over a two-month period under normal circumstances.

Yet, the simple percentage figure is misleading for consideration of the typical slaving voyage, for most individual slave vessels crossing the Atlantic had a lower mortality rate. Captains wanted it so. If they were paid according to the profit of the voyage, which was tied to sales, they strove to keep slave deaths at a minimum. The average is skewed upwards by a small number of vessels that experienced astronomical mortality, often because of an uncontrollable epidemic of measles or smallpox on board. It is skewed, too, by the results of perils at sea that were common to all at the time: shipwrecks, sinkings, pirate attacks. Shipboard slave revolts occurred on about 10 percent of all slaving voyages and typically resulted in the deaths of 10 percent of the captives on board.

Middle-passage mortality declined generally through the eighteenth century—from 15 percent over the first third to 11 percent through the last third—but, again, that of ships bringing slaves to Britain's mainland colonies was consistently higher than the average and did not decline as much: from 19.4 percent to 16 percent for the same periods. The apparent reasons for the general reduced mortality were new ship configurations that allowed vessels to carry more water and catch more from the rains, and innovative methods of producing fresh water by boiling and evaporating seawater. Reducing dehydration of the men and women on board meant lower death rates. And, in addition to learning more about preventing smallpox, after the 1760s captains discovered they could prevent scurvy by feeding people citrus fruits. But, again, none of these innovations reduced slave mortality in the middle passage to the range of that of other groups crossing the Atlantic, either way and at any time.

The very human question remains of how the captive men, women, and children involved in the murderous passage of fifty or sixty or seventy days endured all the hardships it brought them. In *Saltwater Slavery: A Middle Passage from Africa to American Diaspora* (2007), Stephanie E. Smallwood credits "anomalous intimacies" the captives shared. Sometimes all that two individual captives had in common were their circumstance of detachment and their fear of what was to come. African captives "continued to function as . . . persons possessing independent will and agency," Smallwood writes. "Women who exhausted themselves to death in their futile efforts to attend to the needs of their infants; captives who helped care for one another when disease invariably struck; and strangers who facilitated communication between speakers of mutually unintelligible languages . . . demonstrated the determination required to live as a human being rather than exist as an object aboard the slave ship at sea."

Dangers of the voyage were not over with landfall. Africans long inured to a host of diseases endemic to their tropical homes were once again thrust into a new disease environment, one with new foods and different water as well. Some ports required several weeks' quarantine of arriving slaves, and it took days or weeks to arrange for sale. This was always a time of further slave mortality. In colonial Virginia between 1710 and 1718, for example, over 5 percent of the captive Africans died between the time they reached America and their sale and dispersal. Half a century later, South Carolina's governor complained about the "large number of dead negroes, whose bodies have been thrown into the river [and] are drove upon the marsh opposite Charles Town." For that matter, the entire first year and more in America would be precarious for African immigrants: perhaps one-fourth of all newly arrived slaves in the Chesapeake and one-third of those arriving in the Low Country died before that initial year was out. Just two years after he arranged for sale of the slaves off the *John and Betty* in 1729, "King" Carter, who kept close tabs on his recently purchased slaves, complained, "My new Hands are all down in their Seasoning Except one. I must wait with Patience till they recover their strength before I can send them to a distant quarter."

Crews used several days to a week immediately after arrival to prepare the slaves for sale. "[T]he American slave market was as compelling a theatrical stage as any to be found in Renaissance England," writes Smallwood, "for here, where the commodification of Africans bore fruit in the sale of their bodies for profit, packaging and the power of illusion held sway." Lean, tired, raw, discouraged, demoralized men, women, and children had to be "convincingly fashioned into slaves—the human machinery that would plant and harvest the crops of sugar, rice, and tobacco that drove the colonial American economy." This fashioning involved "feeding up" the poorly nourished slaves with starchy foods that would be their plantation fare and sprucing up their physical appearance: shaving heads to remove lice-infested hair, bathing, and then rubbing their bodies with oil to hide wounds and defects and to give them luster.

The sale of slaves worked differently in various ports. In the Chesapeake the experience of the *John and Betty* with colonial grandee Carter was typical. Large slave owners in the region were the central figures in most economic dealings; buying and selling slaves was no exception. Captains of vessels entering the Chesapeake with lists of prominent planters who might serve as middlemen cast around for the best deal. Commissions of 7 or 8 percent were common. The planters evaluated buyers' credit, helped obtain return cargoes, arranged for provisions, and sometimes made deals for leasing slaves. They carried out transactions shipboard, where the Africans remained quartered, or on nearby wharves. After the middle of the eighteenth century—perhaps as profits from investing one's time in agricultural pursuits were proving less promising—some planters would buy lots of slaves from a ship's master and then march them around to settlements and crossroads, reselling them in small bunches. All of this took time: on average it was two months between arrival and final sales for slavers entering the Chesapeake.

It was different for slave ships going to Charleston. The city was an enormous slave mart, the major port of entry for Africans on the North American mainland, importing 43 percent of all slaves brought into these colonies from Africa through the colonial period. African men and women arriving in Charleston were sold more rapidly and in larger lots than those arriving up the coast. Many South Carolina planters had financial interest in local merchant firms, and slaving captains who called regularly could establish relations with one or another of these firms for everything from slave acquisition in Africa to marketing in America. Eighteen such firms did 60 percent of the slaving business in Charleston. Individual merchant houses might at one time have a consignment of several hundred slaves to sell. They did the advertising and most often sold the slaves at public auction for cash or commodities. Some provided credit for needy buyers. If the market was not promising, the firm might hold the Africans until prospects improved, but costs of food and shelter had to be weighed in the decision. Through it all— quarantine, advertising, auctioning—things happened quickly in Charleston, twelve days being the average time between ship's arrival and final sale.

New York and Boston were sites of fewer slave imports, and in smaller loads, than more southerly regions of the mainland, and this affected methods of sale: many took place on board the importing vessels as they were moored at a wharf. (Robert E. Desroches shows, however, in "Slave-for-Sale Advertisements and Slavery in Massachusetts, 1704–1781," *The William and Mary Quarterly,* 3rd series, 59 (2002), a regular, bustling market for African men and women in taverns, at public auctions, and even in homes across metropolitan Boston.) Sales on ships were variously conducted by merchants or captains of the vessels in a process not as rapid as in Charleston. Most advertisements for New York slave sales between 1749 and 1765 appeared for three weeks or longer in newspapers, suggesting low demand or protracted bargaining. Possibly because New Yorkers feared revolt from fresh, adult arrivals, especially after a suspected slave conspiracy in 1741, or because a big part of the urban market was for domestics rather than field hands, a June 16, 1760, ad in the *New York Mercury* for "likely Negro Boys and Girls, from 9 to 12 years of age" apparently brought buyers.

From one of the points of entry, buyers transported slaves across an increasingly wide part of the colonies' Atlantic hinterland. From Charleston, large numbers of slaves moved into Georgia after 1750, smaller numbers went to North Carolina, and coasting vessels carried slaves northward to other colonies. This movement tended to be swift, since the sooner an African man or woman arrived on a farm or plantation, the sooner his or her new owner could begin to recoup the investment with profit from the person's labor.

Arrival on a plantation or a small farm in America meant part of a test for the Africans was completed. Being alive was a victory in itself. From the time of enslavement in Africa, through passage to the coast, across the Atlantic, and to a location of some permanence in America, perhaps half of all the victimized Africans died. But now the black men, women, and children had to do more than survive—they had to learn to get by and eventually to acculturate to necessary degrees in a new land under radically different circumstances. Above all, the newest forced immigrants to America had to learn to perform work as their owners directed, for the vast Atlantic slaving system brought them to the colonies as a commodity of labor. This fact would play the biggest role in directing the lives of the slaves and their offspring in the new land for generations to come.

CHAPTER TWO

Development of Slavery in Mainland North America

No history of slavery can avoid these themes: violence, power, and labor, hence the formation and reformation of classes and race.

—IRA BERLIN

When the first English colonists settled Jamestown in 1607, they did not have in mind establishing an economy and society based on slavery. None of the earliest settlers of colonial Virginia and Maryland intended specifically to import African chattel slaves as their workforce, as the settlers of South Carolina would do just over six decades later. But black slavery appeared in the Chesapeake Bay colonies before the middle of the seventeenth century, and it grew rapidly after 1680. By the early 1700s, over half of all the laborers in Virginia and Maryland were of African origin and enslaved.

The institution of black slavery, which already had appeared as close as Spanish Florida, began slowly in Virginia and Maryland; it caught on there and in other new mainland colonies as the seventeenth century ran its course. In a narrow sense, it came into being around the Chesapeake because English colonists with bountiful land were having difficulty finding an adequate, stable labor force to make their efforts, mostly at growing tobacco, pay. White servitude worked for a time alongside black slavery, but the latter proved more economical and fraught with fewer problems for the landowners.

But, in a larger sense, black slavery began in the English mainland colonies, perhaps inevitably, because the colonies were part of the growing Atlantic colonial economic system that by the seventeenth century was rapidly moving toward production of staples for the European market and reliance on the form of labor that best fit its needs: African chattel slavery. Throughout tropical parts of the New World from Brazil to Cuba, black slavery was spreading. Planters could work Africans harder and control them more thoroughly than they could European servants, and because Africans were inexpensive by comparison with other laborers, they brought owners greater profits. So if colonists in Virginia and Maryland were venturing into something different when, in the last decades of the seventeenth century, they began buying large numbers of Africans to work their lands, they were simply following what by then had become a conventional pattern in the Atlantic colonial system.

The larger picture of English settlement of the North American mainland involved trying to rebound from failed efforts to rival Spain by finding precious metals or a maritime shortcut to Asia. Supported by investors at home, English merchant-adventurers at the start of the seventeenth century sought footholds for enterprise, not only at spots around the Atlantic but also as far away as the East Indies and the Ottoman Empire. Spanish success at staple-producing agriculture in American colonies gave English speculators the idea that they could support similar ventures, and the crown was all for such schemes. Colonial production of staples for the English market would create a favorable balance of trade, as colonists with money could afford to purchase imported manufactured goods from the mother country. The main variation among the colonies was in items produced. Virginia and Maryland grew tobacco at first, and then over time diversified and began producing cereals and livestock, primarily for export to other English colonies. Low-Country South Carolina and Georgia moved in the other direction, exporting livestock and timber before establishing plantations for growing rice and indigo. Along the Lower

Mississippi, French landholders tried with little success to turn a profit from tobacco and indigo. Northern colonies produced foodstuffs, including fish, and all the colonies, but especially the northern ones, participated in a carrying trade. In every sense, export production fueled a need for laborers. The commodities produced would be the most important determinant of the size and type of labor force that the colonists would require.

It is important to recognize that far from existing alone in these enterprises, the mainland colonies had close ties to the islands in the Caribbean. Ships from London, Liverpool, and Bristol serviced England's island colonies as well as those on the mainland. Islanders emigrated to the mainland when opportunities there seemed greater, and mainland colonists, who knew what was taking place in the rest of the Atlantic world, were especially attuned to the Caribbean. By the 1640s, English planters on Barbados and their French counterparts on Martinique were making the change from tobacco and cotton production to sugar cane, and as they did so, they opted for African slave labor over the white servants they had been using. Jamaica and the other English Leeward Islands (Antigua, Montserrat, Nevis, and St. Christopher) and French-controlled St. Domingue followed suit. By the last quarter of the seventeenth century a plantation model, with owners using repressive force to exact extraordinary amounts of work from African men and women held in bondage, existed "next door" to the mainland colonies and was still growing in other colonies up and down the Atlantic rim of the Americas. So it is not surprising that the mainland colonies began to import African slaves in large numbers. What seems more surprising is that they waited so long to begin to do so.

One historian, Ira Berlin, made a particularly important contribution to study of the development of North American mainland slavery in "Time, Space, and the Evolution of Afro-American Society in British Mainland North America," *American Historical Review,* 85 (1980). Black slavery, Berlin pointed out, came into being at different times in various mainland regions; it began for different reasons (though some factors were similar); and through the seventeenth and eighteenth centuries various forms of slave systems developed in different mainland areas. In *Many*

Colonies of the North American Mainland
in the Eighteenth Century

Thousands Gone, Berlin broadens these earlier arguments and provides a schematic for understanding the first two centuries of slavery in mainland North America that is central to understanding this complex matter.

Berlin's clear vision of grand issues and his ability to write about them simply and directly make the heretofore unrevealed seem obvious. He differentiates societies with slaves (in which slavery "was just one form of labor among many") from slave societies (in which slavery "stood at the center of economic production") and charts how and when societies moved from being one to becoming the other. Berlin groups Africans and African Americans chronologically, by their sets of common experiences, into charter generations ("the first arrivals, their children, and in some cases their grandchildren"), plantation generations ("who were forced to grow the great staples"), and revolutionary generations ("who grasped the promise of freedom and faced a resurgent slave regime"). He emphasizes the overriding importance of work in slavery's growth and stresses the effects of the late-eighteenth-century Age of Revolution, which roiled the waters of American slavery. Perhaps most important, Berlin points out that the most consistent agitator of those waters was the constant struggle between master and slave to determine the nature of their relationship. It was a struggle not of individuals of equal power, to be sure, but one between willful humans nonetheless. The struggle persisted in every locale where slavery appeared and was the major force behind the changing nature of the institution and the African-American society that evolved in each region of the colonial mainland.

The Chesapeake

The first English settlers in colonial Virginia in 1607 did not come there to be planters; they came to be traders. Models for profitable English commercial enterprise on foreign soils existed in the Levant and at spots around the Indian Ocean. The initial investors in the Virginia Company pictured warehouses stuffed with "goods, wares and commodities" without a clear idea of what those commodities might be—maybe naval stores or grapes for wine. It was when, for a variety of reasons, the early settlers failed as trad-ers—and this did not take them long—that they turned to planting. Making this possible were their accommodating surroundings. "The mildnesse of the aire, the fertilitie of the soile, and the situation of the rivers," wrote John Smith in *A Map of Virginia* (1612), "are so propitious to the nature and use of man as no place is more convenient for pleasure, profit, and man's sustenance." It was a land "overgrowne with trees" that, in Smith's vision, could "soone be amended by good husbandry." In his experiments with growing and curing tobacco shortly after 1610, John Rolfe became the first noteworthy Englishman to so amend the land. Tobacco was recognized as a noxious weed by some, no doubt, but it was a commodity that Englishmen used more than any other Europe-ans and that, consequently, brought a good price at export. What occurred fairly quickly in Virginia, writes Alison Games in *The Web of Empire: English Cosmopolitans in an Age of Expansion, 1560–1660* (2008), "was a tobacco craze so furious that colonists once again neglected to plant food crops." By 1617 tobacco was the dominant export from Virginia to the mother country.

This turned out to please investors, settlers, and the English crown. If it meant that demand for laborers grew beyond anyone's expectations, England certainly had plenty of potential work-ers. In fact, government and landed men worried over the threat posed by the alarming number of landless, often unemployed Englishmen, unhappy with their circumstances in a society that suffered from declining real wages and generalized turmoil. It was primarily these young men (median age sixteen) who came to the colonies in the early decades to work the tobacco fields. Unable to afford their own passage, the laborers made arrange-ments with recruiters to repay their fare through work in the new lands. Thus, they came mostly as servants—some as tenants working for shares of their crop, some as bondservants, and some as apprentices. All had fairly long (five to seven years) terms of servitude, or indenture.

Early colonial planters were not tied solely to English ser-vants, however. For a time there was hope the colonists could develop a harmonious relationship with Native Americans, whom they believed could benefit from exposure to "English civilizing tendencies." Trade and military alliance formed an element of this envisioned relationship, but so did labor after March 1622, when nearly 350 English lost their lives in a surprise attack on several English settlements along the James River by warriors of the Powhatan confederacy. From then on, those native to the region were "that perfidious and inhumane people," and the idea of enslaving them grew popular among the settlers who remained and new ones who arrived. But Indian enslavement for grueling labor in Virginia tobacco fields, or anything else, never panned out. The Native-American lifestyle was simply not that of a regimented cultivator. Indians balked at the work and ran off or died under its strain.

English mainland colonists imported persons of African descent too, the first in Jamestown in 1619, and they seemed to fit the colonial ideal better. Although the precise status of these early African arrivals is not clear, they were bound laborers in somewhat the same sense as their white counterparts. Most were probably closer to slaves than to indentured servants, and on the whole they seemed to have served for longer stints than did whites. Still, their condition was hardly that of the chattel slaves of the tidewater plantations a century later. By most accounts their lives were not significantly different from those of English servants in the same place at the same time. Being mostly Atlantic creoles familiar with European cultures and the workings of commerce around the Atlantic rim, the early-seventeenth-century Virginians and Marylanders of African descent were not at a disadvantage to the white workers with whom they lived and interacted. Some of them gained their freedom; some eventually owned servants themselves. T. H. Breen and Stephen Innes in *"Myne Owne Ground": Race and Freedom on Virginia's Eastern Shore, 1640–1676* (1980), found that in Virginia's Northampton County there was a time around the middle of the seventeenth century when a number of resourceful blacks purchased their freedom and entered into the class of small planters. "They became part of a complex human network," the authors conclude, "and it was their success in dealing with white planters, great and small, servants and slaves, that in large measure explains their viability."

Stories of some of these free blacks stand out in the records. One Virginia arrival, identified only as "Antonio a Negro" and sold as something approximating a slave in 1621, survived an Indian assault with four others (out of the fifty-six men on their plantation), married an African woman, and by 1650, as Anthony Johnson, had acquired his freedom along with 250 acres and a herd of cattle. Five years later, on advice from his extended family, Johnson successfully sued a white man, Robert Parker, for detaining a slave belonging to Johnson. Part of the Johnson clan moved to Somerset, Maryland, in the 1660s, where they continued to prosper, in a fashion, until the turn of the century. Another free African American, Francis Payne, worked six years to be able to purchase two servants and accumulate 1,650 pounds of tobacco, all of which he traded for his freedom. He then worked seven more years for wages and acquired 3,800 pounds of tobacco, enough to buy his wife and children out of slavery. Yet another black man in seventeenth-century Northampton County exhibited such confidence in his status that he manifested contempt for the law as administered largely by whites. When approached by a warrant-bearing Northampton County Court official while working in his tobacco field, Virginian Tony Longo told the officer, "shitt of your warrant," and Longo's wife offered up to the official "such noyse that I could hardly heare my owne words." Johnson, Payne, and Longo were not alone. In Northampton County between 1664 and 1677, ten of fifty-three black males were free householders. These free blacks lived like the whites who were not of the wealthiest class. They owned land, grew crops, raised livestock, traded, argued in the courts, and had broad social relationships, some legal and moral and some not. But the number of blacks, free or serving, remained small through mid-century. Out of a Chesapeake population of nearly thirteen thousand residents, only three hundred were of African descent.

With some exceptions, the early experience of white and black servants in the American colonies was neither pleasant nor rewarding. Most wanted to come to the colonies, complete their periods of service, work a few years for wages, and then obtain land, acquire their own servants, and gradually enter the wealthier, planter class.

Some were able to achieve their goal. Many did not. Servitude in the colonies was not what they expected, not at all like servitude in England. In order to make the most of the tobacco boom, planters extracted from their servants all the labor they could, far more than young Englishmen were accustomed to. As a consequence, discipline grew harsh and servants soon became, in the eyes of those who worked them, less human and more a commodity. If their status was better than that of African slaves on the larger sugar plantations on Caribbean islands at the same time, the difference was not marked. Furthermore, and no doubt more important for those involved, not many servants lived long enough to become planters on any scale. Regardless of race or status, because of typhoid, malaria, influenza, measles, and smallpox, for most who came to the mainland colonies during the first third of the century, the new land was a deathtrap.

Immigrants to the mainland began living longer after the 1640s, though, and for a time opportunity abounded. However, for several decades tobacco prices had been falling and wages remained low. Large planters and speculators had obtained much of the good tidewater land. Edmund S. Morgan in *American Slavery, American Freedom: The Ordeal of Colonial Virginia* (1975) describes the consequences for Chesapeake laborers. Growing numbers of servants who lived through their indentures were unable to acquire the resources to buy land. Soon there developed a group of young men similar to those feared back in England— poor, landless, restless vagabonds living on the margins of wealthier society. Such were especially dangerous in the colonies, where all men, for their own protection, were armed. They posed a threat to colonial authorities because they resented and envied the ruling, landed gentry. Rebellion was in the air, and it became manifest on several occasions—the best known being Bacon's Rebellion in 1676. Landowners tried several methods of preventing the growth of these poorer classes, including lengthening terms of servitude and seeing to passage of laws preventing the propertyless from voting.

Still, the problem remained. Servitude had provided a labor force, but it had brought with it a disruptive class of hard-to-control young men. The circumstance might have been different had landowners in Virginia and Maryland been able to own and control these men as chattel slaves for the duration of their lives and the lives of their offspring, but strong cultural factors prevented this. Europeans could slaughter one another in merciless wars, burn suspected witches at the stake, hang the corpses of punished thieves on public display, and sell the body parts of murdered religious enemies for souvenirs, but by the sixteenth century they considered chattel slavery a condition appropriate only for others, non-Europeans—"outsiders." So by the end of the 1670s some prosperous tidewater landowners involved in governing Virginia and Maryland probably recognized that a switch to another form of servitude would afford them greater and more permanent control over the labor force, this one from outside Europe.

But it was not only planters' fears of rebellious former servants that cut importation of English bondsmen into the Chesapeake. It was a combination of declining numbers of young Englishmen available and willing to venture across the Atlantic, waning opportunity for such men in Virginia and Maryland, and competition from other new colonies for the limited supply of white laborers. Dropping birthrates in England after 1630 cut the number of potential American migrants after midcentury. So did war. The English Civil War disrupted the flow of servants to America, and rising real wages in the mother country following the war rendered fewer unemployed and footloose men eager to listen to colonial recruiters. A generation later, King William III's War followed closely by Queen Anne's War—leaving England only five years of peaceful respite between 1688 and 1713—led potential servants to find military employment or take the jobs abandoned by those in service. Opportunities in the Chesapeake no longer tempted white servants so much after 1680, either, when a long depression in at least a portion of the tobacco market began, making it still more difficult for poor immigrants to acquire enough money to obtain their own land and labor force. By comparison, opportunity appeared greater in New York (which England took over from the Dutch in 1664) and Pennsylvania (established in 1681). Many of the remaining young

Englishmen willing to venture across the Atlantic preferred to pursue their lives in these colonies rather than in the Chesapeake, and some whites already in Virginia and Maryland left to join them. Through the course of the 1690s more whites left the Chesapeake colonies than entered them, and by 1700 white servant immigration to these colonies came nowhere close to meeting labor needs.

It is a mistake, however, to think that all Chesapeake planters gave up on white servants completely, or all at the same time. Criminals sentenced to labor continued to enter the region as did southern Irish, both being relatively inexpensive. But the decline of sufficient numbers of servants, coupled with the hint of availability of larger numbers of Africans, the result of more English shippers participating in the carrying trade from Africa, helped bring Virginia and Maryland tobacco growers to make the same decision to switch to African slaves that their counterparts on sugar plantations in the Caribbean had made almost half a century earlier. The laborers they turned to were a far cry from the Atlantic creoles of earlier days, persons familiar with European languages and ways. These new workers were persons the English in the Chesapeake considered as "outlandish"— human beings with filed teeth and ritual facial scars who spoke languages and practiced customs that seemed to the English strange and brutish. Yet they were comparatively inexpensive and with sufficient force could be made to work hard in the tobacco fields, harder indeed than white servants who preceded them because conventions that protected English servants from overwork—rest periods in the heat of the day, Saturdays off, and many traditional holidays—need not apply to bonded Africans. Never lost on colonial Englishmen intent on building a family estate was that, unlike the servants, African slaves were permanently bound, through their lifetimes and through those of generations of their offspring, theirs to work or to sell as they might choose. It was thus a combination of factors that led to a plantation revolution around the Chesapeake Bay, over time turning Virginia and Maryland's society with slaves into a slave society and altering the lives and possibilities for advancement of persons of African descent in the colonies.

The transition to black slavery occurred at a varied pace throughout the Tidewater. The wealthy growers of sweet-scented tobacco in York County, low on the west side of the Chesapeake Bay, bought Africans early. By the 1680s four of every five bound laborers there were black. Areas farther north made the switch more slowly. By 1695, however, the rush to buy Africans was on; by 1700, Chesapeake planters had purchased 3,000 Africans, about the same number they had purchased over the previous twenty years. Population figures provide evidence for the switch. In 1660 there were not 1,700 blacks in all of Virginia and Maryland, and in 1680 there were still only about 4,600. But by the end of the century the black population of the two colonies had tripled, to almost 13,000, nearly all of whom were slaves. Free whites still made up the majority of tobacco workers in 1700, but black slaves had become the laborers of choice, and slave labor was rapidly gaining ground on free labor.

Once the institution of black slavery was established, demand took over and pulled slave vessels crossing the ocean from Africa. From 1700 the Atlantic trade would be the major source of labor until the slave population could sustain natural growth, and that would be a while. Mortality rates for "unseasoned" slaves in English North America remained high through the first two decades of the eighteenth century. Also, from Africa came an imbalance of men, which automatically meant fewer offspring than in a sexually balanced population. Then, too, planters who knew they could obtain young male laborers cheaply through the trade saw no need to import women, and they did not encourage (and probably actively discouraged) childbirth, which hindered a woman's ability to work. So the number of slaves imported annually into the Chesapeake region rose steadily to a peak in about 1740. It was just a bit before then that the native-born African-American population achieved a rough sexual balance and began to grow naturally. Once the sexual balance evened out, African Americans showed they could indeed be, as some planters considered them, "a prolifick people." Darrett and Anita Rutman in *A Place in Time: Middlesex County, Virginia, 1650–1750* (1984) write of one "Sharlott," a twelve-year-old girl purchased by Henry Thacker in 1720. Over forty-four years Sharlott had thirteen children of her own, and in 1764 she, her surviving children, and her grandchildren numbered twenty-two persons—all still Thacker's slaves.

The Chesapeake region went through important economic changes as the eighteenth century progressed, some necessitated by the nature of tobacco and its fragile place in the market. Tobacco sapped the tidewater soils of their nutrients. Planters could produce a tobacco crop in the same field for about three years before needing to let it lie fallow for up to two decades. As long as land was plentiful and the population small, this was practical, but it became less so as colonists grew in number, and less appealing in the downswings of fluctuating tobacco prices. Some planters began growing winter wheat to complement their tobacco production in the first half of the eighteenth century, but more turned to grain production in the 1750s and 1760s. North Carolina, too, was entering the mix in a bigger way around the middle of the eighteenth century. That colony's slave economy matured rapidly after 1750, resting on production of naval stores, lumber, grains, and provisions. North Carolinians imported the bulk of their slaves later than the Chesapeake colonies to the north, and more of them directly from Africa. By the time of the American Revolution, the region comprising Virginia, Maryland, and North Carolina had a more diversified economy than other staple-producing regions of the mainland, but all had one thing in common: nearly all the work was in the hands of enslaved men and women whose ancestors had come from Africa.

The Atlantic trade into the Chesapeake leveled off and then began a gradual decline toward the last third of the century, but the overall numbers remain startling. Between 1690 and 1770, Chesapeake planters bought about 100,000 slaves off vessels from West and West Central Africa. On the eve of the American Revolution the nearly 200,000 men and women of African descent living around the Chesapeake made up between two-thirds and three-fourths of all Virginia and Maryland's laborers, and they constituted practically the entirety of the agricultural workforce.

The growth of black slavery to fill colonial labor needs necessitated a legal basis for the institution. Long-standing precedent was irrelevant because English common law did not allow slavery. In fact, more so than almost anywhere else, in England individual rights underpinned much of the law. Nevertheless, the economic and social pressures of English planters to create slavery in order to compete successfully with their New World neighbors from Portugal, The Netherlands, and France led to the legal establishment of such an institution in the Americas. Fortunately for mainland planters, English landowners in the Caribbean had worked through the legal difficulties a generation before slavery became an issue in the Chesapeake. Virginia burgesses and Maryland assemblymen looked to Barbados and Jamaica for legal precedent when constructing their own slave codes.

There was a direct relationship between the changing proportion of blacks to whites in a colony and the sense of need a colonial government felt to develop laws regulating the slave population. Tidewater legislators had not bothered to codify slavery until the number of slaves there swelled and problems with their control arose. Before this time, at least some blacks and whites shared escapades and punishments. In 1649, for instance, William Watts, a white man, and Mary, a black servant, performed the same penance for fornication as would any white couple: they had to stand before the congregation in church at Elizabeth River in Virginia, dressed in a white sheet and holding a white wand. But beginning around the middle of the seventeenth century, colonial judges and lawmakers started stripping away the rights of African immigrants. Precisely when the erosion of blacks' legal status began differs by location. In some places courts were treating individual blacks differently from whites by 1640, as indicated by the sentence handed down to runaway black servant John Punch "to serve his said master or his assigns for the time of his natural life here or elsewhere." The two white servants who ran away with Punch, "one called Victor, a dutchman, the other a Scotchman called James Gregory," decreed the same Virginia court, which apparently was careful to record whites' national origins, had to serve their masters an additional year and the colony three years. Colonial records bear no evidence of a white servant in America ever receiving such a sentence as that of Punch.

In other places blacks like Anthony Johnson held their own in court cases against whites through the 1660s. But the trend was toward the loss of black rights. In the 1640s blacks in Maryland lost the right to bear firearms. In the 1640s (Virginia) and 1660s (Maryland) black women were included in lists of tithables (because those taxed were "all those that worked in the ground," and black women did so, along with white and black men). In the 1660s both colonies meted out stiff punishment for fornication between individuals of the two races. (Maryland decreed in 1664 that all "English women forgettfull of their free Condicion and to the disgrace of our Nation do intermarry with Negro Slaves . . . shall Serve the master of such slaves during the life of her husband.") Recognizing that masters must make slaves fear for their lives—their liberty already lost—to get necessary work from them, and realizing that this required a level of brutality that easily could result in the slaves' death, Virginia in 1669 passed "An act about the casual killing of slaves":

Be it enacted and declared by this grand assembly, if any slave resist his master (or other by his masters order correcting him) and by the extremity of the correction should chance to die, that his death shall not be accompted Felony, but the master (or that other person appointed by the master to punish him) be acquit from molestation, since it cannot be prepensed malice (which alone makes murther Felony) should induce any man to destroy his own estate.

Social practice did not always follow the law, so some free blacks, remaining descendants of the Atlantic creole population that arrived during the first half-century of the colonies' existence, continued to live as viable and respected members of Chesapeake communities and had all manner of relations with whites into the 1670s. But whatever dike held back the flood of legislation and social practice condemning blacks to slavery and ostracism broke with the importation of large numbers of African men and women after the 1680s. In short order, blacks in the Chesapeake lost most of their remaining rights and found themselves completely set apart from whites on all levels of colonial society.

The most important loss to any hope slaves harbored to attain freedom and any social position was the right to hold property. For everyone in colonial America, property was the basis for freedom and dreams of prosperity. In property all persons had legal rights that gave them confidence in their dealings with others. In property all persons had self-respect that manifested itself in a variety of ways favorable to the individual. Removing African Americans' right to own property took away their ability to accumulate wealth and to participate in the quest for betterment that had once included almost all mainland colonists. The loss of their right to personal property undermined the possibility for blacks to have success in personal relations.

Thus, after the first two decades of the eighteenth century, the Chesapeake colonies were well on their way to becoming slave societies rather than societies with slaves. The economic and social system that existed is sometimes characterized in relative terms as one of "smaller plantations," but that seems to refer to the most evident institutions of the Tidewater and does not describe appropriately the variety of circumstances in which African Americans lived at different times and in different places. Until black slavery caught hold, persons of African descent who lived in the Chesapeake were scattered broadly among white servants and free men. Their public contacts were with as many whites as blacks and there was little segregation based on race. African Americans seldom lived on farms with more than a dozen workers of any kind, and only a few lived with more than a handful of other slaves.

With the increase of slavery after 1700, Chesapeake society grew in a direction of having three broad levels based on land and slave holdings. Most landowners lived on family farms of a relatively small size. In Virginia the more prosperous of these might have owned a slave or two or a hired hand, but family members did most of the work. In Maryland by far the largest group of landowners owned no servants or slaves. There also was a middle level of landowners, those with aspirations of becoming big-time planters, who owned a few slaves. These people either succeeded in joining the class of big planters, or else overextended themselves and failed. The middling farmers were thus a group that was economically and socially "transient," and its numbers declined as the century progressed.

The class of landowners that remained relatively small was that of the largest planters, who eventually owned nearly all of the African Americans in the two colonies. Gloria L. Main in *Tobacco Colony: Life in Early Maryland, 1650–1720* (1982) searched probate records from six Maryland counties and found that through the period of her study two-thirds of all slaves worked for just 6 percent of the planters. On the largest plantations owners hired overseers from the group of young, landless white men in the vicinity, and these men drove their workers in gangs and practiced harsh discipline.

The farms, crops, and slaves fell into distinct spatial arrangements. The largest plantations were the tobacco-growing holdings along the Chesapeake Bay and its rivers and inlets. This region formed a tobacco core in the two colonies, with wealth and slaves concentrated on large estates. Around the periphery—the Virginia and Maryland eastern shores, northern Maryland, and areas of Virginia more distant from the water—grain farming and livestock raising increasingly were the basic economic activities. Here smaller land holdings and fewer slaves were the norm.

Even on large plantations slaves did not always live together in a single group of communal quarters. Instead, planters often housed their slaves in small clusters of dwellings located around their holdings; this dispersed herds of cattle and hogs, which the slaves tended, and put laborers close to the fields they worked. Tobacco fields tended to be small and separated because the best tobacco-growing soils were seldom found in large patches. Also, as mentioned, tobacco stripped the soil of nutrients and rendered fields barren for long periods, so once-productive fields in one locale might be grown over in brush a few years later. In Maryland a typical grouping of dwellings might house four or five men or women field hands and one or two women to cook, wash, and care for children. Residents of one such cluster might have thirty cattle and twenty hogs to look after and several fields of tobacco to maintain. One of the wealthiest Maryland colonists in 1681, Colonel Benjamin Rozer, owned a workforce of sixty-nine slaves and servants. Of these he kept fourteen at the "dwelling plantation" on Port Tobacco Creek and settled the others among half a dozen work sites with such names as "Jack's," "Indian Field," and "War Captain's Neck."

Over about a century the establishment and development of black slavery altered nearly every facet of society in the Chesapeake colonies. In 1680 persons of African descent had constituted slightly more than 7 percent of the total population of Virginia and Maryland. A century later blacks made up nearly 40 percent of all the people in the two colonies. As the slave population grew, Virginia legislators stayed busy creating new ways of controlling unruly African Americans in their midst. Mechanisms for such control developed, writes Sally E. Hadden in *Slave Patrols: Law and Violence in Virginia and the Carolinas* (2001), through "a lengthy process of trial and error, experimentation and failure, and often curious digressions." These passed through stages of using overseers and private slave catchers, reliance on the larger white population to guard against runaways and rebels, and eventually movement toward use of militias and organized patrols of armed men. The slave patrols normally consisted of cross-sections of white society and not just lower-class ruffians, as often thought, although the men on patrol were certainly capable of behaving like lower-class ruffians whenever they encountered an African-American man or woman they deemed out of line.

Punishments for violating the law grew harsh. Philip J. Schwarz in *Twice Condemned: Slaves and the Criminal Laws of Virginia, 1705–1865* (1988) relates the story of Jacob, a slave of Martha Flint of Lancaster County, Virginia, who stood trial with his owner and another white woman for stealing tobacco and food from several local whites. The white women received whippings. Jacob, who could have been hanged for his actions, was granted "mercy" because he had acted in the company of "Christian white persons," including the person who owned him. So instead of execution for stealing what turned out to be six pence worth of goods, Jacob was made to stand for an hour at the pillory, to have each ear nailed to the pillory and then cut off "close to the head," and then to receive a "full whipping." Virginian Landon Carter, who struggled in his diary to make punishments administered to his slaves compatible with his notion of himself as a humane patriarch, recorded using "a horse with traces" to overpower a woman claiming she could not work because of her condition—she was quite pregnant—and at least once punished a persistent runaway by leaving him tied, heels to neck.

With the growth of black slavery also came about the almost total disappearance of free blacks, a fact that would have considerable effect on the evolution of African-American culture in the colonies. By the onset of the Revolution, free blacks made up less than 5 percent of the total Virginia and Maryland black population. A century after slavery had become the preferred institution for colonial labor, persons of African descent lived in considerable numbers throughout the Chesapeake; practically all of them were slaves.

The Low Country

If one defines mainland North America's Low Country broadly, as stretching from Cape Fear in the north all the way down past St. Augustine in the south—the area today that makes up the Atlantic littoral of South Carolina, Georgia, and northern Florida, then one recognizes that the English were neither the first Europeans to establishment a permanent settlement there nor the first ones to bring African slaves to the region. As noted, the Spanish were. After Spain decided to establish a military outpost at St. Augustine in Florida in 1565, blacks worked on the fortifications and participated fairly continuously in garrisoning the fort. Over a century later, free blacks and slaves lent their building skills when fear of pirates and rival European nations brought Spain finally to build a huge stone fort on the site, in 1672, and free blacks and mulattos provided six officers and forty-two men to St. Augustine's black militia in 1683. The Spanish outpost at St. Augustine functioned to protect the country's shipping passing between the wealthy colonies of New Spain and the mother country rather than to grow staples for export, as did most of the American settlements. Thus, the population of Africans—or of any persons serving as laborers—in Spanish Florida remained small.

Yet in spite of its size or purpose, the Spanish settlement of blacks, whites, and Indians at St. Augustine would be a thorn in the side of English efforts to create a slave-based plantation economy in southern parts of the British mainland after 1670. For religious and humane reasons, doubtlessly reinforced by political and military factors, Spain's Charles II in 1693 granted freedom to slaves escaping from the English colonies who made it to the Florida outpost. Thereafter, Spanish Florida became a direction for escape and a potential refuge for black men and women fleeing the tightening bonds of English plantation slavery. Initially Spanish authorities reneged on the crown's promise and sold some of the early fugitives back into slavery to benefit the financially strapped colony, but after 1738, when St. Augustine's new governor reinforced the royal edict, prospects for runaways brightened. In that year, with the governor's permission and under the leadership of a black militia captain named Francisco Menendez, thirty-eight fugitives from the English colonies established the first free-black town on the North American mainland some two miles due north of St Augustine. They named the village Gracia Real de Santa Teresa de Mose; it would be abandoned and then rebuilt and occupied until the Spanish lost Florida to the English in 1763. Throughout the village's existence, according to Jane Landers in *Black Society in Spanish Florida* (1999), "the continuing lure of Mose" would draw slaves from England's southernmost mainland colonies while its free black residents would find a way "to shape a village community under extremely difficult conditions."

The slaves fleeing in the direction of Mose and St. Augustine were coming from the thriving slave societies in South Carolina and, later, Georgia. These milieus differed considerably from the Spanish settlements in northeastern Florida, but they differed as well from the English colonies of the Chesapeake.

More early English migrants to the mainland Low Country came from other English colonies, Barbados especially in the beginning, as opposed to the British Isles. Like their counterparts to the north, they came intent on producing for an English market, but the Low Country was not tobacco country. For the first thirty years of settlement these newcomers concentrated on providing sustenance for themselves, and then livestock and timber for the English in the Caribbean and deerskins for those "back home" in

England. After that they turned, gradually at first but then almost totally, to rice production.

The first South Carolina settlers arrived after 1670 with a clear sense of who would be doing the major work of production. African slavery had been thriving in the sugar cane fields of Barbados since the 1640s. Two of South Carolina's Lords Proprietors had been successful Barbadian planters and several others were directors of the Royal African Company, which looked to making its profit off the delivery of slaves to the Americas. The first Englishmen acquiring land along the South Carolina coast noted "the aptnes of Negroes and other servants fitt for such labor as wilbe there required." So black slaves, mostly Atlantic creoles, were present in South Carolina in the year of the colony's founding, and after a generation of settlement persons of African descent constituted a majority of the Low Country population. The extension of settlement and agricultural production in coastal South Carolina, then, would mean the spread of an economy and society based on slavery, regardless of what else the founders and first settlers may have had in mind.

Another important difference between the Low Country and the Chesapeake had to do with environment. The lowland region was subtropical, a land of summer heat and humidity, malarial swamps and pine forests. It was more like the islands of the British West Indies or the homelands of many Africans than any part of the British Isles or the more northerly mainland colonies. Adult slaves whose ancestors had acquired in Africa some resistance to malaria or yellow fever had advantages over their masters in staying healthy, and whether they came from the West Indies or West Africa, they knew something of raising and caring for plants and animals in a subtropical clime. This meant that for the early years of Low Country settlement, at least, the enslaved segment of the population had something significant to offer to the mix beyond physical labor: skills of husbandry and technical know-how. For this reason, English masters in this region may have been more dependent on their slaves than their counterparts elsewhere in the colonies.

From its birth as a colony in 1670 through the first thirty years of its existence, South Carolina was as much a child of Barbados as of England. Its first settlers were from both places, its economy soon became geared to supplying Barbados with provisions, and the model lifestyle of the South Carolina landowner was that of the English gentleman with an eye on the Barbadian planter. By 1650 the English island in the Caribbean was seriously overcrowded and most of its arable land was under cultivation. Freed servants on Barbados now lacked opportunity and the population needed provisions. So in the last third of the century there was considerable migration from Barbados to other English colonies in the New World. In 1670 a mix of wealthy planters, freed servants, and slaves of African descent left the island and, following word previously gathered from native Cusabo on the benefits of their Ashley River home on the North American mainland, settled near what is now Charleston, where the Cooper River meets the Ashley. They first followed the Cusabos in growing maize and beans for their survival; then, they began to produce other foods, raise livestock, and harvest timber for the island market.

Whether slavery was to be part of South Carolina's economy and society was never in question. Its proprietors granted generous amounts of land to those bringing black slaves with them to the colony: "To the Owner of every Negro-Man or Slave, brought thither to settle within the first year, twenty acres; and for every Woman Negro or Slave, ten acres of Land; and all Men-Negro's or slaves after that time, and within the first five years, ten acres, and for every Woman Negro or slave, five acres." The 1669 Fundamental Constitutions of Carolina, written by John Locke and meant to guide the colonists in their new settlement, accepted slavery as a way of life. It was unequivocal in stating, "Every Freeman of Carolina, shall have absolute power and authority over Negro Slaves, of what opinion or Religion soever."

Taking advantage of the situation were such individuals as John Coming, distant ancestor of Edward Ball, about whom Ball writes in his black-and-white family history, *Slaves in the Family* (1998). Coming was a sailor from Devon in southwestern England, who in 1669 signed as first mate on the vessel taking the first colonists to Carolina. After wintering in Barbados, where they picked up more colonists and their slaves, the group made permanent settlement at the confluence of the Ashley and Cooper rivers. Coming married an Englishwoman, Affra, on the voyage, set up residence at the new settlement, and then spent the 1670s as captain of a vessel carrying servants from England to Carolina (thereby earning himself a headright to Carolina land) and hauling cargo among England's American colonies. Ball suspects some of this cargo consisted of enslaved men and women, Native Americans from Carolina taken to Barbados and Africans purchased on Barbados and taken back to Carolina.

In 1682 Coming retired from sailing, turned in enough warrants for land to obtain a 740-acre plot located twenty-five miles up the Cooper River, and with his wife began building the equivalent of an English farm—on a much grander scale. To perform much of the work, Coming began buying Indian and African slaves. Through the 1680s these men and women built a house for the Comings and African-like quarters for themselves, the latter with earthen walls and thatched roofs. They then felled trees and drained the land, selling off the timber or, later, extracting tar and pitch from it, and raised cattle for beef and hides on the cleared fields. Coming died in 1695, Affra in 1699, without having had children. Ownership of the estate was split between Affra's nephew, John Harleston, and her husband's half-nephew, Elias Ball of Devon. Ball arrived in South Carolina in 1698, ambitious and profit hungry. Perhaps above the odors from the cattle and the tar kilns he could smell prosperity of a different sort in the balmy breeze. Like most New World endeavors, Ball's would be based on the labor of others; these, increasingly, would be enslaved Africans.

If Coming's experience was typical, then most of the slaves passed on to his and his wife's heirs were persons of African descent rather than natives of the region. Through these early years, between one-fourth and one-third of the individuals coming to South Carolina were enslaved blacks, predominantly men. Their importance to colonial enterprise in the Low Country was considerable from the beginning. Some West Africans were experienced breeders and keepers of cattle, and over the years of the seventeenth century they brought their animal-husbandry skills and techniques to the West Indies, where, with input from experienced Spanish cattlemen, they blended into a workable cattle-keeping culture. The early English settlers to South Carolina relied largely on the expertise of the slaves they brought from Barbados to develop thriving herds. The methods of tending cattle in the colony's free-grazing environment included seasonal burning to freshen grasses and nighttime penning of cattle for protection.

The planters' readiness to adapt to the strange (to them), swampy, Low Country environment in whatever way they deemed best, and especially their willingness to blend into their ideas of the best practices of English husbandry the agricultural techniques of any or all of the non-English folk in their midst to make the swamps and their surroundings pay, set them on a course toward a plantation economy and, through it, abundance. By the late 1690s there was a hint that the basis of that abundance would be rice, and after a quarter of the next century had passed there was no longer any doubt about it.

"The story of rice's rise," writes S. Max Edelson in *Plantation Enterprise in Colonial South Carolina* (2006), "cannot be separated from the cross-cultural search for food on Britain's subtropical colonial frontier." Every newcomer to the Low Country, master and slave alike, had reason to want to produce and consume the tasty grain, which they preferred to maize-based foods. Also, soon after Carolina's founding, its English settlers had gone through the same search for a staple as had Virginia colonists half a century earlier. Once slaves cleared land, the planters performed systematic experiments with cotton, silk, tobacco, indigo, sugar cane, naval stores, ginger, olives, and wine. They experimented with rice also, primarily to eat, but through the mid-1690s they did not have much to show for their effort. Then, sometime near the end of the century, Carolinians began to succeed in growing and processing rice. The grain was inexpensive, filling, and easy to store, making it popular among poorer European families as well as a preferred grain for feeding armies and gang workers. This gave it market possibilities that were not lost on the enterprising planters. With the demand for food high and the European population inching upward, in time a "rice revolution" struck the Low Country, with effects every bit as profound as tobacco's had been on the Chesapeake—and, as it turned out, with the same kind of foreshadowing for African slaves who would be the workforce producing the commodity.

For a brief time after 1700, South Carolina had one of the most diversified lists of exports in colonial America. Then rice overtook all the others. South Carolina exported 1.5 million pounds of rice in 1710, 6 million pounds in 1720, and 20 million pounds in 1730. By the 1720s rice was the major Low Country export, surpassing pitch and tar. When around the middle of the century Carolina planters introduced a "tidal flow" method of rice production that regulated water on fields and prevented poor yields from drought, rice, and in particular a strain known as Carolina Gold, became the Low Country king. "The only Commodity of Consequence produced in South Carolina is Rice," noted the colony's governor, James Glen, in 1761, "and they reckon it as much their staple Commodity, as sugar is to Barbados and Jamaica, or Tobacco to Virginia and Maryland." By Glen's time the popular grain was accounting for 60 percent of all exports of the region.

The beginning of rice production created a demand for labor that would cause South Carolina to import more slaves than any other mainland colony through the rest of the eighteenth century. Ball's ancestors would ride this wave: by the end of the 1720s the Ball plantations would cover 4,328 Low Country acres, worked by forty-three slaves. "Rice would become the manna of the Balls," he writes, "and the bane of thousands of blacks."

Geography limited rice culture and affected the direction of its spread. Rice grew readily only in the lowest coastlands where tidal rivers irrigated the fields. This restricted its cultivation to a strip along the Atlantic seldom more than twenty miles wide. Southward along the Carolina coast, rice culture spread rapidly, but that spread halted at the Savannah River, below which ownership claims with Spain were not clear.

It was along those more southerly coastal lands in 1732 that England chartered Georgia, a colony that was to reform England's dispossessed and criminal elements and be the basis for a society that saw virtue in hard work, temperance, and Christian morals. The Georgia Trustees banned slavery from the colony by legislation in 1734 because they believed it would hinder development of the virtuous, egalitarian society of small landholders they expected to create. So Georgia was free of slaves, more or less, through the first two decades of its existence.

Slavery might have come to Georgia eventually no matter what, but its introduction there was hurried along by the failure of the inadequately prepared and poorly skilled white colonists to succeed at producing anything (wine, silk, and more) the trustees wanted. South Carolinians in particular began pressing Georgia's trustees and the English Parliament to make slavery legal in the colony. The trustees experimented with a more humane system of forced servitude in the 1740s, but by mid-century it fell before economic expedience. Thereafter, Parliament rendered Georgia free of restriction on slave holding. Land-hungry South Carolinians were the first migrants into Georgia's coastal regions after 1750. They brought with them their know-how for producing rice and their preferred labor force. Other groups followed and moved southward toward the St. Mary's River following Spanish cession of disputed land after 1763.

Low Country Georgians got most of their slaves via the South Carolina market until the middle 1760s. After that they began importing slaves directly from Africa. Like other colonies, Georgia had to wait until its market could dispose of entire cargoes before fully laden slavers bothered to put in at its ports. But by 1773 Georgia had a black population of around 15,000, roughly equal the size of its white population. As in South Carolina, in Georgia's rice-producing region blacks outnumbered whites considerably. Because of the confinement of rice culture to the narrow coastal strip and the difficulties Georgians had finding staple products to grow in the backcountry, slavery in colonial Georgia remained exclusively a Low Country institution. Georgia's 126-mile-long Rice Coast was also its Slave Coast.

The transformation to rice production in South Carolina and its spread to coastal Georgia brought about plantation agriculture on a scale and concentration not before known on the North American mainland, and the large plantation operations affected the working lives of the slaves. More than any other mainland area, the Low Country began to resemble the sugar cane islands in the

British West Indies. Small farms were not as efficient as large, specialized plantations, so the latter became the norm. By the end of the eighteenth century, in spite of disruptions associated with the American Revolution, two Ball brothers owned plantations totaling nearly 15,000 acres worked by 500 slaves.

If this were not enough, the Low Country developed a secondary staple, indigo, which one planter termed "an excellent colleague Commodity with Rice." The early growth of English textile production in the 1740s and the demand for the blue dye that indigo rendered brought a thirty-year-long boom in the crop. Indigo is a delicate plant that requires attention during its growth and then timely and extensive processing at its harvest, but it has a short production cycle, just seven months, so planters could integrate it with other operations—production of naval stores, for instance, or even the growing of rice.

Under these circumstances, the Atlantic trade was asked to bring in enormous numbers of Africans to provide the workforce needed for the plantation enterprises, and it responded to the demand. Between 1706 and 1776, 92,000 slaves entered Charleston harbor for sale and disbursement throughout the Low Country. By 1740, in the oldest plantation areas north and south of Charleston, black slaves made up 90 percent of the population. The largest plantation owners grew exceedingly wealthy and spent time away from production, in Charleston or Savannah during winter months and perhaps in New England through the heat of the summer. In their absences, managers and overseers saw to the running of the plantation.

The difficult working and living conditions brought on by the switch to intensive staple agriculture led to rising rates of slave mortality in the Low Country. South Carolina physician Alexander Garden notified the Royal Society of Arts in 1755 of the situation:

. . . Tilling, Planting, Hoeing, Reaping, Threshing, Pounding have all been done merely by the poor Slaves here. Labour and the Loss of many of their Lives testified the Fatigue they Underwent, in Satiating the Inexpressible Avarice of their Masters, [who] . . . pay . . . dear for their Barbarity, by the loss of many . . . Valuable Negroes, and how can it well be otherwise, the poor Wretches are Obliged to Labour hard to Compleat their Task, and often overheat themselves, then Exposing themselves to the bad Air, or Drinking Cold Water, are immediately . . . Seized with Dangerous Pleurisies and peripneumonies . . . which soon . . . End their wretched Being here.

The wealthy planters were not particularly mindful of the results. Prices for imported Africans dropped with increased supply, so masters could more readily purchase healthy Africans to replace the deceased. When prices for rice fell, as they did with the rising production, planters' instincts were to clear more land, grow more rice, increase crop yield, and exact still more labor from the existing workforce—all of which meant worsening living conditions and greater morbidity for the slaves. Not until the eve of the American Revolution did the Low Country slave population begin to sustain itself, and "salt water" slaves continued to flow into the region in large numbers—over four thousand per year through the first half of the 1770s.

As in other colonies, when the proportion of slaves to free persons began to rise, or even portended to do so, white anxiety mounted. The result in South Carolina and Georgia was the steady erosion of rights for blacks until they faced the strictest laws with the harshest punishments of anywhere in the English mainland colonies. The process took place first in South Carolina, where in the 1690s the Assembly began borrowing from the slave codes of its "parent" colony, Barbados. White fears rose particularly, though, after the mid-1720s, when slave imports into the colony topped 1,000 per year. As the Lords Commissioners for Trade and Plantations put it, "ye whole Province was lately in danger of being massacred by their Owne Slaves, who are too numerous in proportion to ye White Men there." "Suspicious gatherings" of blacks in the streets of Charleston set whites on edge, prompting the organization in 1721 of a "Negro Watch" to stop slaves on sight (with instructions to shoot any black not halting on command) and to confine blacks found on the street after 9:00 P.M. In the same year the colonial militia took over previously irregular patrols in rural areas. Powers of patrolmen were arbitrary and almost without limits. They could administer twenty lashes to a slave found off the plantation without authorization, search slave dwellings indiscriminately, and kill suspected runaways who resisted or fled. A system of justices of the peace for minor offenses and panels of justices and freemen for felonies maintained the appearance of formality in the seemingly contradictory realm of "slave justice." Punishments for those judged guilty were swift, severe, and frequently inhumane. They included castration; nose-splitting; chopping off of ears, hands, or toes; branding; or burning at the stake. Overseers and masters administered their own justice and punishment on the plantation, and those acts varied from more reasonable to arbitrary and depraved.

Beyond the law, however, was social practice, which limited slaves' lives and took away from the quality of their existence. Tension between the minority of white workers and the black majority manifested itself in the setting apart of specific jobs for each group. Whites limited blacks in the practice of skilled trades and designated certain jobs as fit only for persons of color. Consequently, blacks, often the young, collected and disposed of all refuse, built most roads and cut canals, served as carters and stevedores, and even had duty as roughnecks to collect debts or settle masters' scores. Tensions naturally mounted between white and black men over sexual relations. White preoccupation with the notion of a black man raping a white woman grew through the century. The *South Carolina Gazette* tended to overlook the ravishing of black women by white men, as happened with regularity, but it devoted front-page space to instances of rape committed by black men alleged to have occurred in distant colonies.

Even still, there were hidden social and cultural advantages for blacks living on the isolated Low Country plantations. Rice production, which required individual, demanding work on separate, quarter-acre plots, lent itself to a task system of labor. Overseers gave individual slaves specific tasks to complete for a day's work. When finished, the person had free time. This free time, which men and women worked hard to gain, enabled rice plantation slaves to do things on their own, among fellow slaves, and usually away from the eyes of white society. They raised their own crops and poultry, made crafts, hunted and fished, sold their surplus wares or produce, and spent time socializing with their peers. The effects of this intermittent isolation and limited free time were important in the development of a distinct culture among Low Country slaves—a culture that included much more from their African heritage than that of other blacks who were less isolated and had less personal freedom.

Can we identify the principal agents of the original turn to rice production and the eventual development of a way of life—a "rice culture"—in colonial South Carolina and Georgia, where the grand rice-producing plantations dominated economy and society, and the plantation owners dominated politics? Historians writing on the subject through the mid-twentieth century believed they could. Dashing the myth that rice and its methods of production were accidental discoveries, this group gave full credit to English colonists determined to make the most out of the region's location on the edge of the Atlantic economy. But a long revisionist trend, which began with Peter Wood's *Black Majority: Negroes in Colonial South Carolina from 1670 through the Stono Rebellion* (1974), was reinforced by Daniel Littlefield's *Rice and Slaves: Ethnicity and the Slave Trade in Colonial South Carolina* (1981), peaked with Judith A. Carney's *Black Rice: The African Origins of Rice Cultivation in the Americas* (2001), and has been advanced again recently by Edda Fields-Black in *Deep Roots,* credited men and women from rice-growing areas of West Africa with introducing both the grain and the elaborate technology for producing it in the swampy, Low Country landscapes. (Ball agrees, suspecting "that during the first years after his immigration, Elias had only a vague idea how to manage his copious inheritance, and that he was forced to put himself under the apprenticeship of his slaves").

But recent studies raise questions about the "Black-rice thesis" and point toward a process at once more complex and less clearly attributable to one or another group. "Wherever rice grew," writes Edelson, "members of both groups [English planters and African slaves] staked out interests in its production and consumption that brought together desires to eat and sell it, methods to cultivate and process it, and experience doing so in Low Country swamps—all critical factors in the crop's future as a staple commodity." The planters were less tradition bound and more innovative than given credit; the captive workers had know-how—like the laborious processing of the rice that involved pounding it with heavy pestles in deep mortars and fanning it, using African-style grass baskets, both standard methods used through the first half-century of Low Country rice production. "As Africans and Europeans pursued material comfort in the most basic and intimate ways through food," Edelson continues, "they set in place customs for labor, land use, and material exchange that shaped this society's later development. Satisfying small desires during the colony's formative years set precedents that reverberated with unanticipated force as African and European cultural aspirations converged on rice in early South Carolina." The convergence brought the planters to have goals that often included living in opulence in colonial Charleston, while it left the slaves little more than the ability to cling to certain African cultural patterns in some of the mainland's most unhealthy conditions—the drained swamps and fields they tended on the massive Low Country estates.

The Lower Mississippi

The experience of persons of African descent in the lower Mississippi River Valley (or Lower Mississippi) differed in many ways from that of blacks in other parts of the North American mainland. France and Spain were the major European colonial nations involved in the region through the colonial period (England would control West Florida after 1763), and the Lower Mississippi remained marginal in the ambitious New World colonial designs of each. The French tried early to create a slave-based, staple-producing economy, but it never took hold and thrived as it would in other parts of the southeastern mainland. Thus, what by 1730 was a slave society, where persons of African descent outnumbered whites and where rigorous enforcement of rigid slave laws meant harsh discipline, had become a more open setting by mid-century. What evolved was a mingling of Indians, whites, and blacks that allowed individuals in each group greater movement, more social and economic interaction, and for blacks some opportunity for freedom, even as it continued to manifest the typical harsh living and working conditions that were a function of slavery in all parts of the New World. After 1763 Spanish control meant more efforts to stimulate plantation production with white settlers and black slaves, but Spain provided ambitious blacks still more opportunities to gain and thrive in freedom. All of this led to a greater mixing of blacks, whites, and Indians in the Lower Mississippi than anywhere else in the colonial period.

Frenchmen from Canada established the first European settlements in the seasonally-steamy lower Mississippi Valley in 1699, intent mainly on securing a back door to the Indian fur trade. At the time, with slave-based sugar plantations thriving on the French Caribbean islands of St. Domingue and Martinique, French authorities saw little reason to try to duplicate that success along the Mississippi with African or Indian slaves. But following establishment of New Orleans by the French crown in 1718, settlers with an eye on plantation agriculture raised the pressure to allow importation of African slaves, and a year later the government relented. So between 1719 and 1731 the French *Compagnie des Indies* brought 7,600 slaves directly from Africa into Louisiana. Over 80 percent of these people came from Senegambia; the French referred to some as Bambaras, not so much an ethnic identifier—as it is now—as a term for captive or soldier from the Senegambian interior. Other African arrivals came from the Bight of Biafra and Angola.

Louisiana was an unhealthy place and many of the new migrants did not live long, but in time Louisiana's African population began to survive—better than the whites in the region. By 1727 blacks outnumbered whites in the colony. Those Africans who remained around New Orleans constructed levees, built buildings, and worked on the farms and plantations that abutted the small town. Outside of New Orleans slaves felled trees, cut roads, constructed levees, built dwellings, and provided the labor to create tobacco and indigo plantations on huge estates lining the Mississippi from New Orleans north to Point Coupée.

French slavery in the New World already had a legal basis in the *Code Noir* that King Louis XIV had decreed in 1685; his successor, Louis XV, merely issued a similar code for Louisiana in

1724. Unlike English laws, the French code called for Catholic instruction for slaves and placed church and state in a position to guarantee meager rights for slaves, but it never worked that way. Rare was the plantation slave who received sacraments beyond baptism; rarer still the abused slave who resorted to the law for protection or compensation. Reflecting the typical fears of a white minority, punishments of slaves for wrongdoing were as severe in the Lower Mississippi as they were anywhere. In *Mammon and Manon in Early New Orleans: The First Slave Society in the Deep South, 1719–1819* (1999), Thomas N. Ingersoll writes of the retribution leveled against slave rebels from 1730s New Orleans: "As late as 1800 there were living whites and blacks who remembered the sounds of bones breaking on the wheel and the cries of the victims as the sun slowly put them out of their misery high above the Bayou Road." Jesuits, who were thought to be present at least partly to look after the well being of slaves and indigenous folk, owned and worked slaves on one of the largest plantations. Thus, in the teeming heat of long summers, in a disease environment that included yellow fever among the other subtropical plagues, and in a budding plantation economy demanding hard work and meting out punishment most severe, the lot of slaves up and down the Lower Mississippi was particularly mean.

As everywhere else in the New World, blacks in the Lower Mississippi were not the only ones maltreated by the European colonists. Indians, some of whom the French enslaved also, were threatened by the expanding plantations. French authorities were continually afraid that runaways from Louisiana plantations would make common cause with the Indians, and small numbers of them did. There even existed a handful of maroon settlements where Africans, Indians, African French, and African Indians organized banditry raids, traded goods stolen from the French colonists, and planned ways to halt the expansion of plantations. In 1729 Natchez Indians aided by fugitive slaves rose up in districts north of New Orleans and killed over two hundred French settlers, liberating slaves in the process. New Orleans's governor armed fifteen trusted slaves from the city, who joined the Natchez's enemies, the Choctaw, to quell the rebellion. Two years later, a group of fugitives the French labeled "Bambaras" planned another insurrection with local Indians, only to be defeated by another French force augmented by slaves. In such a threatening environment, French authorities rewarded blacks who fought for them with their freedom and then formed a small black militia to protect the colony and ensure the loyalty of its black population in the future. Over the next several decades that militia helped protect the settlement against more groups of Indians and prepared to fight various European enemies when rumors of invasion spread.

The frightening insurrections, coupled with fear of a larger and potentially unruly black majority, brought French authorities to stop importing African slaves into the Lower Mississippi after 1730. With that, the expansion of tobacco- and indigo-producing plantations slowed and the colony began to diversify its export economy. Thus, at the very time that Africans were beginning to pour into the Chesapeake and Low-Country colonies, where plantation agriculture was holding its own (in the former) and thriving (in the latter), demands and constrictions on Africans and African Americans in the Lower Mississippi began to loosen. As creoles began to replace African-born slaves, more men (especially) and women were finding ways to gain their freedom. Once they did, they joined the broad spectrum of the Franco-American-African-Indian population that exchanged goods and services with one another in a broad, freewheeling, subsistence-based exchange economy that the French could do little to control.

Eventually, slaves participated in the economy, too. In place of providing their bondspeople food and clothing, some masters began allowing them time to work for themselves, and many of them marketed the foods they had grown on their own behalf or game they had trapped and hunted. Some slaves prospered from services they provided as boatmen along the bayous and backwaters. Eventually, masters permitted individual slaves to hire out their own time. Assisting in service as the guardians of society, as well as a police force, in New Orleans and on the remaining plantations were free black militiamen. The more integral their service became in securing the colony's residents against foreign and domestic threats, the more these men gained in individual respect and status. Thus, by 1760 a unique creole society had formed in the Lower Mississippi. The slaves in this society had greater independence than their counterparts in Anglo-America, and the smaller number of free blacks within it found more opportunity. Harsh punishment and discrimination continued to exist there, to be sure, but along with such treatment was opportunity for some and a modest amount of respect for at least a few.

The takeover of Louisiana by Spain and West Florida by England, as dictated by the 1763 Treaty of Paris, altered this arrangement at least in degree. Both new rulers had intentions of trying again to create a staple-producing economy—and they did bring in more settlers and slaves and increased indigo production—but both had their hands full simply maintaining order in their new colonies, so society and the economy remained fluid. The black militia helped authorities put down a revolt by unhappy French planters in 1769 and then stood more strongly than ever as a force to quell unrest. This prompted Spanish authorities to keep paths to freedom open for Louisiana blacks, who might augment their small number of supporters. It was during the period of Spanish control that New Orleans's population of free blacks increased in number and advanced socially and economically. For the remainder of the colonial period mostly creole blacks, speaking a unique French-African language, worked hard in the Lower Mississippi heat, above all, but they also played and mixed in New Orleans and up and down the great river.

Thus, what had begun as a slave society had become a society with slaves, where work in particular and life in general were difficult for the vast majority of blacks who remained in slavery, but where an openness in marketing and movement and a level of white-black-red interaction not known elsewhere—one even including limited opportunity—prevailed through the rest of the colonial period. Not until planters began growing sugar there after 1795 would conditions change significantly for African Americans in the Lower Mississippi. By that time, New Orleans had the foundations of a unique creole society in its sizable free-black population. Those who remained in slavery and the many more who followed formed the backbone of a workforce that would turn nineteenth-century Louisiana into a land of commercial agriculture based on sugar cane.

New England and the Middle Colonies

After considering black slavery from the Chesapeake to East Florida and in Louisiana, one tends to think of the much smaller number of blacks in New England and the Middle Colonies as relatively insignificant. After all, in 1770 there were barely 50,000 individuals of African descent north of Maryland, not quite 4.5 percent of the total population, whereas in the same year from Maryland southward some 400,000 blacks made up 40 percent of the total number of persons. Blacks were only 2.5 percent of the New England population and 6.5 percent of the people in the Middle Colonies on the eve of the American Revolution.

But figures alone fail to give an accurate picture of the importance of slavery to the economy of the area north of the Chesapeake and especially to particular regions of it. In some of the most agriculturally productive rural areas of Connecticut, Long Island, the lower Hudson River valley, and southern Pennsylvania blacks made up as much as half the workforce in the decades after the middle of the eighteenth century. Certain industries—ironworking in Pennsylvania or tanning in New York, for instance—relied heavily on slave labor, and slaves worked in the carrying trade and around shipyards in Rhode Island and Massachusetts. In New England, blacks were concentrated near coastal urban centers and along river systems, with a particularly heavy concentration in Rhode Island. In these places they did work for white elites, freeing their masters to pursue lucrative mercantile ventures. The Middle Colonies had black urban populations of considerable size, where they moved from serving the gentry to assisting tradesmen. "New York was a slave city," Jill Lepore asserts plainly in *New York Burning: Liberty, Slavery, and Conspiracy in Eighteenth-Century Manhattan* (2005). Thus, in certain areas the black population was a significant proportion of the total and critical to the regional economy. In these places blacks did not live in isolation from others of African descent and the demands and customs of whites did not totally dominate their lives.

In addition to sheer numbers of people involved, slavery in New England and the Middle Colonies was different in other obvious ways from the institution found on the mainland from the Chesapeake southward. Plantations never formed from Pennsylvania northward. If the typical southern African American after 1750 lived and worked with a fair-sized group of other slaves on a large tobacco or rice plantation, the typical northern slave lived alone or with one or two other slaves, perhaps in a dwelling with the family of the owner, and worked on a small farm, in a small industry, as a domestic, or at a trade in an urban area. The origin of most northern slaves was different, too. Before about 1740 it was rare for captives to arrive in a northern port immediately after the voyage from Africa. Most of the early imports were Atlantic creoles who came from the West Indies or one of the southern mainland colonies. Only between 1740 and 1770 was there significant, direct importation of men and women from Africa into northern markets, and even then their numbers never approached those in the plantation colonies.

Reasons for the considerable differences of slavery in the northern colonies have to do with the region's economy. New England and the Middle Colonies never devoted most of their resources to production of a major staple for export. There was simply not one in demand that they could produce. Instead, over time, northerners became efficient at a variety of tasks that, when combined, brought them the export credits they needed to keep in check their balance of trade. These tasks included grain and livestock farming, whaling and fishing, and the carrying trade. None of these tasks involved the same economy of scale that southern planters exercised. Even those northerners producing food for export did so efficiently on small farms. There were exceptions, of course, but most producers relied on their own and their families' labor, and they tended not to gain the extraordinary wealth that would enable them to buy many laborers and considerably expand operations.

Why, then, did settlers of the northern colonies get involved with black slavery in the first place, even in the relatively small numbers they did, and why did northerners continue to purchase slaves all the way to the eve of the Revolution? The answer to the first question has to do largely with their early and extensive participation in the carrying trade, and to the second with their need for labor and its availability. Both show how much their decisions and actions were bound up in the Atlantic economy in which they operated.

Dutch colonists rather than the English were the first to import slaves north of Maryland. The Dutch West India Company, which carried out settlement of New Netherland along the Hudson River, established posts there in the mid-1620s for participation in the fur and timber trade. The company may have desired development of a stable, agriculture-producing colony along the lower Hudson as well, but it refused to invest enough initially to prompt a sufficient number of colonizers from the Netherlands to settle there. Instead, it brought in workers before farmers. Always eager to introduce chattel slavery to New World colonies so it could enhance its carrying trade in slaves, but also in need of laborers to build the necessary forts and roads and to raise food for the Dutch garrison in New Amsterdam, the company began in 1626 to import blacks into its own mainland colony. Most of these people had African, Portuguese, or Dutch names and came from Curaçao in the Dutch West Indies or from the holds of Spanish ships, removed from these by pirates. Eventually, the company put its slaves to work clearing land along the Hudson. By mid-century enough slaves had entered the colony and rendered enough land arable to alter the nature of New Netherland. Only then did Dutch colonists arrive intending to settle permanently, using the cleared land for growing grain and keeping livestock. Farming replaced fur trading as the principal colonial activity.

A fair number of the earliest slaves, largely Atlantic creoles, used their knowledge of the Dutch Atlantic mercantile world to their advantage: many gained baptism in the Dutch Reformed Church (believing—in the end mistakenly—that church membership might help them in their quest for freedom), established families, accumulated property, and pushed for their rights under law. Some obtained their freedom (though not necessarily that of their offspring) from the company and gained title to farmland about one mile north of the company's fort on lower Manhattan Island—in the area where Washington Square is today. Thus, the 1640s found free-black men and women trading at a weekly New Amsterdam market and frolicking in taverns with Indians, Dutch, and Walloons, resulting in a melding of cultures.

But access to freedom closed quickly to persons of even partial African ancestry in New Netherland. Dutch authorities used the promise of the availability of slaves as a lure to attract more white farmers. In the 1640s a slave bound for lifetime cost about the same as the wages, provisions, and lodging for a free worker for a single year. In addition, noted Governor William Kieft in 1644, "Negroes . . . accomplish more work for their masters, and at less expense, than [Dutch] farm servants, who must be bribed to go thither by a great deal of money and promises." Thus, from coastal African ports newly opened to Dutch shipping and from older, established markets in the Caribbean came more slaves. The Dutch Reformed Church helped move along acceptance of slavery in the colony by halting slave baptism and curtailing emancipation there. By the 1660s one in eight citizens of New Netherland owned slaves and persons of African descent made up a quarter of the colony's population.

The takeover of New Netherland by the English in 1664 did not alter the status of slaves there. If the new colonial government took a while to express itself on the prescribed status of Africans in bondage and the future of slavery in the colony, white colonists already knew what they wanted and moved fast to effect it. "[T]he want of hands and the Dearness of the Wages of hired Servants," New York slave owner Cadwallader Colden would later put it, "makes Slaves at this Time, necessary." New York whites continued to seek enslaved men and women to do the variety of tasks needed in the growing urban port on lower Manhattan and to work the farms that were spreading along the lower Hudson. Eventually, English laws in New York recognized slavery as a legal institution at the same time they restricted white servitude. As they did, demand for slaves increased. The slave trade from the islands flourished, if in imports of a few at a time, and New York's black population grew. By 1700 the colony had 2,000 slaves in a total population of about 19,000 and by 1750 the number of those enslaved had grown to 10,000 out of 75,000 total—more than any other mainland colony north of the Chesapeake.

Many of these Africans and African Americans lived in the vicinity of New York City. As the city's population grew, from 5,000 to 13,000 over the first half of the eighteenth century, so did the proportion of African Americans residing there, from 14 to 21 percent. Because of their frequent use as domestics in the city, black women outnumbered black men among the city's slave population. A low rate of fertility among these women, the result of their hard work, malnutrition, and discouragement to reproduce by their owners, meant the city's black population growth was tied to continued slave importing. After a suspected slave conspiracy in 1741, which some blamed on acculturated slaves, New Yorkers looked to Africa for slaves.

New York was not the only Middle Colony to which the Dutch West India Company brought slaves. Its ships carried blacks in small lots to settlements along the Delaware River after 1639 and to the west bank of the Hudson that became part of New Jersey in 1664. English proprietors of New Jersey eventually authorized slavery and encouraged the importation of slaves by offering prospective settlers up to sixty acres for each slave they brought to the colony. By the end of the century, Perth Amboy became one of the main ports of entry for northern slaves.

There were slaves in Pennsylvania, too, even before there were Quakers living there. A handful of farmers owned and worked blacks along the Delaware River as early as the 1660s, and the arrival of English, Irish, and Welsh with William Penn in 1682 did not change that. The English slave trade was just picking up to meet the growing mainland demand as Penn and those joining him in his "holy experiment" settled along the western bank of the Delaware, and the new migrants took advantage of the situation. While still living in temporary housing, in 1684, Philadelphia Quakers snapped up 150 Africans off a slaver to work clearing trees and erecting houses. Penn himself preferred black slaves to white servants "for then," he reasoned, "a man has them while they live"; he owned and worked about a dozen black men and women on his estate. Philadelphia carriers in the Caribbean trade soon were bringing slaves as part of return cargoes. By 1700 one Philadelphia family in fifteen owned slaves. Pennsylvania laws began treating slaves differently than servants early in the eighteenth century, and in 1726 the colonial legislature codified the laws governing slavery and free blacks. While these laws were not as rigorous as slave codes in most other colonies, they nevertheless installed race as the basis for a caste system in the colony. Through the first two-thirds of the eighteenth century, as Philadelphia more clearly became a major port city and cosmopolitan center distinguished from its rural hinterland, so did slavery in the colony take urban and rural forms. Bonded black workers were more important in Philadelphia's early years, as they helped build the city, labored in and around the bustling port facilities as well as on ships, and worked for the city's artisans, merchants, and professionals. Other slaves grew increasingly important as agricultural workers on the farmlands of southeastern Pennsylvania after 1750.

New England had fewer African Americans than any other region of the mainland colonies. Black slaves had been in the region since before 1640, however, and in some places they were important elements of the economy and society. Most black men and women came there because of coastal New England's interdependence with the West Indies and its heavy participation in the Caribbean trade. Ships arriving in New England ports from the British West Indies often carried half a dozen slaves. Some were "refuse" slaves (the infirm or ailing, who could not be sold profitably in the island markets), exiled offenders of various sorts, or those purchased to work the voyage northward and then sold upon its termination. More New England slave imports were African by birth than this implies, however. Slavers sometimes used the Caribbean islands as way stations, selling some captives and then passing on to New England with partial loads of Caribbean produce and the remainder of their slaves. New England masters seemed to care less than Tidewater planters about receiving the "bad lot" of slaves from the Caribbean, just as they showed less concern for place of origin of the Africans they purchased. They believed they could train blacks individually and instill proper Yankee traits in even the most reluctant slave.

After about 1740, northern slavery took on a much greater African cast. In a fashion similar to what happened regarding the decline of servants in the late-seventeenth-century Chesapeake, increasing opportunities in Europe and occasional blocking of European shipping lanes by warfare cut the immigration of white laborers to the northern colonies, prompting labor-hungry Yankees to purchase slaves. Demand was great enough to entice whole shiploads from Africa, so the new entrants were not predominantly Atlantic creoles, as before, but men and women fresh from the ocean crossing and not long out of a West-African society. This change in the nature of the slave trade would affect everything from the ability of black men and women to build families and conduct orderly domestic lives to the marked infusion of African elements in northern African-American culture and the waning of the region's free-black population.

Regardless of where the slaves came from, the distribution of African Americans in the northern colonies was uneven. This was particularly true in New England, where, because of the ties of slave imports to colonial shipping, major ports held concentrations of African Americans. In 1754 three quarters of Massachusetts's black population of 2,700 lived in coastal towns in only three counties. At the same time, blacks made up good portions of the population of Rhode Island's Narragansett ports—20 percent of Newport, 30 percent of South Kingston, and 40 percent of Charlestown.

Slavery in northern towns and cities from Salem to Philadelphia was different from most other forms of slavery in the colonies. In 1767 one in every six Philadelphia households owned slaves, their total being close to 1,500. For many owners the bondspeople were a symbol of status. Merchants and shopkeepers owned one-third of the slaves, professionals owned 10 percent, innkeepers or tavern owners about 5 percent, and widows and "gentlemen" another 5 percent. Nearly all slaves from this last group were household servants. Artisans and craftsmen or men involved in maritime ventures owned the other half of the city's slaves. Bakers, ropemakers, brewers, millers, shipwrights, blockmakers, sailmakers, goldsmiths, and ferrymen also used slaves in their work. Some slaves had particular skills: Boston newspapers in the eighteenth century carried ads for a chocolate maker, a soap boiler, a ladies hair dresser (a man), and a woman who specialized in "turtle dressing." A surprising number of ship captains and mariners (10 percent of all owners) purchased slaves with the intention of having them work on board ship as sailors.

None of this should give the impression that northern slavery was entirely, or even primarily, an urban experience. As elsewhere, the vast majority of northern blacks lived and worked in the countryside. Most were agricultural workers on small or middle-sized farms, with the heaviest concentrations in Connecticut and Rhode Island, on Long Island, and in northern New Jersey. These farms raised provisions and draft animals, primarily for export to the West Indies. Even here, white laborers made up a good part of the workers on seasonal crops. Through most of the year, African Americans worked around the masters' houses and stables. As in the cities, owning a slave was a mark of wealth and status.

Because African Americans were in much smaller proportion to the total northern population, control of slaves in most locales was less of a problem than it was in the southern colonies. Absence of laws regulating slavery did not reflect this so much as did lax enforcement of those already on the books. Slave codes in New England were probably the least stringent of all. There, slaves walked a fine line between being persons with certain rights on the one hand, and being pieces of property on the other. The result was ambivalence in colonial statutes. Massachusetts taxed slaves as persons and as property; Connecticut and Rhode Island taxed them as they did livestock. New England slaves could own, transfer, and inherit property at the same time their masters could sell and bequeath them. Puritan masters were especially inconsistent in dealings with their bondspeople. To them the slave was part of the family, so Massachusetts Puritans saw to it that their slaves had "all the liberties and Christian usages which the law of God, established in Israel concerning such persons, doth normally require." However, Puritans regarded persons of African descent in Biblical terms, too, which meant, in the words of Cotton Mather, they were "miserable children of Adam and Noah." Strict in their response to all sexual matters, Puritans held particular abhorrence of miscegenation. The Massachusetts law banishing—usually to the West Indies—blacks guilty of fornication with whites was the most severe miscegenation law in any continental colony.

The increase in the number of slaves with a greater African presence alarmed some northerners by the mid-eighteenth century, prompting some colonies to tighten laws regarding manumission and slave control. In the Middle Colonies, where larger numbers of African Americans tended to congregate in cities, authorities had more difficulty controlling slave populations. Curfews and laws forbidding the serving of alcohol to blacks were common; punishments for those who broke these laws were severe. New York had the most difficulty of any northern city. It experienced panics over slave conspiracies in 1712 and 1741. The latter led to the arrest of 54 blacks and execution of 31 of them.

In spite of the body of legislation that governed northern slaves, their lives were not so proscribed as those of slaves in southern colonies. It was difficult in any town or city where slaves worked as deliverymen, errand runners, or hired artisans to restrain their movement and assembly. It was not so much easier in the countryside, where slaves found time to work for themselves and to participate in petty trade at crossroads and in town markets. So urban authorities gradually grew tolerant of curfew violations and gatherings of African Americans that did not appear to presage trouble. Still, lack of enforcement did not reduce the total effect of the northern slave codes. "They cast a shadow everywhere," writes Edgar J. McManus in *Black Bondage in the North* (1973), "reminding slaves they were a caste apart, living on sufferance in a system amply geared for their destruction."

Beyond jurisdiction of the slave codes was a body of African Americans in the North who were free. Numbers of free blacks in the northern colonies were small, on par with the numbers of free blacks in the southern colonies. In material ways, the lives of these free people were not considerably better than those of the slaves in their midst. In some ways the very presence of slavery hindered free blacks. Slaves who rose to responsible positions under their masters' employ posed no threat to white society, but free blacks who achieved important positions by themselves did. So whites took care to see that northern free black persons remained in menial jobs. Free African-American shopkeepers had difficulty getting credit. Free black artisans were not always welcome in shipyards or at building sites. For those who were destitute life was more difficult in freedom than in slavery. In Boston in 1742 there were 110 free African Americans in the almshouse and 36 in the workhouse, this out of the city's total black population, slave and free, of only 1,500. If other immigrants to the mainland received rewards for hard work, thrift, and steady movement toward assimilation, Africans in colonial America suffered for such behavior at the hands of a white population that saw African-American advancement as a serious threat to the established order.

Slavery and Racial Prejudice

Consideration of the origins of slavery in the English mainland colonies leads to critical questions about the relationship between slavery and racial prejudice: Was English racial prejudice against black Africans the main reason slavery began, or did the enslavement of Africans come first for economic reasons, with the condition of slavery for blacks then leading to racial prejudice against those enslaved?

Investigation to answer these questions has long centered on the Chesapeake, where English mainland colonists made the first legal commitment to black slavery and first practiced it on a large scale. The major problem investigators encounter has to do with the lack of acceptable evidence showing clear trends for the period before 1660. Good historians have examined existing evidence and concluded that English landowners treated their black and white servants similarly. Others equally good have used the same evidence to find that the early English settlers had strong feelings of racial prejudice against Africans, concluding that this racism was the basis for the eventual development of black slavery as a major economic and social institution in the colonies. In his classic study,

White Over Black: American Attitudes Toward the Negro, 1550–1812 (1968), Winthrop D. Jordan offers a middle ground. Enslaving blacks was an "unthinking decision," according to Jordan. "Slavery and 'prejudice' may have been equally cause and effect, continuously reacting upon each other, dynamically joining hands to hustle the Negro down the road to complete degradation." But not everyone has since agreed with this part of Jordan's book.

Lately, historians have broadened their focus to the larger Atlantic world in which the early mainland colonies existed, and have joined Joyce E. Chaplin in arguing, in her chapter on "Race" in *The British Atlantic World, 1500–1800*, ed. by David Armitage and Michael J. Braddick, 2nd ed. (2009), that "racism in its present form is a specific product of Atlantic history." Certainly a level of prejudice toward darker people existed among the early Europeans who ventured down the Atlantic coast to sub-Saharan Africa and then across to the Americas. In the most recent of his many studies on slavery, *Inhuman Bondage: The Rise and Fall of Slavery in the New World* (2006), David Brion Davis finds the roots of American racial prejudice stretching back through the millennia across the Euro-Asian world in, among other things, Islamic-Christian conflict, the biblical "Curse of Ham," and Spanish fears of "contamination" of their blood by intermixture with Jewish converts and then by blacks. "[T]he dishonor, contempt, and dehumanization always associated with human bondage," Davis concludes, "were [in the fifteenth and sixteenth centuries] being transferred to the scores of African ethnic groups that Arabs and Europeans had begun to perceive as a single race."

Such cultural and intellectual air was part of the emotional atmosphere surrounding the early English settlers of the Chesapeake and had considerable effect on the colonists' attitudes. For matters concerning race, the first English colonists were inheritors of experiences and attitudes of the Portuguese and Spanish, but, as Chaplin shows, they had less oversight from the home government than their Iberian colonial neighbors and thus were freer to develop their own ideas about the Indians, and soon the Africans, they encountered. Once settlers craved Natives' land, a handy, hostile-savage-without-civilization image gained acceptance. Colonists assuaged their guilt over taking these lands by thinking of Indians as many Europeans thought of Africans: brutish, uncultured, areligious, nearer to beasts than to human beings. They witnessed Native Americans being violent in the futile—though wholly justifiable—defense of their lands, which only reinforced English conceptions. By the 1620s, following massacres of encroaching settlers by local Indians, Virginians were describing Native Americans as "by nature slothfull and idle, vitious, melancholy, slovenly, of bad conditions, lyers, of small memory, of no constancy or trust . . . , never looking what dangers may happen afterwards, less capable then children of sixe or seven years old, and less apt and ingenious." All of this added to ideas inherited from Iberians, based on how quickly Native populations died off upon contact with Europeans, that they were physically weak, unable to withstand hardship, and incapable of rigorous work (as the early Europeans had in mind). Similarly, such ideas of a people physically different from the English developed rapidly throughout the mainland colonies.

English ideas about Africans affected settlers' thoughts and actions, too. Before confronting Africans in America, most English already shared with other Europeans some standard, negative preconceptions of blackness and black people. In the English world, black signified things dark, sinister, evil and foul, whereas white suggested purity and virtue. Most sub-Saharan Africans the English encountered were not just darker than they, as were Mediterranean people, but many were among the darkest people in the world, odd-looking individuals to the English, with customs they found strange. These Africans were not only un-Christian but seemingly without religion to an English mentality that found its basis on earth and beyond in Christianity. And Africans appeared to be savage folk who dressed in few clothes, ate strange foods without utensils, and lived among odd and ferocious beasts. But Iberians had already proved Africans' physical toughness. Unlike Native Americans (and, to a lesser extent, Europeans), Africans proved themselves capable of surviving long hours of work in the hot tropics. So no matter where African immigrants arrived on the mainland, they stepped into a narrowly defined world charged with strong feeling about the natural differences of themselves and others of color, namely those native to the land.

But was it primarily this racial prejudice that led English settlers to adopt slavery as the permanent condition for African immigrants to the mainland? As Jordan argued four decades ago (in a
book that has stood the tests of changing interpretations about as
well as any), whites' cultural background was only part of the story; there was a strong economic element as well. "[The colonists']
actions revealed an early propensity to seek labor and use it by any
means possible," Chaplin writes. Their failure to find elsewhere
in North America the long-term, stable labor force they needed to
fulfill their economic ambitions, coupled with the availability of
large numbers of Africans at inexpensive prices, brought about "an
'unthinking imitation' of Iberian enslavement of Africans, a little-
questioned tendency to lean toward enslaved African labor whenever [they] could afford it." Racial prejudice would more clearly
help the English justify enslaving Africans some time later, when
they needed to do so, just as it helped them rationalize taking land
from Native Americans.

And once slavery became a permanent condition for Africans
in America, its effect on strengthening the existing racial prejudice was considerable. One racial group could hardly keep another
in bondage without developing negative feelings about those they
had forcibly enslaved. When it proved necessary to punish slaves
beyond the limits English law allowed—as when in March 1707
Robert "King" Carter got an order from the Lancaster County
(Virginia) court to cut off the toes of "two incorrigible negroes of
his named Bambarra Harry and Dinah . . . for the better reclaiming
the said negroes and deterring others from ill practices"—justification came in labeling the persons of African descent as different from the white English. Their physical toughness helped them
withstand such treatment, for that matter. "It was not necessary
to extend the rights of Englishmen to Africans," writes Edmund
Morgan, "because Africans were 'a brutish sort of people.' And
because they were 'brutish' it was necessary 'or at least convenient' to kill or maim them in order to make them work."

Across all classes of white colonial society, negative feelings
toward Africans and African Americans grew with their increasing numbers in enslavement. Moreover, the very existence of black
slavery provided a sense of separateness and unity to whites of

gentry, middling, or commoner classes. It gave whites a common identity and then intensified their attitudes toward one of the other major identifiable groups on the mainland. The result within a few generations was a white society manifesting a racial prejudice that would soon intensify and last for centuries, and a black population caught in a labor system that must necessarily keep them at the bottom of America's economy and society. Gary B. Nash summarizes African Americans' plight in *Red, White, and Black: The Peoples of Early America,* fifth edition (2005):

Irrevocably caught in the web of perpetual servitude, the slave had little opportunity to prove the white stereotype wrong. Socially and legally defined as less than humans, African-Americans became a truly servile, ignoble, degraded people in the eyes of the Europeans. This was used as further reason to keep them in slavery, for it was argued that they were worth nothing better and were incapable of occupying any higher role. In the long evolution of racial attitudes in America, nothing was of greater importance than the enslavement of Africans.

CHAPTER THREE

African-American Culture

Subject to grinding daily exploitation, caught in the grip of powerful forces that were often beyond their power to control, slaves nevertheless strove to create order in their lives, to preserve their humanity, to achieve dignity, and to sustain dreams of a better future.

—PHILIP D. MORGAN

Frederick Douglass, the gifted African American who escaped from slavery in 1838 and became one of the country's leading abolitionists, was born in Talbot County, Maryland, in 1818. Many know of Douglass and the difficulties he faced as a slave from *Narrative of the Life of Frederick Douglass, an American Slave,* which he wrote in 1845 to further the abolitionist cause. Much of the book concerns his relationship with white masters and mistresses. There is little in the narrative about his family or the black community in which he lived.

In the late 1970s, Dickson J. Preston began investigating Douglass's early life to determine how much of the *Narrative* he could verify with independent evidence. In *Young Frederick Douglass: The Maryland Years* (1980), Preston shows that Douglass

had not sprung full-grown out of nowhere, as his contemporaries seemed to think; his black ancestors, for a century or more before his birth, had been a strong and closely knit kin group with family pride and traditions that were handed on to him by his part-Indian grand mother, Betsey Bailey. His roots were anchored deeply in the earliest American experience.

Douglass's family was part of a black subculture of Maryland's Eastern Shore, itself a variant of a greater Chesapeake African-American culture. Both were set into the broader unity of black culture in America and of blacks around the Atlantic basin. Both were tied closely to the Euro-American culture of whites, among whom African Americans lived, worked, worshiped, and played. Douglass was not unique among mainland North American blacks of his time in his family origins or cultural surroundings. Throughout the mainland for several generations before Douglass was born, African Americans had been living in families and participating in different but related subcultures that were stable products of a long evolution in the colonies—part of a broader cultural mixing and melding occurring up and down the Atlantic side of the Americas and at Atlantic ports in Africa and Europe. The black American subcultures that appeared long before Douglass's birth were the result of interactions among Africans, Native Americans, and Europeans. What emerged were patterns of behavior and social customs that were distinctly African American.

African-American culture did indeed come to absorb many elements from the cultures of Europeans and Indians. But any idea that acculturation in colonial America moved in a single direction—from Anglo-Americans to African Americans or Native Americans without spreading in reverse—is one that treats culture narrowly and fails to hold up to careful examination of the evidence. Not until the last few years have historians begun to realize just how much African Americans have influenced important aspects of Euro-American culture. In *The World They Made Together,* Sobel shows the extent of the interdependence of Anglo-Virginian and Afro-Virginian subcultures in colonial times. The two groups from different preindustrial worlds shared many of the same values and held many of the same ideas—especially in their thoughts of time, space, worldview, causality, family ties, and death and the afterlife. In this environment, Africans had considerable influence in the shaping of Euro-American culture. More recently, William Piersen, in *Black Legacy: America's Hidden Heritage* (1993), has argued that the colonial foundation for such cultural interdependence persisted in the southern states in particular. "The evidence is compelling," he writes, that white southerners adopted much from the culture of blacks who raised their children and who lived alongside them. In speech patterns, in traditions of manners and honor, in the region's ways of cooking, work habits, religious styles, in southern 'superstitious beliefs,' holiday celebrations, and music, the white American South developed a distinctive and African-American way of life.

That until recently historians were unaware of this sharing of values, habits, and ways of life between blacks and whites is largely a factor of their sources. White people, who kept most of the records on which historians must rely, simply failed to realize how much black thoughts and values altered their own ways of doing things and looking at the world.

Africans in America

Not all persons of African descent who arrived on slave ships in colonial America were "raw Africans"—persons fresh out of West-African farming or herding communities for whom coming into contact with whites on an American farm or plantation was a shocking experience. As Berlin shows in *Many Thousands Gone,* many of the earliest slaves in mainland American locales were Atlantic creoles, products of the long-standing commercial world of the Atlantic rim of four continents, people familiar with European languages, religions, and ways of living. Some of these individuals used their linguistic facility and cultural knowledge to their advantage. Fitting into the patterns of life in British mainland North America was not easy for them, but it was easier for them than it would be for the Africans who would follow. And Africans followed in abundance. Atlantic creoles were nowhere in great numbers, nor were they long in the majority among mainland slaves. At different times in different places, but certainly widespread by the time slavery began growing rapidly in a number of mainland regions after the early decades of the eighteenth century, "outlandish" Africans made up the overwhelming majority on the slave vessels arriving in South Carolina, Virginia, New York, or Louisiana. For them, nothing would be easy.

Africans went through considerable change in the process of becoming African Americans. Slaves just arriving after the grueling Atlantic crossing were stepping into completely new physical, social, and cultural settings. Tired, sore, probably sick and malnourished, and likely separated quickly from other Africans they had come to know on the voyage, they must have been bewildered and frightened of what was to come. And many were certainly angry. Over a short time they had been forcibly detached from the kinship networks that had been their social, economic, and psychological underpinnings in Africa. Never would they be more alone. Yet by 1770, most African Americans throughout the mainland colonies were living in families with extended ties of kinship in greater black communities, and they were practicing a culture of their own. The development of African-American families, communities, and a common culture took place during the first two-thirds of the eighteenth century in the English mainland colonies. These activities set the basis for black life in America from that time forward.

Slaves' early experiences were among the most difficult they faced once in America. Simply getting by in the harsh circumstances of their new surroundings was a tall order, and adaptation came slowly. In trying to cope and build new lives, the uprooted Africans tended to cling to their own cultural traditions and ways of doing things. These included a sense of personal identity; a language; a worldview that usually involved a religion; ideas of time and space, family life, and work; social customs; historical traditions; and a good bit of general know-how. Because slaves came from such a broad range of West and West Central Africa, as a group they brought with them a variety of languages, customs, and traditions. Individually, therefore, relatively few of them could simply join with others and practice group survival on the basis of a common heritage. Still, most Africans held in common enough ideas that they could mingle certain aspects of their respective cultures. For many this process seems to have begun soon after capture in Africa or aboard a ship. Once they arrived in the English colonies they continued this amalgamation even as they began applying "old ways" to new circumstances. This process of clinging to and adapting certain of their traditional customs while borrowing heavily from Anglo-American and Native-American ways would result, over time, in the development of a hybrid African-American culture.

But just how African was it? This is a question that has perplexed historians and anthropologists at least since E. Franklin Frazier expressed doubts about the persistence of African cultural elements in America in *The Negro Family in the United States* in 1939. Two years later Melville J. Herskovits countered by drawing attention to New World black culture's essentially African nature in *The Myth of the Negro Past*. The disagreement flared again in the 1990s when Sidney W. Mintz and Richard Price re-emphasized in *The Birth of African-American Culture: An Anthropological Perspective* (1992) a point they had made sixteen years earlier about the "randomizing" of African groups in the Americas, which led more easily to their creolization without the long survival of cultural manifestations of particular African groups. At the same time, John K. Thornton in *Africa and Africans in the Making of the Atlantic World, 1400–1800* (1992, 2nd ed., 1997), argued that across the tropical and subtropical Americas the Atlantic slave trade was not so random as widely thought, but instead brought persons of like ethnicity to particular New World regions, even to particular plantations in these regions, where they formed "a base from which many elements of African culture could be shared, continued, and developed in America." Agreeing with Thornton as the theory applies to mainland North America is Michael A. Gomez, who argues in *Exchanging Our Country Marks: The Transformation of African Identities in the Colonial and Antebellum South* (1998) that "[t]he development of African American society through 1830 was much the product of contributions made by specific ethnic groups," as well as Gwendolyn Midlo Hall, in *Slavery and African Ethnicities in the Americas: Restoring the Links* (2005).

These studies joined exchanges on the Internet and in print (see articles by Douglas B. Chambers and David Northrup in *Slavery and Abolition* between 2000 and 2002) questioning ethnic identification, then and now, and raising issues about determining Africanisms in American culture. Some argued that Africans did not identify themselves with large ethnic groupings the way

Europeans did. Given the nature of the evidence, it was the white slave traders and the men and women who owned slaves in the Americas who spoke of Africans in ethnic terms—a person was a "Bambara" or an "Ibo" in the eyes of the enslaver rather than the enslaved. And by what ethnic terms did seventeenth-century Virginia or Maryland planters identify those Atlantic hybrids like Antonio Gomez, who already were cultural products of more than a century of borrowing and mixing? Transmitting their ethnicity to the New World or uniting with others of some broad grouping in America to maintain their cultural ways was not necessarily the highest priority of most enslaved men and women from Africa. And although statistics show that slaves who ended up in certain parts of America might have come from particular regions of West or West Central Africa at certain times, there was a randomizing tendency in the Atlantic trade—the ports on both sides of the ocean were funnels, bringing together persons speaking different languages and holding different beliefs from broad hinterlands on the African side and dispersing them in reverse fashion from ports on the American side. The experience of enslavement, separation from kin, and movement over thousands of miles uprooted African men, women, and children from their ways of life, and forces in the Americas worked against survival of many particular (and purely) African traits. "Africans in Virginia found themselves purchased in tiny lots, dispersed onto widely scattered estates, resident on small plantations, soon surrounded by a majority of native-born slaves, and brought into close contact with whites," writes Philip D. Morgan in "The Cultural Implications of the Atlantic Slave Trade: African Regional Origins, American Destinations and New World Developments," in *Routes to Slavery*. "All of this was not conducive to the reconstitution of an African ethnic identity."

With this said, however, there is evidence that in some regions through certain times, particular African cultural groupings were dominant among a slave population. In the Virginia Piedmont in the middle decades of the eighteenth century, for example, because of extensive importation of "Calabar slaves" from the Bight of Biafra, the culture that developed among slaves in that region did so from what Douglas B. Chambers in *Murder at Monticello:*

Igbo Africans in Virginia (2005) identifies as "a diasporic Igbo base." African-American subcultures in other regions may have developed likewise from a basis of one or another African group. Chambers offers a schematic for "primary, secondary, and tertiary creolization" in seventeenth-century Virginia that, if limited spatially, is useful for considering the process. During the Atlantic crossing (primary), "enslaved people would have learned that they were Eboe, probably for the first time," he writes. Men and women of the following generation (secondary) tended to choose the more general term "Guinea" when identifying where they had come from, using it in names of people and places, whereas by late in the eighteenth century (tertiary) individuals seem to have identified themselves still more generally as Africans.

Of course, there was a broad African basis for the African-American culture that would exist by the end of the colonial period, but that result was a rich and complex hybrid, the product of a heterogeneous Atlantic world in which persons from four continents continually interacted and mixed. As with all thoughts of culture change and formation around the Atlantic rim in the seventeenth and eighteenth centuries—whether along the Gambia River in West Africa, inland from the Cape of Good Hope at Africa's southern tip, in the Atlantic hinterlands of northeastern Brazil, or on the islands of the Caribbean—when considering African-American culture, Morgan continues, "the emphasis should be on heterogeneity, on fluid boundaries, on precarious and permeable zones of interaction, on hybrid societies, on mosaics of borderlands where cultures jostled and converged in combinations and permutations of dizzying complexity." In the United States the combinations involved broad African and European cultural traits, along with those of the indigenous persons the Africans and Europeans lived among.

The complexity was so dizzying, in fact, that often the tendency has been to see only how Africans acculturated and adopted European ways. But another perspective is that of Sobel and Piersen, who focus on such less obvious cultural traits as ideas and ways of thinking. In this regard, Sobel does not ask "How 'African' was African-American culture?" but, instead, "How 'African' was the broader culture of colonial Virginia?" Her answer, after examining many commonly held notions of the time, is "more than we might think."

Demography, Community, and Culture

Not all newly arrived Africans experienced culture change in similar fashion or at the same time and pace. For individuals the rate of acculturation varied according to a combination of factors including their local circumstances, the strength of their particular African cultural tradition, and their personal willingness to change. For groups the process varied more widely because individual survival did not require formation of a group culture. However, a single, and simple, principle dominates consideration of the development of African-American culture in colonial America. It is that blacks in America first had to have extensive social contacts with a substantial number of other blacks—they had to exist in black communities—before there could be real development of group values, ways, and beliefs. The conduit for passing these manifestations of culture along to subsequent generations was the black family, in which adults could teach their children ways of doing things and values considered important for survival and good living.

For more than a century of black existence in the English mainland colonies, the obstacles to African-American community development and family formation were myriad. Simple demographic configurations—the number of blacks and the relative numbers of blacks and whites in specific locations—affected social relations. These numbers were determined largely by the nature of the economy and of the slave trade in any given region at any given time. In addition to sufficient numbers of African Americans within proximity, blacks required a certain amount of freedom to interact outside the supervision of whites.

Proximity to white colonists also affected African-American social and cultural development. Contrary to the traditional image of American slavery, in many places in colonial America blacks lived, worked, and interacted daily and fully with whites. This was true not only in New England, but as far south as urban Charleston or rural Virginia. In the latter colony, even the wealthiest masters spent hours each day with their slaves, directing, working, punishing, cajoling, teasing, arguing, relaxing, laughing, and worshiping. African slaves who had such close relationships with whites learned English and practiced Euro-American customs—all with an African cast—more quickly than those who did not. Those living and working with larger numbers of blacks and fewer whites in more isolated conditions—on Low Country plantations, for example, where blacks were in overwhelming majority—had more extensive social relations among themselves and better retained their African customs. For them, naturally, acculturation toward an Anglo-American "norm" was slower and less complete.

Demographic configurations between American slaves born in Africa (and hereafter referred to simply as Africans) and those of African descent born in the New World and partly acculturated (the true African Americans or American creoles) also were important factors in community development and cultural change. Where slave imports from Africa were heavy over several years and a good proportion of the black population comprised slaves born in Africa, the Africans tended to remain separate, keep more to themselves, and retain more of their African ways. Where the trade was light or involved a majority of Atlantic creoles or "seasoned" slaves from the Caribbean, there was more unity among the partly acculturated black population and less adherence to unadulterated African customs.

Demographics and the slave trade also played a role in the ability of black populations to grow by natural increase and maintain stable families. As long as the Atlantic trade was bringing large numbers of slaves every year to a particular region of the mainland, black men continued to outnumber black women there. Knowing they could more cheaply purchase and train a male adult laborer from Africa than rear one, owners in these regions often did little to encourage marriage, procreation, and family life among their slaves. They worked women as hard as they did men and allowed minimal time off for bearing or rearing children. In addition, slaves suffered in the new disease environment, and with replacements coming so cheaply, many owners cared little of the human beings they owned. So when the slave trade was heavy, slave mortality rates were high and birth rates low. Under such circumstances a slave society could not replace its numbers naturally. And for some time the slave trade continued to bring in twice as many men as women from across the Atlantic. With more black men than black women present and with interracial marriage illegal, it was impossible for most slaves to achieve a normal family life. Through the first half-century of mainland settlement, because of unequal sex ratios and high death rates, few males, black or white, were able to marry. When the slave trade from Africa declined, slave populations began increasing their numbers through natural means and sex ratios became more balanced. Only then could families provide the foundation of slave communities.

Different circumstances for living and working affected community development, too. Slaves living on isolated plantations that functioned as self-contained production units had less contact with Anglo-American culture than such persons on small farms growing provisions for local markets. Plantation slaves working under the task system had more control of their lives than those working in gangs under more watchful eyes, and this degree of autonomy enabled them to hold onto more of their African culture. Over time, in certain regions, plantation life grew settled and slaves enjoyed mobility among plantations. Once this happened, even those African-American communities centered on one plantation could broaden to include others in the vicinity.

Urban slaves generally enjoyed greater autonomy than their rural counterparts, but they also lived more closely with whites. Some were permitted to attain skills, live on their own, and hire their own time. In the urban atmosphere, where work requirements led to laxness in enforcing controls, black men and women mingled with white men and women at work and play. For them acculturation—or, actually, cultural borrowing, in both directions—took place regularly. James Sidbury in *Ploughshares into Swords: Race, Rebellion, and Identity in Gabriel's Virginia, 1730–1810* (1997) shows that in the rapidly growing, more open, urban Chesapeake settings—late-eighteenth-century Richmond is his example— black perceptions of individual and community identity involved not simply race and status in bondage, but gender, skill, religion, and current ideologies. The worlds of black and white, enslaved and free, women and men in the urban Chesapeake overlapped and grew snarled. In the welter of cross-cutting influences, personal and community identities grew remarkably complex.

And, finally, some groups of blacks found themselves in situations that offered them a unique existence that affected their acculturation. A group with as much autonomy as urban blacks, or perhaps more of it still, was that of African Americans working as boatmen and seamen. Not many did so through the first third of the eighteenth century, but from the 1740s on (through Revolutionary times and beyond) blacks, many of them slaves, worked the lighters and river craft that carried goods in the colonial economy and served on civilian and military ships at sea. Some of these individuals had an Atlantic creole heritage. Most of them were accustomed to the ways of whites but also conscious and proud of their own traditions, which they maintained and passed on to those around them.

Thus, as different levels of slave importation (from the West Indies and from Africa) and different systems of slavery developed at various times in the separate regions of the North American mainland, and as colonial American culture matured generally, variant forms of African-American culture grew and matured. And within the separate African-American cultures of each region, one could make obvious and subtle distinctions in different localities and at various times.

For the first seventy-five years of settlement in Virginia and Maryland, planters made such distinctions more on the basis of class than race. Chesapeake blacks, mostly Atlantic creoles, suffered the same hardships as white servants. Some of each group who lived long enough attained freedom and ownership of land. Blacks interacted with whites of their class in work, play, and sex. But a more open racial society did not last. The importation of large numbers of Africans after 1680 altered any rapid acculturation. By 1710 three-quarters of Chesapeake blacks were Africans, mostly men. The sexual imbalance made opportunities for black family life difficult and cut birth rates. Furthermore, Virginia planters often sent new arrivals to the piedmont frontier, where they lived isolated from the tidewater area and most creoles. The smaller number of creoles remained closer to their masters, working as domestic servants and skilled artisans, freer to travel and more comfortable in an Anglo-American culture. Thus, through the 1740s Virginia and Maryland had distinct African and creole slave societies.

But whatever potential there was in the Chesapeake for a long-term African-creole split did not last. Allan Kulikoff explains why in *Tobacco and Slaves: The Development of Southern Culture in the Chesapeake, 1680–1800* (1986). In response to the growing number of blacks, planters in the region forged a unity with lower-class whites. They lumped all blacks together, stifling creole opportunities. Then, beginning in the 1740s, the slave trade from Africa declined and a long period of black natural increase ensued. The population grew with a more balanced sex ratio and African-American creoles—blacks born in America—soon predominated. At the same time, planters brought more slaves together on larger plantations and turned over some areas to wheat production, giving African-American men and women seasonal variety in their work and opportunities to learn new skills and make broader social contacts. This, and the development of a network of roads and markets, enabled slaves from different plantations to interact. Eventually, black families with links going back through generations and reaching broader slave communities existed.

Thus, in some parts of the Chesapeake by the time of the American Revolution, there existed an African-American community with its own ways of life and the time and space to practice them. Race remained a primary determinant of the behaviors of the members of that community; most individuals still did not have great latitude in their personal actions. Many blacks lived near their masters and under the watchful eyes of the white majority. In language, formal religion, and family structure they were more like Anglo Americans than were most slaves to their south. However, by this time many African Americans had close, broad kinship relations, had incorporated many African ways into their religious practice, and enjoyed their own forms of music and dance, diet and dress, and work and play—all of which made their culture identifiable and distinct.

If the African-American population of the Chesapeake drew together and became increasingly acculturated through the middle of the eighteenth century, its counterpart in the Carolina and Georgia Low Country separated into distinct parts. For the first thirty years of coastal settlement, the mostly seasoned, imported slaves worked closely with their white owners and a seemingly mutual cultural exchange transpired. In early South Carolina this exchange may have been more reciprocal and symbiotic than any other in the English colonies.

But such a large-scale blending of cultures as took place in northeastern Brazil or on certain islands of the Caribbean was not long lived in the Low Country. The massive African imports that gave the Low Country its black majority after 1720 changed the direction of the evolution of African-American culture there. In Charleston a creole slave community emerged. These largely mulatto men and women lived close to whites and were more privileged and more thoroughly acculturated than their rural counterparts. In rural areas the slave trade was continually renewing a growing black community—not with Atlantic creoles or "seasoned" slaves of any sort, but with men and women straight from Africa. Individual segments of this group centered on the rice plantations; its members were independent and self-reliant. Working on the task system gave these slaves more time to socialize with fellow blacks, away from white authority. Their relative isolation and independence enabled them to hold onto more African speech patterns (thus developed a mixture of English and certain West-African languages that made up the distinctive form of English known as Gullah), religious practices, social customs, music and art forms, cuisine, and folk tales than could any other African Americans on the English mainland. By 1770 the two groups of Low-Country blacks, urban creoles and plantation slaves, lived a more separate and different existence than did many other groupings of whites and blacks in the Chesapeake.

A handful of books—those by Kimberly Hanger and Gwendolyn Hall, Thomas Ingersoll and Daniel Usner—collectively make the argument that it was in the Lower Mississippi, rather than the Chesapeake or Low Country, that the greatest cultural mingling took place over the longest time on the colonial North American mainland. Europeans had difficulty bringing order to the large region, and around the periphery of the narrow colonial control, whites, blacks, and Indians worked and played and fought with one another as they hunted, trapped, herded, and farmed in a frontier setting. Even where administrative controls were tighter, as in New Orleans, an openness existed that provided slaves greater opportunity than elsewhere and led, in Ingersoll's words, to an "interweaving of white and black lives" that produced "two communities, one creole society." It is not clear whether Indians played a greater role in the cultural mixing in the region than elsewhere, or whether French and Spanish keepers of records in the Lower Mississippi were simply more aware of the indigenous presence than were the English along the eastern seaboard. But in any event, powerful Indians and weak indigenous slaves; European soldiers and sailors, planters and peddlers; and African slaves and *libres*, traders, and maroons melded their farming, herding, and hunting techniques; shared their notions of how to build dwellings, cook foods, make music, and bring others harm; blended their ways of speaking into a regional patois; and to a considerable extent mixed their DNA. The result by the end of the colonial period was a creole culture shared by many that had an easily identifiable African element at its heart.

North of Maryland, a century of importing small numbers of mostly seasoned slaves brought about, by 1740, a stable society of African Americans largely attuned to Yankee ways. Unlike early black arrivals in other areas, northern slaves increased their numbers through natural procreation, lived in family groups, often slept and ate in the house of the master, and more than in any other region lived in a world dominated by white society. Those who worked on farms did not do so in gangs with other Africans and had considerable freedom of movement. Also, a far larger proportion of black men and women in the northern colonies lived and worked in urban areas, with all the freedoms that situation afforded.

However, between 1730 and 1770, increased importing of Africans reoriented northern blacks' tendencies away from a more

complete Anglo assimilation. Standing apart from northern creoles, the "raw" imports reacquainted African Americans with
aspects of their African heritage. As a result, communities of
northern blacks consciously incorporated African social customs
and practices—especially in ceremonies, folklore, singing, dancing, and leisure activities. The greater autonomy of northern blacks
enabled them to maintain, even readopt, certain African customs
while conforming more than any others to the white culture surrounding them. And their smaller numbers relative to the regional
population made it possible for them to do so without threatening
their owners or white society.

Does this mean that by the end of the colonial period blacks
on the North American mainland had a sense of being "African"?
For a few, at least, the answer is probably yes, to some degree.
James Sidbury demonstrates in *Becoming African in America:
Race and Nation in the Early Black Atlantic* (2007) how events
transpired over the second half of the eighteenth century to bring
some of the earliest African-American and African-British writers
to identify with others they considered "Africans." By the 1760s
and 1770s, as the number of native English-speaking creoles was
on the rise, more and more people began to question the morality
of human bondage, and the rare master was providing a talented
slave opportunity far beyond the norm, a tiny group of African
Americans found it possible to get their writing into print. Phillis
Wheatley, who lived in Boston, and Ignatius Sancho of London
became the first persons of African ancestry outside of Africa to
have their English-language poetry (Wheatley) and letters (Sancho) published. In different ways, they voiced in their writings the
earliest recognition of connection with other Africans.

An ironic element of this circumstance was that the authors
were tied to British intellectual currents and knew little about
West African societies and cultures. They accepted their identity
as "Africans" largely because that is how others thought of and
referred to them. Several writers, including the African-American
autobiographers Olaudah Equiano and James Albert Ukawsaw
Gronniosaw, followed Wheatley and Sancho in the literary tradition. Their "claims to a kind of 'blood' kinship and claims to a

sense of allegiance that rested on oppression originating in slavery and the modern diaspora," Sidbury writes, "became an animating force in the early black discourse on African identity." If Sidbury is correct, then it is not a stretch to extend the idea of pan-Africanism and a diasporic identity among Africans on all four continents bordering the Atlantic and push back its origins well before the emergence of such influential African-American writers of the nineteenth and twentieth centuries as Marcus Garvey and W. E. B. Du Bois. It was African Americans in the colonial era who hatched the notion and offered it up for subsequent generations to broaden and solidify.

Yet for most Africans and African Americans across the colonial period, identity remained flexible and fluid. Within each of the broad regions of colonial America's African-American society, variety existed in individual communities and in local customs and practices. Work routines, family practices, religious thought and modes of worship, circumstances of daily lives, personal interactions, and modes of resistance to bondage differed depending on a host of local circumstances. Examination of these manifestations of African-American culture provides a sense of the variety within a culture group that for most of the last century historians so easily lumped together and considered as static and virtually homogenous.

The Daily Toil

If one thing dominated the daily lives of African Americans in colonial America, it was work. English traders brought persons from Africa and colonial landowners and businesspeople purchased these men and women to constitute the colonial labor force, so work they must. It was the rare master who did not want to get as much labor from his slave as he or she possibly could. But Africans received none of the rewards of their labors, so they naturally lacked incentive to work. What had to result was a form of accommodation between master and slave that got neither exactly what he or she wanted, but turned out to be a livable situation.

Complicating accommodation was this: although colonial English master and African in bondage shared preindustrial concepts of time, relying on the sun's position, phases of the moon, crop cycles, and the seasons to measure time's passage, the two brought different ideas about the proper pace of work and the amount of daily or weekly toil one human being could expect another to perform. By the seventeenth century, English landowners and shopkeepers were becoming increasingly aware of the need to use time efficiently and make a strict accounting of time spent at work. They expected their servants to work from dawn to dusk with breaks only for meals. Before coming to America, upper-class English had difficulty getting what they considered a decent amount of labor out of their "lazy" workers, whose more popular, traditional, quasi-medieval notions of the length of a day's work and its pace differed considerably—and probably naturally—from those of their employers. West Africans' ideas of work were more like those of English servants than those of the gentry. And Africans' approaches to work were practical for the heat of the tropics, based on patience and slow movement, and purposely allowing time to relax and socialize. Where possible work was communal and involved singing and talking. It also involved resting. In many West-African societies, women did the heavy agricultural labor and worked more steadily than men throughout the year. While men did some such field work, they protected their villages and served in positions that required them to manage family and village affairs. A general and widely accepted goal for African men—especially for those of the higher classes—was not having to do great amounts of physical toil. It is not surprising, then, that English planters agreed generally with Virginia slave owner Landon Carter's assessment of it being "almost impossible to make a negro do his work well. No orders can engage it, no encouragement persuade it, nor no Punishment oblige it."

As it turned out, the appropriate amount of work for an enslaved man or woman varied with the situation and was subject to almost constant, if often tacit, negotiation. White slave owners went to great lengths to exact work from their bondspeople, who normally entered the workforce between the ages of eight and ten (though some did so earlier) and exited it with death. Instructions to overseers were explicit on how to do so: it required vigilance and punishment. (In the 1750s, the same Landon Carter records ordering his slaves "Correction" over "three days running" for not threshing oats as thoroughly as he judged proper, and notes casually after that: "They have been severely whipd day by day.") But sometimes overseers could push too hard, and when they did slaves had chips for the bargaining. Too much coercion often resulted in sick workers, broken tools, and purposely sloppy (thus costly) work. Sometimes the consequences were more serious. The *South-Carolina Gazette* reported on October 14, 1732, that after rice planter James Gray "work'd his Negroes late in his Barn at Night" and "next Morning before Day, hurried them out again," he found the barn containing his harvested rice "burnt down to the Ground."

Compromises over work took into account the varying, and seasonally determined, labor requirements of the regional staple. Some crops simply required longer and harder work than others and had different "down times." Masters and slaves came to know and live by these crop cycles, the former altering their work requirements and the latter the amount of work they would do accordingly.

"Rice was a roller coaster," writes Morgan in *Slave Counterpoint*, "tobacco a slow-moving train." By all accounts, rice was the staple grown on the English mainland that required the hardest work in the unhealthiest settings. (While sugar cane truly holds that dubious distinction, only in a few, isolated spots did black slaves grow sugar on the North American mainland during the colonial period.) The rice cycle had peaks of intense work and valleys of less-strenuous toil, however. Continual weeding with heavy hoes in the hottest and most humid summer months made June, July, and August the months during which most slaves chose to run away in the rice-growing regions. Late summer and fall brought a respite as women and men cut, dried, stacked, and threshed the grain, only to be followed by the most exacting work of all: pounding the rice in tall mortars to remove husk and film. From mid-November to mid-January and beyond, writes Edward Ball of his ancestors' South Carolina rice plantations, "a constant sound of *thrup, thrup, thrup* came from the rice barns." The *thrup-thrupping* might have been a soothing sound to the folks in the master's house, but it must have been a harrowing one to anyone who had ever been forced to do the physically exhausting pounding. According to one observer in 1760, the mortar-and-pestle work "costs every planter the lives of several slaves annually." Slaves then separated rice grains from the hulls with winnowing baskets or fans and bagged or barreled the rice for shipping. Over the latter half of the eighteenth century, such mechanical inventions as horse- and water-powered pounding mills, and such technological innovations as using tidal flows to irrigate rice, alleviated the worst of the pounding and hoeing, making the lot of Low Country slaves somewhat easier.

Tobacco had a shorter annual cycle than rice and required less heavy work at given times, but the work on tobacco was steadier, lacking the peaks and valleys of rice growing. Tobacco is "a very tender plant," in the words of one eighteenth-century Virginian, and its workers had to pamper it with regular attention, even if the individual tasks—transplanting, debugging, "topping," "suckering," curing, and packing—were not so arduous. Further, tobacco growing lent itself to plowing and the use of carts for hauling. All of this meant, in Morgan's comparison of slaves in the Chesapeake and Low Country, that the former "were more favored" in their basic working conditions.

Other crops required generally less work. Indigo had a shorter growing season than either rice or tobacco, but it required nearly constant attention between April and August, hoeing and removing insects from the plants. Then indigo had to be processed hastily in the fall, before the first frost, with fairly constant stirring and beating as it fermented in vats—the stench of the fermenting plant matter attracting flies. Wheat growing, which expanded greatly in the Chesapeake in the late colonial period, required less labor than the other staples, two weeks at harvest being the most intense work involved.

Of course, none of this should suggest that the cultivation and processing of any given crop was all that slaves did during any given season. A list of the myriad tasks that enslaved black men and women had to perform during the colonial period, regardless of staple grown or time of year, would fill pages. Fields needed clearing. Fences, ditches, roads, and buildings needed maintaining. Food crops needed to be grown—often at the same time on the agricultural calendar when the most intensive work was required on the export staples—and cattle needed tending. But through it all, a day's work was longer and harder at peak times, and those peak times did vary. If owners accepted "sunup-to-sundown" as the normal work routine in principle, the rigor of its application varied with the crop cycle.

The differences in crop requirements and growing techniques led masters and slaves to work out different ways to organize the slaves' labor. Basically, African-American men and women worked at specific, individual tasks on Low Country rice plantations and in supervised gangs nearly everywhere else—even when producing indigo next to the rice fields in the Low Country. Slaves almost certainly did not garner the benefits of the task system in return for teaching the early English planters how to cultivate rice, as some have suggested. Instead, the system grew into local custom between 1720 and 1740, most likely out of the inclination of the first generation of Low Country masters to allow their captive laborers the autonomy to provide for their own sustenance. As rice production grew over the first decades of the eighteenth century, masters set out tasks for their slaves to make sure the laborers were allowed time—minimal though it was—to produce their own food. By the time masters realized that providing their slaves rations lent stability to the plantation operation, tasking had become a custom and, more than with any other crop, rice production lent itself to the task system: men and women working in rice did not need constant supervision and their duties were easy to measure. Individuals were given specific daily or weekly tasks to complete, and once they had done so, their time was their own. Failure to accomplish one's tasks would be grounds for a beating. Of course, there was constant negotiation of a sort over what were deemed reasonable tasks for a day's or a week's work, but by late in the colonial period most accepted common standards—a quarter acre of rice weeded (extended to a half acre once planters began using the tidal method of growing) or seven mortars full of rice pounded daily. Once they accomplished their task, slaves were free to hunt or fish or rest. Many used such time to work in their own gardens, growing corn, pumpkins, potatoes, or melons for their own consumption or sale. Masters were happy to turn over land for such use. It was cheap incentive and, along with fish and game, the vegetables added to the slaves' diet.

Tobacco was such a touchy crop, needing constant, careful attention to produce the high-quality leaves packed for export, that it lent itself to gangs of workers under close supervision. Once employed in the Virginia and Maryland tobacco fields, the supervised-gang system spread much more widely. Gang laboring was more of a sunup-to-sundown system and held little incentive for individuals to work quickly. Thus, it is more Chesapeake tobacco planters than South Carolina rice growers who complained of their slaves' penchant for inactivity. If ganged slaves worked less briskly than did tasked slaves, persons working in gangs had less free time and its attendant benefits—like much smaller garden plots for themselves. Often, it was only on Sundays when Chesapeake slaves had time to grow things on their own or to hunt, fish, or play.

Slaves seem to have worked more steadily on small farms, where they toiled alongside the master. On large plantations where overseers were involved, slaves became adept at manipulating the rate at which they completed their work. If allowed to work at their own pace they appeared satisfied, but they troubled overseers who drove them hard and complained to their masters of misuse.

But no matter where they lived, a good bit of the Africans' inherent sense of time and pace persisted. No less famous a Virginia planter than George Washington knew of the dangers to plantation efficiency and production of allowing blacks to set the pace and ways of work. He instructed a new manager to be wary of

an error which I have felt no small inconvenience from; and that is, that rather than persevere in doing things right themselves, and being at the trouble of making others do the like, they will fall into the slovenly mode of executing work which is practiced by those, among whom they are. I have experienced this not only from European tradesmen, but from farmers also, who have come from England and none in a greater degree than Mr. Whiting, and one Bloxham, who preceded him; and who, tho' perfectly acquainted with every part of a farmer's business; and peculiarly so . . . in the management and use of Oxen for the Cart . . . , finding it a little troublesome to instruct the Negros and to compel them to practice of his modes, he slided into theirs. . . ."

It was rare when slaves did not get evenings and Sundays to themselves. On this day they could practice their religion, rest, tend their garden plots, and go visiting. Holidays worked into the compromise, too. The biggest holiday that blacks and whites celebrated together was "Harvest Home." Traditionally both West Africans and English always had their biggest feasts once the crops were in, and the two peoples had coinciding celebrations that involved eating, drinking, and merriment.

A common misconception is that rural slave women, in serving as house servants, had an easier time of it than their male counterparts. The opposite is closer to the truth. Many West African men and women came to the New World with entrenched ideas about women's place: it was in constant, fairly heavy labor. And African Americans seem to have joined masters in perpetuating this idea in the colonial world of work. In the plantation colonies nearly all black women worked in the fields, plowing, hoeing, and harvesting. "A good Negro woman has the same day's work as the man in the planting and cultivating of the fields," wrote Johann Martin Bolzius in 1751 from a settlement on the Savannah River in Georgia. "The men fell the trees, and the women cut the bushes and carry them together." By the time Bolzius was writing this, perhaps one slave woman in twenty from Maryland to South Carolina was strictly a house servant. The proportion was greater on larger plantations and practically nil on small farms. As more enslaved men gained opportunity to perform skilled work away from the fields, enslaved women filled in the difference.

As one might suppose, a slave woman's productive functions regularly took precedence over her reproductive ones. Pregnancy did not significantly remove a woman from her tasks in the fields and thus made the condition especially difficult to endure. A study from Antebellum plantations shows pregnant women, as late as between one and four weeks prior to giving birth, picking three-quarters the amount of cotton picked by nonpregnant women, and studies from colonial times tend to bear out the same pattern.

For that matter, colonial slave women bore children under extremely difficult circumstances. Many black midwives coated the umbilical stump with mud, a practice sometimes transmitting

tetanus, and stood the woman erect and shook her violently immediately after giving birth to deliver the placenta. It is not surprising
that the death of the mother in childbirth was common. Women
cooked for their families (in an age, lest we forget, when "cooking" meals included building fires after hauling wood to do so, in
addition to hauling in water, and took considerable time and effort
in preparation with rudimentary utensils) and cared for the young.
Not surprisingly, few slaves made it to what today we would consider "old age," but those women who did so earned no respite.
Elderly male slaves might "retire" to the homestead when their
field-working days were over, but old slave women more often simply got moved to domestic work, child caring, weaving, spinning,
or dairying, to free younger women for work in the fields.

Many similarities existed among the regions in the evolution
of the black workforce and in the tasks that slaves performed. With
the exception of Africans who brought with them such usable skills
as rice-growing, livestock-tending, weaving, or fishing and boat-
ing, unseasoned Africans knew the least about their labors. Masters had to teach them to perform simple tasks and then keep close
watch on them. Creoles were more aware of how to perform jobs
and they knew more about the harsh treatment that awaited those
who resisted. Masters gave creoles more autonomy and sometimes
more authority over their work, so that physically and emotionally
their working lives were better than were those of most Africans.

Slaves practiced skilled trades at different times throughout
the colonies, but two generalizations apply to consideration of
black Americans and skilled work. One is that opportunities for
nonfield labor expanded steadily throughout the eighteenth century as mainland economies matured and required a greater diversity of goods and services. The other is that work outside the field,
skilled or not, was not available equally: men had the only real
shot at practicing the growing range of skilled tasks; women had
only domestic work to remove them from the fields. Thus agricultural work became even more the work of women as slavery grew
in America. In that regard, and ironically, slavery from the Chesapeake southward took on an African cast, since women dominated
crop production in many West African societies.

Slave men on small farms or urban areas in the North always did a variety of tasks; some were the original jacks-of-all-trades. The more diversified economies of northern colonies or urban areas required a broader range of skills, and whites in these places often felt less threatened if the African Americans among them performed skilled work. Lists of skilled roles slaves played are long and range from barber, blacksmith, and bookbinder to watch-maker, weaver, and whitesmith. Around the docks and boatyards of northern port cities, shipbuilders, ship chandlers, merchants, bakers, brewers, and tavern keepers needed workers with a variety of skills and found them in enslaved African Americans.

Farther south, because plantation size was related to the division of tasks, opportunities for skilled slaves existed earlier, and on a greater scale, in the Low Country than in the Chesapeake. In 1733, when one of every six Low Country male slaves worked at something other than crop production, nine of every ten slave men and probably all slave women in one Maryland county were field hands. Eventually, as larger proportions of the slave populations became native born and as the growing plantations demanded craftsmen of all sorts, black men began practicing a wide range of skilled work. Even in the Virginia tidewater, but especially on the Low Country rice and indigo plantations, by the middle of the eighteenth century large plantations were becoming self-contained production units with slaves doing the necessary artisanal work as well as producing the crop. In 1768 James Grant of South Carolina could write, "In established Plantations, the Planter has Tradesmen of all kinds in his Gang of Slaves, and 'tis a Rule with them, never to pay Money for what can be made upon their Estates, not a Lock, a Hing, or a Nail if they can avoid it." Woodworking was the first and most widely held plantation skill. In addition to the need for dwellings, there were barrels and hogsheads to be made, cart bodies to be constructed, and boats to be fashioned. Blacksmithing, butchering, leatherworking, and sewing eventually became skills essential to most farms and plantations, and over time slaves on the larger units began weaving, cobbling, making and laying bricks, and distilling. Some of the products of these skills—pots and baskets made on Low Country plantations, for instance—evinced

African styles and motifs. By the time of the American Revolution, African Americans were performing some or all of the above types of skilled labor in all of the English colonies.

The rise of urban areas brought increased opportunities for more diversified slave craftsmen—even for craftswomen. In Charleston slaves dominated stalls in the public markets. A particular group of skills, those related to the water, was one that many Atlantic West Africans brought with them to the mainland and used all along the coastal settlements from the earliest times. In New England blacks worked as sailors, while Carolina plantations had "fishing Negroes," and throughout the southern lowlands African Americans manning skiffs and lighters were the heart of a transportation system that carried plantation goods to market, brought imported wares back from ports, and ferried whites across the maze of coastal waterways and landings.

It was as houseservants that male and female slaves served in nearly equal numbers, though still largely without equal status. African-American men around the house—manservants and grooms—had the greater chance of gaining whites' attention and appreciation. Women did the routine, and less-noticed, household work, including cooking, cleaning, dairying, marketing, and repairing clothing. Late in the eighteenth century, partly out of necessity caused by the cutoff of imports during the Revolution, slave women began doing much more carding, spinning, and weaving of "homespun" cloth. Yet, most planters continued to believe that women were best employed in crop production, so that even as specialization rose toward the end of the eighteenth century, no more than 5 percent of slave women served in and around the house. Throughout the colonial period, the African-American woman's place was in the field.

As the eighteenth century wore on and the colonial economy grew, slaves played increasingly diversified roles in it. W. Jeffrey Bolster in *Black Jacks* shows how growing numbers of blacks took to the sea after 1740, some skippering small coasting vessels, some serving as cooks or stewards, and more hoisting and trimming the sails of Atlantic vessels as common jack tars. These men met racial discrimination and difficult working conditions on the one hand, but found much greater possibilities for freedom and, at least for a time, enhanced their status in the black community on the other. African Americans in general also assumed more tasks as colonial industries grew. In New England, blacks worked in shipbuilding and such related industries as rope and sail making. They were involved in much of the building construction in towns or rural areas. They also mined coal and iron and worked many of the iron forges and furnaces in the colonies. By the 1770s slaves were performing most of the skilled and manual labor in Chesapeake iron industries. Larger than most tobacco farms, these industries employed 1 percent of all adult slaves (women as well as men) in the Chesapeake. If the ironworks were representative, industrial slaves were the most privileged black laborers in the colonial period. They worked five-day weeks on average, were paid for work they did on the other two days, had access to goods in company stores, and had more freedom of movement than typical persons in bondage.

By the eve of the nineteenth century, slaves simply did a lot more. Where there was work to do, unskilled or skilled, simple or complex, requiring a few minutes or half a year, slaves did it. There was such a variety of slave work that it defies easy generalization. Any individual, any group, any civic body in any British mainland colony that had work to accomplish could purchase slaves to perform it. The military was intricately involved with slave labor. Ranking officers normally had slave valets; the artillery department in Charleston owned forty-two slave women and their children in 1782, using them to cook and wash for the troops and to tend to horses; and British troops occupying Philadelphia during the Revolution had a "Company of Black Pioneers," a group of fifteen slave women made to "assist in Cleaning the Streets and Removing all Newsiances being thrown into the Streets."

As everywhere, technology was a factor in the working lives of slaves. Early technology in most places was simple and seemed to be of mixed English and African origin. English had ways of doing agricultural work they thought best, but so did Africans. It was difficult for masters and overseers to dictate the kinds of tools the workforce used, and for a long time they did not do so. Africans devised tools for rice production based on their experience, and they clung, sometimes proudly and tenaciously, to their ways of threshing with hooped poles instead of "proper flails" until overseers stopped trying to coerce them out of it. African workers had "perseverance" and "Greatness of Soul," overseers noted, referring to their adherence to their own farming methods. Slaves on some Chesapeake lands did not use carts and plows, as English farmers had done for centuries, until after 1750. Once carts and plows became commonplace, though, slaves were better able still to regulate the pace of work, working slowly for periods and then catching up quickly through use of the new implements.

Still, no matter how or how much slaves were able to manipulate the pace of work in their favor, no matter how good the enslaved black men and women became at their work, no matter what personal skills he or she acquired, the crux of slavery was that the fruits of the labor belonged to the master. If a slave reached a level of proficiency in a skill in great demand, or if field labor came to be in oversupply, as it did on some plantations after 1750, the master might "hire out" a slave to another party to provide additional income. Hiring out was especially prevalent in northern colonies or in grain-producing areas where landowners had seasonal labor requirements and could not afford to keep large numbers of slaves yearlong. In some areas, masters hired out women slaves more frequently than men. After the 1750s in the Chesapeake, a small but growing number of slave artisans hired their own time—that is, they were allowed to live by and fend for themselves, finding their own work and paying their masters a weekly or monthly amount from the wages they earned. Blacks normally received lower wages than whites for the same work, but it seems clear they liked hiring out their own time. In doing so they worked and mingled with a wider range of people, and they appreciated the relative freedom the situation afforded them.

Although masters controlled slaves and held almost boundless legal authority to exact labor from them, no statutes or pressures could bring humans to perform endless toil. What developed were patterns of labor that did not fully satisfy either master or slave, but evolved, through fairly constant negotiation, to accommodate both. If the African-American men, women, and children had to work, the master alone could not define the quantity and quality of that labor. Colonial America was largely a black world of work, so African Americans had something to say about the setting of the standards in that world.

Family

African-American culture hardly could perpetuate itself in identifiable form in colonial America until black families came into existence. The family was the place where community began. It was also the unit for educating and socializing the young. If adults were to create and adhere to common values and customs, it was the family that transferred these to subsequent generations.

Of course, it was not in America that the family first became central to blacks' existence. In West Africa kinship was the basis for all social organization. The extended family on the village level and kinship links across wider areas gave Africans their individual and collective identities. These institutions united people separated by space and provided material and psychological support essential for daily living. Loss of the kinship network was probably the most disruptive force in the Africans' enslavement and movement from the homelands. It follows, then, that for Africans, recreating the family in America was especially important.

Yet, African-American families were destined to be different from the families that had been such a key part of the men and women's lives in Africa. West-African families tended to follow single lines of descent, through males or females, but not both. This enabled brothers and half-brothers, sisters and half-sisters, aunts, uncles, and more distant relatives—all who shared a common ancestor—to identify with an enormous group of kin. Marriage united two such kin networks in relationships of obligation and responsibility, so Africans arranged marriages carefully and bound them with family pressures and payments of bridewealth. Thus across West Africa, bridging whatever linguistic or ethnic divides that may have existed, was a grid of related kin groups that held society together much more tightly than political authority or national loyalty. Even if slaves in colonial America could have practiced African-style unilineal kinship, it would have taken generations, and complete freedom in marriage and residence, to do so. In the end it was impossible.

Not that Africans did not try. Even on slave ships they began seeking relatives. Children called friendly adults "uncle" or "aunt," and men and women tended to look after younger children whether or not they were related. Where slaves existed in some numbers on the English mainland there developed a broad pattern of slave children addressing all older slaves with kinship titles and regarding them as the equivalent of relatives. Younger slaves respected their elders in the African fashion. And those children who developed bonds to fictive kin had a broader community of support and were better able to cope following the death or sale of their parents or other blood relatives.

Eventually, however, not fictive kin but real family relationships provided the foundation for the African-American community. Although regional differences in the process, as well as progress and retreat, were considerable, it was during the eighteenth century that the black family came into existence and matured in English mainland North America. Once demographic circumstances—sufficient numbers of blacks in roughly equal proportions of men and women—made black families possible, what emerged was an English-style nuclear family with monogamous marital relationships that traced descent through both parents. This occurred earliest in the Chesapeake and then later—after midcentury—in the Low Country and Lower Mississippi. In each region, for the nuclear family to prevail, black Americans had to overcome considerable obstacles, the greatest of which was the regular movement of slaves at the hands of their owners and thus the separation of married adults from one another and parents from children. Kulikoff describes a continuing process of slave household and family development and redevelopment in eighteenth-century Virginia and Maryland, variants of which were probably typical of other areas:

A young [white] man tended to receive slaves from his parents or purchase them on the open market, thereby separating [slave] family members. If economic disaster did not intervene, his slaveholdings grew through natural increase, slave families were reestablished, and extended family networks developed. When the master died, the family's slaves were divided among heirs, and the process began again. Only during the second stage [of family building in a new location] were slave families even relatively secure. At the same time, as generation followed generation, households, or adjacent huts, became increasingly complex and sometimes included grandparents, uncles, aunts, or cousins as well as the immediate family. Since other kin lived on nearby plantations, geographically dispersed kinship networks that connected numbers of quarters emerged during the pre-Revolutionary era.

But because of the obstacles to smooth family development for blacks, and because of remnants of African family patterns, black families in America only partially resembled the nuclear families of English colonists. It was common, for instance, for African-American families in the Chesapeake to live apart. Men often lived in separate households—out of necessity in areas of small black population or few concentrations of slaves on the same plantations. In Virginia there even was a term for this sort of arrangement, "marrying abroad," which meant marrying someone off the home farm or plantation. In these cases, women frequently played the most important role in child rearing. Men tended to be older than their wives and to be domineering in marital relationships, a possible throwback to African customs that fit well in colonial America. Some blacks did not have attitudes toward sex and monogamy in accord with the wishes, if not the actions, of their Christian masters. Premarital sex in limited practice was the norm in some West-African societies, and so were freer sexual connections in polygynous marriages. Some African Americans seem to have clung to African sexual customs in their largely monogamous relationships, often to the consternation of their masters, white church officials, and others who believed promiscuity a flawed part of the black's natural makeup.

Few masters thought it necessary to bother with legality in slave marriages, but many of the African-American men and women involved regarded the ceremonies as important and binding. Marriage rites varied and seemed to mean as much as the couples desired. Christian marriages occasionally took place for blacks, especially in New England, but common-law marriages, called "Negro marriages," were the norm. Farther south, slaves conducted their own wedding ceremonies, often at night, sometimes with good-sized crowds in attendance and much merriment. Though there is no evidence of it having taken place anywhere in colonial America, the practice of "jumping the broomstick," thought of as a popular, symbolic way of uniting slaves in marriage in the nineteenth century, may have had its roots in unrecorded practices much earlier.

Better than anyone else at the time or since, slaves knew how tenuous was their family security. Such seemingly unrelated matters as the death of a master or an economic downturn could mean sale of loved ones and separation from them. As the master-slave relationship moved in the direction of paternalism over the course of the eighteenth century, more masters professed greater concern for slave families and reluctance to separate family members through sale. But evidence shows that neither the professed concern for the mother-father-child relationship nor plaintive appeals from those involved mattered when the breakup of a family was deemed "plantation necessity," or even when it merely promised greater profits. Masters sometimes would regard the African-American mother and her young children as a unit, separating them from their husband and father with little concern, but at other times a callous, even casual attitude about separating mothers and children existed. Contemporary newspapers carried such advertisements of slaves for sale as, "likely Negro wench, about 22 years old and a child about four years old . . ."; "likely Negro wench with a likely male child, ten months old . . ."; or "A Negro woman age about 24 years, and her child, a girl about five years." The *Boston News Letter* of May 1, 1732, listed for sale a nineteen-year-old African-American woman and her infant son, to be sold "together or apart." Masters were known to ponder what to do with the "future increase" of women they owned.

Yet in spite of the difficulties they faced, it is inaccurate to describe slave marriages or slave families as "unstable" with the implication that contemporary white marriages and families were necessarily more "stable." Granted, not as many black husbands as white husbands lived with their wives and children, especially on small farms, and black families were always liable to forced separation, a master's sexual incursions, and more, but the older and more established colonial African-American society became, the more black husbands lived with their families. However, the circumstance alone of a man, black or white, residing with his wife and children did not mean necessarily that he cared greatly for any of his coresidents, nor did cohabitation automatically make for a "stable" or "secure" family. It is also not fair to assume that a man living apart was one who cared little for his family or failed to nurture a loving group. White husbands of the time were not ones to involve themselves in child rearing. Many white men who resided "at home" spent hours or days away from it. William Byrd of Westover, Virginia, spent more waking time with those he called "his people," his black workforce, than with his white family. Conversely, some black husbands who lived in quarters removed from their families found ways to visit at nights and on Sundays and holidays, giving them, perhaps, as much intimate contact as some whites who resided with their families. In addition, some African-American women seem to have had especially close ties with their children that were rewarding for both. One should not suppose that white women did not have such close ties, but tendencies of upper-class whites to hire nurses and nannies for their young children imply that some white women did not experience as close and fulfilling relationships with their children as did some black women—the specter of forced separation notwithstanding.

Ties between black marriage partners, parents and children, brothers and sisters, and even distant kin a generation or more apart tended to be strong. The best evidence is in advertisements for runaway slaves. One-third of the slaves mentioned in 589 Virginia advertisements before 1775 ran off to rejoin members of their families who lived in the vicinity, and the proportion of Maryland slaves who stole away for the same reason between 1745 and 1779 may have been higher still. "His parents are free and live in Port-Royal," read one Virginia advertisement; "he is about Mr. Samuel Thomae's in Warwick County, where he has a father and grandmother," read another; and a third read, "supposed to be harboured by Colonel John Snelson's Negroes . . . among whom he has a wife, or by his Brother, John Kenny, a Mulatto Slave belonging to Mr. Thomas Johnson of Louisa." According to Gerald W. Mullin in *Flight and Rebellion: Slave Resistance in Eighteenth-Century Virginia* (1972), "owners' understatements [in advertisements] indicate a depth to slave family life—and the whites' tacit recognition of that life—that up till now has not been dealt with in interpretations of American Negro slavery."

Religion

Religion was the heart of African-American culture in colonial America, but through much of the period the form of religion most blacks practiced was minimally Christian. African slaves came to the New World with strong religious and spiritual beliefs and thoughts of the afterlife. In the American colonies they encountered masters and Christian ministers, Puritans and Anglicans, Methodists and Baptists, Quakers and Moravians, some of whom were intent (in varying degrees, at different times, and often where they perceived it useful to their own ends or to white society) on turning slaves into Christians. But religious belief is personal, often developed individually, and the private world of religion was a sanctuary to which slaves could turn during the periods of anxiety and stress that were such a large part of their lives. Religions that could not accommodate their preferred cosmologies and customs, based in part on their African heritage, were of little interest. Thus, slaves kept their distance from Christianity for much of the colonial period, and when they did take more notice of it, they did so by blending Christian tenets into African religious practices and beliefs. But regardless of the form it took, religion was a source of individual strength and collective security for African Americans as their culture matured.

African religions were not at all alike, but West and West-Central Africans held some patterns of belief in common. It is probably important to note that in some manifestations of this belief—spirits, magic, taboos, and use of amulets, for example—Africans shared ideas with common English people of their day. The living bodies of many Africans held their spirits, which, upon death, returned to a greater spiritual world where they joined those of their ancestors. They believed spirits were also about in inanimate objects—trees, rocks, hills, rivers—and that these forces controlled much of the workings of their everyday world. The spirits of ancestors also intervened in the world of the living. Acts of placation, magic, and taboos were important in controlling spirits. So workers of magic, diviners, and healers were manipulators of spirits, often through the manufacturing of amulets and charms, and as such were powerful people in the African world. Beyond this, many West Africans had a sense of there being one or more hegemonic deities involved with creation and events of the world beyond the local realm. These powers, naturally, were less personal, less intimate, and more difficult to manipulate. It was to these sorts of religious beliefs and practices that Africans and African Americans clung through the first half of the eighteenth century and beyond.

In the New World, blacks received Christian teaching in more or less strenuous doses at different times and in various locales. Some owners opposed attempts to make slaves Christians, masking fear of loss of control of their property with arguments of insufficient black intellect for an appreciation of religion or the inappropriateness of the doctrine. But following the lead of New Englanders like Puritan divine Cotton Mather, who expressed a desire to prepare "A Catechism" for "Negroes in this World. . . towards their welfare in the World to Come," some whites came to believe that slavery was part of God's plan for bringing "heathens" out of Africa and giving them "knowledge of the True God." In this spirit, Protestant evangelicals began filtering through colonial America after the first quarter of the eighteenth century, attempting to instruct slaves in the "proper faith." To slave owners amenable to such activity, this was a selection of Christian teachings that stressed meekness, humility, obedience, discipline, and, indeed, work. Brotherhood of man and the escape of the Hebrews from bondage were noticeably absent from the Gospel according to the master.

An ironic but instructive axiom about slave conversion is that, generally speaking, the more closely blacks worshipped with whites, the less they wanted to become Christians. Those who did worship with whites and still converted, however, practiced a form of Christianity that paralleled closely that of their Anglo-American fellow Christians. The opposite was also true. Where there was greater distance between master and slave in religious practice, blacks were more eager to become Christian, but their Christianity was different, much more a blending of African and European religious practices and beliefs.

In New England, for example, where social interaction was greatest and Christian proselytizing strongest, the majority of African Americans remained outside the white church. Only 3 percent of Newport, Rhode Island, blacks were Christians in good standing in 1775, and only a quarter of them attended church at all. This was so because, in spite of proselytical intentions that seemed noble, New England whites segregated blacks in church and in worship treated them as second-class Christians. Requirements for the baptism of a black person were especially rigorous. They included demonstrable theological knowledge on the part of the would-be convert as well as "a Christian demeanor." Sermons to African-American congregations justified the proper relationship between master and servant. Most important, slave owners refused to allow their bondspeople to worship by themselves for fear of "mongrelization" of Christian practices, meaning the infusion of African-based religious practices they thought bound to occur. The failure to make good Christians of more than a tiny minority of African Americans "was not so much that Yankee masters did not tell their servants about Christianity," observes William D. Piersen in *Black Yankees: The Development of an Afro-American Sub-culture in Eighteenth-Century New England* (1988), "but that the Christianity they offered was self-serving and neither emotionally nor intellectually satisfying to most Africans and Afro-Americans." Moreover, adds John Wood Sweet in *Bodies Politic:*

Negotiating Race in the American North, 1730–1830 (2003), "the closer Indians and blacks came to converting and becoming civilized, the more adamant settlers grew about drawing new lines of exclusion." Those African Americans who did not convert continued to practice their own folk religion or a blending thereof.

The situation was not significantly different in the Middle Colonies. The Society for the Propagation of the Gospel in Foreign Parts had been busy working to bring Anglican Christianity to blacks in the region since 1701, and in southern New York the society baptized on average some twenty African Americans per year into Revolutionary times. But as the century progressed, blacks followed their New England counterparts in keeping to themselves in religious matters, and they began to manifest a renewed respect for traditional African ways. A Philadelphia minister complained that the city's blacks "gathered on Sundays and holidays and were seen dancing after the manner of their several nations in Africa, and speaking and singing in their native dialects." African Americans continued to congregate for funerals at their own, separate burial grounds and prepare the dead for eternity in ways that reflected African customs.

Farther south, African Americans learned of Christianity most frequently from their fellow slaves, but also from their masters, evangelical missionaries, and regular clergy. Worship often was with lower-class whites. An important difference from their northern counterparts was that southern whites either allowed their slaves more freedom to worship alone in ways they chose, or, as in the Chesapeake, accepted enough African religious practice themselves, if unwittingly, to help form a blend of Christian worship satisfactory to both. In Maryland and Virginia especially, the middle decades of the eighteenth century was a special time for slave conversions and the blending of African and English modes of worship. Although historians debate the scope and reach of the so-called Great Awakening, a series of revivals that perhaps was neither so widespread geographically nor concentrated chronologically as some have argued, an element of religious fervor does seem to have spread, to a greater or lesser extent, through the lands of southern slaveholders. During this mid-century period poor blacks and whites, inspired by the inclusive public preaching of Evangelicals, joined in worship and song as members of crowds at revivals and in small prayer houses throughout rural Virginia. Together they "proclaimed" and "witnessed" and had emotional religious experiences. A burst of African-American conversion occurred around the Chesapeake between 1785 and 1790. Still, the increasing black acceptance of Christian doctrine did not result in rising church membership among slaves. By the last decade of the eighteenth century not one in twenty blacks was a member of the Methodist or Baptist church, the two denominations with the largest African-American membership. In the Low Country, the number of black church members was smaller still. Only in towns did evangelicals have any real success among blacks. But wherever southern slaves became Christians, they practiced a blended religion like the African-American folk variety extant in New England.

One religious blend of special note was the Afro-Catholicism practiced in New Orleans. West African women in the 1730s and 1740s, write Emily Clark and Virginia Mecham Gould ("The Feminine Face of Afro-Catholicism in New Orleans, 1727–1852," *William and Mary Quarterly,* 3rd series, 59 (2002), 409–48), "perhaps predisposed by their particular religious and social traditions and responding to a unique female ministry in colonial New Orleans, were drawn into the orbit of Catholic ritual." An inordinately large number of enslaved women were baptized in New Orleans, and then they and their creole offspring, through godparenting, religious instruction, and benevolence, became leaders and perpetuators of the city's Afro-Catholic faith.

African Americans everywhere tended to hold onto the idea that upon death one's soul went to one's homeland, almost always in the ground rather than in the sky. Funerals prepared the deceased's spirit for entry into the world of the ancestors. The services this practice of folk religion entailed were not at all the somber functions of most whites, but loud, raucous, joyous affairs with music, singing, dancing, laughing, and drinking. African Americans' practice of worship could also involve soft singing. Presbyterian minister Samuel Davies, who was important in bringing Christian religious fervor to blacks in Hanover County, Virginia, at the middle of the eighteenth century, recorded how African Americans' religious singing affected him spiritually: "March 2, 1756. Sundry of them have lodged all night in my kitchen; and, sometimes, when I have awakened about two or three a-clock in the morning, a torrent of sacred harmony poured into my chamber, and carried my mind away to Heaven. In this seraphic exercise, some of them spend almost the whole night."

But such religious ecstasy was more characteristic of organized services. Leaders of African-American congregations exhorted their listeners and sought emotional response. Singing and dancing, standing and shouting were important parts of the services. In these assemblages, blacks (and whites) frequently had spiritual experiences—visions of ancestors, journeys to other times and places, encounters with God or the devil, views of heaven or hell. A common experience was spiritual death and rebirth, bringing about heightened religious feeling. Efforts to control spirits were manifested in magical practices, many involving wearing of amulets and charms for protection. Black mediums who made the charms became powerful persons in the black community—sometimes in the white community. Through frenzied worship and spiritual experiences, African Americans were able to select from Christian worship the stories from the Old Testament that made them, too, feel a chosen people and allowed them to love their fellow humans in situations where being loving was not a natural tendency.

Folk Culture

When assessing the ways of life of enslaved men, women, and children in colonial mainland North America, it need always be remembered that setting down many, though not all, of the rules they lived by and providing the basic elements of a material culture were their owners. These were men, and sometimes women, who owned slaves primarily to improve their social status and their economic situation, the latter, according to late-eighteenth-century observer Richard Parkinson, to be "pinched and screwed out of the negro."

The idea that most slaves lived in "Negro quarters," clusters of small, individual dwellings set off by themselves and resembling tiny villages, is out of time and place for most of mainland North America through most of the colonial period. Permanent groupings of slave quarters existed only on the largest plantations, and individual dwellings or duplexes were a development signaling the maturing of slave societies—by the mid-eighteenth century in most places, though likely earlier in the Chesapeake. Masters no doubt saw the utility of separating Africans from creoles or allowing slave families to live by themselves, or recognized that diseases spread more quickly among persons living in the same quarters, but they also lived and functioned in a greater English Atlantic world, across which alien laborers were slowly being expelled from a landowner's "polite house." As age-old, live-in relationships that allowed easy interaction between farmers and their servants gave way in England to separate accommodations for members of different social classes, so, too, did slaveowners in the colonies want to visibly improve their social standing by removing their enslaved laborers to more-distant and less-gentile lodgings.

Slaves not long in the colonies often lived in quartering houses, which were dormitory or barracks-like structures that held the most people for the least expense—and offered the least privacy and comfort. In tobacco-growing Maryland of 1720, slaves tended to live scattered about the countryside in relatively isolated groups of half a dozen adults and their children. Even on large Chesapeake plantations before 1750, masters divided their lands into separate units and housed groups of slaves on each to allow easy access to the fields they tended and spread grazing livestock around their holdings. Small planters' field hands slept in barn lofts, tobacco houses, or other outbuildings.

Some slaves, especially in South Carolina and Georgia, relied on African building styles as much as English forms in constructing their dwellings. Houses tended to be small and square, twelve by twelve feet on average, and seldom were they permanent structures, allowing for movement with seasonal crops, fallowing, or removal from waste pits. In the Chesapeake, they built houses of wood mostly—clapboard structures early and then log constructions. In the Low Country more dwellings had mud walls or walls of a cement-like mixture of lime, crushed oyster shells, sand, and water called "tabby." With thatched roofs, these took on a distinct, African look. Slaves typically slept on straw bedding set on earthen floors and cooked by open fires or under wooden chimneys. They fetched water from springs, which were sufficient for most locations. Dwellings tended to grow in size and improve in construction—with such amenities as brick fireplaces—during Revolutionary times, but slave families were larger then, too. Thus, the amount of room per individual seems to have changed little through the eighteenth century, and that amount was almost always small.

With cramped, dark, and often smoky quarters, it is not surprising that much activity went on outside, in yards surrounding the houses. "Gathering around a fire, pipes in hand," writes Philip D. Morgan in *Slave Counterpoint,* "singing, dancing, and telling stories in communal yards; congregating in front of a cooking pot—these images probably convey much of the domestic life in the slave settlements." Many of the yards seem to have been grassless, in the fashion of a West-African compound. Fires were aburn outside most evenings and tended to be the focal point of group interaction. Chickens and dogs were part of the assemblage; garden plots surrounded the yards; and garbage heaps were nearby, sometimes close enough to smell.

In northern colonies, many slaves lived with their masters, sometimes in back rooms or attics of the same houses and sometimes in small outbuildings. Late in the eighteenth century, as Boston, New York, and Philadelphia grew, blacks moved into the cheaply constructed tenements that began to appear. By the end of the colonial period one could see the beginning of the movement of blacks into the southern part of Philadelphia, presaging a larger movement that would plant the seeds for the city's nineteenth-and twentieth-century black neighborhoods.

Slaves' material standard of living was lean, but not static. Enslaved men and women were not allowed to own property in most places, but many did. The longer they remained in one place, the more material goods—clothing, furniture, utensils—they made or acquired. Masters intended slave clothing to be fairly standard. They supplied clothing or plain cloth, perhaps five to ten yards annually per person, of coarse, unbleached linen or heavy, durable, often imported, and sometimes unbearably warm wool. Planters often hired tailors to make the slaves' clothing: jacket, shirt, and breeches (often of leather) for men; jacket and shift for women. In Revolutionary times, when imports were restricted, more slaves wore homespun and made their own clothes.

If coarse, drab, tough, functional clothing was the master's intention, it was not necessarily the slave's, and the latter found ways—sometimes theft, more often cajoling masters out of their castoff items or buying garments in a quasi-licit market—to acquire additional items more to their liking. The color of garments varied widely, but all turned drab with wear. Nonetheless, black men and women often did their best to remedy the situation. Responsible for keeping their own clothes in adequate repair, slaves tended to patch them with bright colors and express themselves by adorning their shirts with distinctive cuffs and collars. Men wore hats while working in the field, women handkerchiefs. Shoes supplied by the master were ill fitting and thus not worn for fieldwork or in warm weather. No one considered undergarments a necessity, socks were a luxury. Perhaps because of their tropical-African ancestry, slaves tended toward being cold rather than hot. They complained of the cold and damp, and their earliest personal acquisitions often were coats and blankets. Wherever scorching heat made clothing a burden, much of it was shed, men sporting breechcloths and women shirts and wraparounds in the fields. Slave children went naked much of the time, anyway.

Wealthy masters dressed personal servants better, in waistcoats and petticoat breeches, and rewarded some slaves with clothing for exceptional work or behavior. Artisans often earned enough to buy finer cloth and generally to dress better. Those who could afford to do so brought an African eye for color to their garments. Piersen notes in *Black Yankees* that African Americans' style of dress in New England "celebrated life in bright colors, demonstrating joy in physical attractiveness." Plantation slaves demonstrated that joy, too, but they had to concern themselves more with function and warmth.

Slave cabins were sparse in their furnishings. An inventory of one in Henrico County, Virginia, in 1697 shows "several chairs and a bed, an iron kettle weighing fifteen pounds, a brass kettle, an iron pot, a pair of pot racks, a pot hook, a frying-pan, and a beer barrel." Its occupants probably had been in the cabin for some time. It was common for slaves to start out with little more than a single iron pot and one frying pan. Enslaved men and women were not resourceless, however. They could purchase or barter for household items, and as the eighteenth century progressed, more cabins contained tables, linens, chamber pots, and a means of interior lighting. Raised beds remained a luxury that few enjoyed.

What and how slaves ate varied greatly from one farm or plantation to another, depending on the regional produce and the ideas of the master. They varied over time, too. Analysis of archaeological sites in the Chesapeake suggests that through most of the seventeenth century masters provided food for their slaves daily and communal eating was the norm, but late in the century, as part of a strategy to have slaves bear the costs of food procurement and preparation, this changed. The existence of subfloor pits for food storage and evidence of more pork (which was easier to preserve) than beef in the slaves' diet indicate that by the early eighteenth century masters were giving slaves weekly food rations. That they ate out of bowls rather than plates suggests that most of their meals were of the slow-cooked, stew variety.

Most colonial slaves existed on a basic core of meal and meat or fish with a few supplements. If the diet was sufficient in quantity—and this is nearly impossible to measure—it was lacking in quality. Advertisements for runaway slaves are full of references to physical problems associated with nutritional deficiencies: bad teeth, crooked legs, knocked knees, eye problems, poor posture, jaundiced or splotchy skin. Slaves in the Chesapeake were better fed than those in the Low Country, masters in the latter region giving their bondspeople less than their Chesapeake counterparts, expecting them to make up the deficit through gardening or hunting. This resulted in Chesapeake slaves being generally taller and experiencing a lower rate of infant and child mortality than Low Country slaves.

The idea that slaves existed on a "hog and hominy" routine is fairly sound, though there were local variations and free blacks and of African languages. Colonial masters deemed arriving Africans slow learners of a usable language (which had to have a basis in English, since whites were not at all willing learners themselves). This varied with age, of course—younger immigrants finding language acquisition easier than older ones—and with the amount of contact the newcomers had with English speakers. Still, it was practically axiomatic in the colonial Low Country that almost no adult Africans having resided there for less than a year spoke any recognizable English, and that some of those who had "been above twenty years in this Province," lamented one white South Carolinian, "can hardly speak even common things, so as to be understood." The situation was slightly different farther north, where saltwater slaves had more contact with creoles and whites.

The linguistic challenge was indeed a difficult one. Because West Africans spoke many mutually unintelligible languages and because most slaves in mainland North America were sufficiently dispersed as to be rarely in close contact with same-language speakers, few newcomers could talk easily with other slaves. Thus, over several generations African Americans developed their own ways to communicate.

Across most of the mainland colonies, blacks held onto common elements of African languages—certain grammar, words, sounds, and tones—as they fashioned their own variants of English. This resulted in sharp local differences in earlier periods, followed by regional variation, with a language closer to standard English being spoken farther north and more of a creole tongue, lingering longer, farther south. Where African slaves were relatively isolated for a long time, they spoke what are often regarded as wholly different languages—"Gullah" in the Sea Islands off the Low Country and an African-French-Portuguese creole along the Lower Mississippi.

Voice was a factor in music, too. West Africans surrounded themselves with music that had a deep heritage, and music was always important in the lives of African Americans. African influence was evident in the forms that black music took. A host of stringed instruments, most notably the banjo, certain fiddles though this style melded quickly with that of the European violin, tambourines, flutes, xylophones, and drums rested on African

slaves made adaptations when they provided their own food. Most masters allowed a weekly ration of cornmeal—a peck (or about a pound) a day for each slave was standard—and pork, often salted and commonly the least desirable parts, in small amounts. There were regional additions. African Americans in the southern Low Country ate the rice that was broken in the cleaning process and thus unsalable, and also chickpeas, but they still consumed more corn than rice; those in the Chesapeake in later years had greater access to wheat flour, from which they baked biscuits, but they preferred corn and cornbread and their masters preferred giving it to them. Adult African Americans did not drink milk because of their genetic intolerance for lactose, and they ate little beef because it did not preserve well. Few slaves in colonial times supplemented their diets with peas, beans, sweet potatoes, or greens, as they may have done in the Cotton South of later times. Most masters allowed slaves to raise produce, poultry, and pigs, but many did so to barter for tobacco, alcohol, or better clothes rather than to improve their diets with fruits, vegetables, and more meat. The most popular (and dietarily useful) supplements were fish and game, the former easiest to get in the Low Country and around New England ports. Blacks in Gracia Real de Santa Teresa de Mose ate fish, shellfish, deer, rabbit, raccoon, and turtle.

Kenneth F. Kiple and Virginia Himmelsteib King in *Another Dimension of the Black Diaspora: Diet, Disease, and Racism* (1981) show that blacks had two major difficulties relating to diet and nutrition. Over centuries they had become adapted for survival in the African tropics, so once removed from that specialized environment they faced particular nutritional requirements that could not easily be satisfied in the British mainland colonies of North America. But regardless of their special needs, the diet they received in America, if sufficient in bulk, was not sufficient in balance. Under such circumstances, many blacks in colonial America lived a nutritional nightmare. The majority of slaves received insufficient protein of good quality and insufficient amounts of the vitamin B complex, vitamins C and D, and calcium and iron. Among the results were frighteningly high rates of infant and early-child mortality, at times and in places up to 60 percent. "The mortality of negro children," wrote one commentator, "is as two to one when compared to whites." Of course, mothers' rigorous work, up to the point of childbirth and soon again afterward, when added to the problems caused by inadequate diet, resulted in high rates of mothers' deaths in childbirth as well. Also related to poor nutrition were development of personality disorders and a host of debilitating and often fatal diseases in the slave population—what masters called "the Negro diseases"—that were largely foreign to whites: rickets, pica (referred to as "dirt-eating"), hookworm, and pellagra ("black tongue"). Malnutrition also made slaves more susceptible to common diseases and more vulnerable to secondary infections when wounded or suffering a common virus.

Diet was the largest factor in African-American children faring as poorly as they did. In fact, the old image of throngs of thinly-clad children playing gayly about the slave quarter must be laid to rest. The more one learns about slaves' diet, their disease environment, and work patterns of slave mothers and children—the elements most directly affecting infant and child mortality—the more one accepts Richard H. Steckel's statement that the experience of enslaved children was "dreadful." In "Women, Work, and Health under Plantation Slavery in the United States" in *More than Chattel: Black Women and Slavery in the Americas,* edited by David Barry Gaspar and Darlene Clark Hine (1996), Steckel summarizes data from just after colonial times that show the effects of diet, work demands, and disease on infant and child health as manifested in height. In a word, slave children were tiny. At age five the average height of enslaved blacks did not make it into the first percentile of modern height distribution. Steckel writes, "The slums of Lagos, Nigeria, and urban areas of Bangladesh provided environments for growth superior to those faced by slave children." Once they reached adolescence, mainland slaves largely caught up, height-wise, with their white peers, likely the result of increased protein from meat distribution that came with the onset of work.

Given the nature of medical treatment in colonial times, which included the letting of blood, application of leeches, administration of harsh purgatives, and lancing with unsterilized instruments,

slaves who were unwell frequently were better off when masters did not summon professional medical advice. Blacks maintained their own medical system in the form of plantation or neighborhood "root doctors," men and women who combined knowledge of herbal remedies and ritual skills with a holistic approach to devise therapeutics for many ills. Actually, practitioners of folk medicine in Africa long had been adept at matching the medicinal properties of plants to the symptoms of diseases. Also, the psychological benefit of believing in the healer, as African Americans seemed to do in their "root doctors," may have been as important as the medication.

Closely tied to black medical practice was another group of activities important to black folk culture that included magic, sorcery, and witchcraft. Belief in individuals with special powers to manipulate the spiritual realm to effect good and evil was widespread in West Africa, where it moved beyond the religious and into the secular world. Africans brought such traditions to colonial America and melded them into a body of beliefs and practice sometimes called "voodoo" or slave magic. Most sizable gro of African Americans comprised one or more individuals, called "conjurers" by whites, who worked their magic to he harm people as requested. One of the most frequently used cal practices was the wearing of amulets or talismans to w illness or misfortune. Blacks visited conjurers to ascertai to get even with evil overseers or cruel masters, or to g mis'ries" to fellow slaves who had done misdeeds. In in the African-American community practiced divinir included discovering lost property and predicting the fut in ghosts was also common. It is important to note that America such African-American folk beliefs were cl of whites of the time and place. New England slaves es nearly as much as whites did, and many a white Y a black medium for protection against ghosts or to some affliction.

Speaking to spirits was one thing; speak was another. To do this, African Americans le oped forms of English comprising, to varying technology. Blacks played these instruments in times of joy and sorrow; they sang together while hoeing crops, grinding corn, or rowing boats; they sang relatives to the afterlife in funerals; and they joined together on moonlit nights to sing "sweet chants." African-based call-and-response forms of song served a variety of purposes. Finally, folk narratives merged with song to provide instruction to children while entertaining them. Storytelling ranged from the amusing to the raunchy, depending on the audience.

Though there is little evidence of the forms of African-American dance in the colonial period, it was clearly a major part of celebrating. On holidays, recalled New Englander Jane Shelton, groups of women "shuffled and tripped to the sound of the fiddle." African-style ring dances were popular, and some dances were raucous, noisy affairs that whites neither understood nor appreciated. Thomas Hazard seemed not to care for the dancing style of the Rhode Island slave Sam, "who had a way of his own of fetching a terrific screech like a catamount, and then dashing forward to the middle of the floor." Likewise, Pierre de Laussat wrote that slaves in South Carolina celebrated the Christmas holiday in dance by "distorting their frame in the most unnatural figures and emitting the most hideous noises." When African Americans persisted in gathering at William Grimes's "upper room" in New Bedford, Connecticut, dancing late into the night, Grimes's neighbors complained until his landlord revoked his lease.

African Americans knew how to enjoy a holiday or an evening away from work. Alcohol regularly had a place in relaxation and merriment. Low Country slaves enjoyed boat races; blacks in port towns from Charleston to Boston liked to drink and play dice, especially "paw paw," an African gambling game. A black/Indian/lower-class-white tavern culture existed in cities of any size. White authorities did not approve of much of what went on in and around the taverns—they were places where the poorer folk could fence stolen goods and, with boldness enhanced by spirits, plan acts of resistance—and neighbors disliked the noises that accompanied tavern revelry. As early as 1692 New York's Common Council ordered the sheriff to give twenty lashes to any slaves "making any hooting or disorderly noise in the Street on the Lords Day." Such efforts tended to be in vain, however. Among the biggest single celebrations in colonial African-American culture was Election Day in New England, when slaves took a holiday to elect their own "kings" and "governors" in a satire of white society. Free of normal restraints, slaves dressed elaborately and celebrated the day with parades and "inaugural" parties. The officers elected became important personages in the black community. In coastal slave communities, mainly in the Low Country, Christmas-time extravaganzas called John Canoe festivals (seemingly named after a mythical or historical figure from the West-African coast) served the same purpose. Some slaves attending these mixtures of African and Anglo-Saxon celebrations dressed in animal masks, others wore headdresses shaped like houses or ships, and music and dance prevailed everywhere.

Whites and Blacks, Men and Women, Humanity and Inhumanity

Of a work so grand in scope and stature as Morgan's *Slave Counterpoint,* it is probably inappropriate to highlight any one particular element. But among the things that set the book apart from many others is Morgan's illumination of the relationships between and among different groups of whites and blacks in colonial America. Morgan not only describes these relationships, but shows how they changed over time and how such changes affected African Americans. After all, blacks in a subordinate position in a society had to relate constantly with white people considered above them, and how they did so affected much about their existence. So too, of course, did the fact that some of those white people owned them, making them at once pieces of property, like farm implements, and human beings with souls and feelings and minds of their own.

Into the early eighteenth century, a social model of patriarchy was dominant in the minds of persons of power—and, they hoped, others—in British mainland North America. In a perceived social hierarchy, male father figures existed at the top, from which lofty position they protected the weak, demanding obedience and loyalty in return. Colonial planters, the patriarchs, regarded slaves as property, made decisions about them with profit in mind, and applied discipline impersonally and severely to exact work from their physically close but socially distant subordinates. Yet many of these same masters could not overcome the notion that it was their duty to look after the well-being—in the lights of that time and place—of their dependent underlings, who were part of the planter's household in its broadest sense.

After the middle of the eighteenth century, the more austere and less emotional patriarchal relationships began to change and become, on the surface at least, softer and gentler, less authoritarian. Morgan cites the rise of evangelicalism, romanticism, and humanitarianism, among other things, as reasons for this shift to a more "enlightened patriarchalism." Eventually, masters who had dealt with members of the same slave families for several generations developed closer relations with them, perhaps cared more for them as individuals, and treated them more humanely. Masters also grew increasingly concerned with their reputations for benevolence: some of them made efforts to ameliorate slave codes and to provide their bondspeople better food, clothing, and housing. Through all of this, whites expected loyalty from their slaves and grew to develop a false sense that the men and women they owned and worked were grateful to them and happy with their lot. It was as if persons of African descent, who earlier were regarded as unfortunate (and perhaps dangerous) beings of a lower order, became perpetual children. The change was not equal across colonial America. It came more slowly and to a lesser degree in the Low Country than in the Chesapeake; in such venues as North Carolina, where the slave system matured late and African imports rose after 1750, it hardly appeared at all. But by the end of the colonial period, master-slave relations were moving toward the out-and-out paternalism that would characterize black-white dealings through much of the nineteenth century.

Lower-class whites generally did not share these views, and in earlier times blacks and whites worked together and interacted considerably. The evidence of white servants running away with enslaved blacks in the seventeenth century is extensive, and on the fringes of plantation country and in the growing urban settings of eighteenth-century colonial America, blacks and whites worked together, drank together, prayed together, and produced offspring together outside the law. In time, however, forces worked to separate African Americans and lower-class whites. The economic condition and status of plain whites rose, if haltingly, and poorer whites began to see blacks more clearly as potential competitors in the economic sphere. At the same time, members of the white gentry, for a multitude of reasons that included the need for greater control in societies that contained a great many slaves, courted poorer whites to identify and align themselves with their wealthier and more powerful neighbors. The result was a steadily growing antipathy between black slaves and white laborers. "The eighteenth century was a crucible in which the deep and increasingly reciprocal contempt felt between lower-class whites and blacks was forged," writes Morgan. "The contempt had not emerged in fully polished form by 1800, but the essentials were in place."

There was never enough antipathy to keep blacks and whites entirely apart in sexual relations, however. The considerable number of persons of mixed black and white parentage is mute evidence of such activity. Sex between white men and black women, and black men and white women, was bound to occur in societies that had such thorough contact. Inter-racial sexual relations probably took place more—at least per capita—in earlier colonial times than later, because strictures against such activity—public condemnation and ridicule often the most effective—grew stronger with the heightened religiosity of the late eighteenth century and the movement toward creation of a common white identity. They also took place more frequently in some places—along the Lower Mississippi or around the Chesapeake, for instance, than in the Low Country. But colonial America was a place where men and women of both races were together frequently and alone sufficiently for sex to take place. And it did.

Black-white sexual relationships in the colonial period could indeed be caring and affectionate. Edward Ball found evidence that his eighteenth-century Low Country ancestor, the planter Elias Ball, had a long and seemingly caring relationship with his slave Dolly, thirty-six years his junior, which produced two children, Edward and Catherine, the only of his slaves to bear English forenames and the only ones to be granted their freedom. The elder Ball summoned a physician for a house call when Dolly took ill—a momentous occurrence indeed—and hired a cobbler to make her expensive shoes that were a far cry from the "Negro shoes" allotted to the rest of his slaves. Other evidence from various places shows white and black men and women living together as man and wife. A white woman in Northampton County, Virginia, paid a fine and served a six-month prison term in 1738 so she could marry a mulatto man.

Of course, a good portion of the inter-racial sexual activity must have been less caring. Sex for money was certainly known in colonial times, and as cities grew larger, toward the late eighteenth century, blacks and whites met in "disorderly houses" and did as they would, in spite of the law. Out on plantations, some masters and their male offspring could be downright predatory in nature toward female slaves. It is not clear how frequently these liaisons constituted violent rape, since such incidents did not come before the law.

But that some of the sexual unions between white men and black women were violent in nature should hardly be surprising, given that slave societies were based on violence. Wherever one turned and regardless with whom the slaves were dealing, the world of master and slave was one of violence. It was corporal punishment that coerced the African-American men and women to work for another's gain, and such punishment and the threat thereof maintained order in the larger slave societies. Plantation justice, meted out on the spot by a master or his agent to an offending slave, was the most common form of "correction." Often, this involved whipping, a punishment done in public for the deterrent effects of the display and one that brought the danger of infection with the slicing action and pain of the cowhide. More serious crimes invoked a greater number of lashes or escalated beyond whipping to dismembering. Perhaps it was only economic practicality—the wariness of losing a working hand—that kept plantation justice from resulting in larger numbers of deaths. Death-by-punishment is evident in the more formal court systems. Marvin L. Michael Kay and Lorin Lee Cary analyze criminal justice in North Carolina in *Slavery in North Carolina, 1748–1775* (1995) and leave no doubts about the barbarity of the system. All whites executed by order of North Carolina courts were hanged, but slaves, whose rate of execution exceeded that of whites by thirteen times, faced sadistic treatment before meeting a savage death. Half the slaves whose mode of execution is known in North Carolina between the mid-seventeenth century and the outbreak of the Revolution suffered clear brutality. "One was chained alive in a gibbet to die slowly and horribly," write Kay and Cary as they describe some of the executions: "Six were burned, two were castrated and then hanged, five were hanged and decapitated with their heads displayed on poles, one was hanged and burned . . . , two died as a result of castration, seven slaves . . . were shot or beaten to death when captured, and five outlawed runaways drowned themselves to avoid capture and sadistic treatment."

In populated areas from New York City to New Orleans, such executions often were prolonged and public. African-American men and women accused of plotting a rebellion might be burned alive—or, in the case of one person executed after the 1712 slave uprising in New York, slowly roasted to death over a low fire—or killed "at the wheel," a torturous medieval device that broke the person's limbs and left him or her outdoors to linger in pain before dying. For the purpose of teaching appropriate lessons, white authorities left bodies hanging in gibbets or severed heads atop poles, about town or at busy crossroads, until they decomposed.

Such brutality had to affect all elements of slave societies. One need not wonder where the men who wrote the United States Constitution in the 1780s came up with the idea for strictures against cruel and inhuman punishments.

Resistance, Escape, and Rebellion

A spirit of resistance and the potential for escape or rebellion ran deep in the colonial slave population. Masters who were honest with themselves never harbored any notion that the men and women they held in bondage were a contented lot. They lived in a world where African Americans were daily expressing rebellious disgust for their situations in dozens of little ways, and one where the potential for uprising was always present.

Proof of this is in the body of laws that existed to prevent such action. As slave populations grew, suspicion, distrust, and fear filled the minds of white colonists and became manifest in colonial statutes. Eighteenth-century slave codes limited the number of blacks who could meet in groups, forbade their carrying anything resembling weapons, kept blacks on the farm or plantation and off streets after dark, and even outlawed their possession of drums or horns, "which may give notice to one another of their wicked designs." Capital offenses included arson, poisoning, repeated theft, inciting insurrection, and resisting interrogation. Police kept a close eye on urban blacks, slave patrols guarded rural areas, and white colonists remained vigilant. Local justices could resort to the equivalent of medieval torture to keep the slave population docile, but it was masters and overseers who most frequently corrected slave misbehavior in the myriad ways the law allowed. Colonial statutes permitted branding, flogging, burning, amputation of limbs, hamstringing, and execution. Records of administration of these punishments are wondrously matter-of-fact. Middlesex County, Virginia, in the first twenty-five years of the eighteenth century was probably typical. During that period the government saw to the sale of eight blacks to the West Indies (with compensation for their owners) for "frequent disorderly meetings." A minister and two accomplices beat to death the clergyman's slave for running away. A vengeful slave owner castrated one slave for "running away, lying out and distroying peoples Stocks"; cut off the toes of another for "lying out and doing Severall Misdemeanors"; and pilloried and cut off the ears of a third for a second offense of stealing. Another Middlesex court executed a slave for treason, dismembering him and hanging one of his quarters in a public place.

In the face of such punishments, slaves were imminently practical. Forms of resistance ranged along a continuum from acts of forgetfulness (failure to remember critical parts of a message, for instance) or carelessness (which might result in breaking a tool, ruining a plant, harming a pig, or burning a stack of hay); to feigning illness or malingering; to mocking whites (masters in particular) in clever words, songs, and actions; to stealing; to running away; and ultimately to organized, armed rebellion. The particular form resisting slaves selected at any time or place depended on its chances for success, but the extent of slaves' acculturation and the kind of work they did had a bearing on how they resisted.

"Saltwater" slaves had a tendency on arrival to run away with others who spoke the same language—or even, sometimes, with shipmates. It did not take them long to grasp the reality of their situations, however. Africans not long in the colonies, lacking command of English and living an isolated existence with few other slaves, resisted in subtle ways. They ruined crops, broke tools, malingered and balked, feigned sickness or stupidity, or stole goods or animals to sell on the black market. Household slaves under closer supervision worked slowly, acted surly, or got drunk. Most blacks not fully acculturated who did run away were more truant than long absent. Their limited ability to exist unnoticed in white society made them "outliers," hiding in the woods, close to the people they knew.

But more often than people at the time wished to admit, African men and women headed for the near or more distant frontier and attempted to form settlements of runaways—called "maroon" settlements (from the Portuguese *cimarrón,* for runaway). It was harder to do this in the Chesapeake, given the African minority and a topography that did not lend itself to hiding, but the Low Country, with its black majority and a terrain difficult to cross, with more places to remove oneself and go unnoticed, was the scene of more maroon camps. Once Spanish authorities established the town of freed Carolina slaves at Gracia Real de Santa Teresa de Mose near St. Augustine in 1738, more Low Country slaves lit out southward to gain their freedom. Some, who chose not to attempt the difficult passage all the way to Florida, built their own settlements. A 1765 expedition against a maroon group up the Savanna River found the escapees inhabiting a small "town" surrounded by a swamp. Members of the force of whites sent to run off the residents, a group that included "two Negroes on a Scaffold one Beating a Drum and the other hoisting Colours," found "a square consisting of four Houses 17 feet long and 14 feet wide, that the kettles were upon the fire boiling rice and about 15 bushels of rough rice." White colonists were intent on rooting out these settlements and taking steps to prevent their further establishment. At the Savanna River town, they gathered up "Blanketts, Potts, Shoes, Axes, and many other tools all of which together with the Town they set fire to."

The more assimilated slaves became, the wiser they were to the ways of whites and thus the more capable of finding more subtle, but still satisfying, intellectual responses to their condition in bondage or, in more extreme cases, fleeing it. Runaway advertisements provide unintended evidence of African-American expressions of resistance and contempt for whites through such normal manifestations of feelings as body movements. Colonial masters described fugitives who, "when speaking looks you full in the face," or who possessed "a sneaking down look," a "sour countenance," or "a Swaggering Air with him in his Walk." Piersen in *Black Legacy* calls attention to "more civilized and more common forms of social pressure based on the African predisposition for wry humor and verbal cleverness" that blacks regularly used in mocking white figures of authority. One observer found whites in such a situation "good naturedly submitting to the hard hits leveled against themselves." Outside of Charleston, South Carolina, in 1772, a white man who sneaked a view of African Americans at a Saturday night country dance failed to find it so funny. "The entertainment was opened by the men copying (or taking off) the manners of their masters," he reported, "and the women those of their mistresses, and relating some highly curious anecdotes, to the inexpressible diversion of that company." Songs of colonial Louisiana slaves could be more biting still:

> Negro cannot walk, without corn in his pocket,
>   It is to steal chickens.
> Mulatto cannot walk without rope in his pocket,
>   It is to steal horses.
> White man cannot walk without money in his pockets,
>   It is to steal girls.

Perhaps it was those less clever with words and better with their hands who took to flight. Skilled artisans who were fully acculturated and moved freely between rural and urban environments were the ones most likely to try to escape from slavery altogether. Carpenters, "fishing Negroes," and boatmen were especially apt to run away for good. In the colonial era there was no northern bastion of freedom to run to, but these runaways often headed for towns where they could get lost among the handful of free blacks and lower-class whites that made up the substratum of society. The North Carolina piedmont, populated by nonslaveholding whites, was another haven for fugitives, as was Spanish Florida. Black artisans ran away alone, many to rejoin relatives, and they relied on their skills and savvy to get jobs and carry on new lives.

Outright rebellion occupied the extreme end of the resistance-rebellion spectrum. Herbert Aptheker in *American Negro Slave Revolts* (1943, rev. ed. 1969) notes that periods of widespread slave rebelliousness came in waves every generation or so, "as though anger accumulated and vented itself and then a period of rest and recuperation was needed before the next upsurge." There seem to have been waves of general slave unrest, which may have corresponded with slave rebelliousness in the Caribbean and the greater Atlantic world between 1710 and 1722, 1730 and 1740, 1765 and 1780, and 1790 and 1802. If full-scale rebellions did not occur regularly every few years, when they did occur they gained notice in colonial society out of proportion to their significance. Here, again, chance of success was a guiding principle. African Americans greatly outnumbered by whites thought better of joining insurrections. Because this was frequently the case in the mainland colonies—different from most other New World slave societies, where slave rebellions were more common—incidents of open rebellion were relatively rare. Still, since colonial publications did not spread word of conspiracies and insurrections, more were probably planned than most white colonists (and, subsequently, most historians) perceived. Evidence from such widely separated locations as New York City, Charleston, and New Orleans suggests that Africans, or blacks who were able to create some real or artificial African identity with other slaves in this country, were involved in some of the largest conspiracies and rebellions. The urban setting, where enslaved men and women had greater freedom of movement and broader choice of their contacts—and where blacks met with all sorts of people in back-alley taverns where rum flowed freely, was particularly conducive to organized rebellion. Benjamin Franklin seems to have captured the general tone of some urban slaves when he described Philadelphia blacks as being of a "plotting Disposition."

Indeed, plotting that occurred in New York City and its environs bore fruit that was deadly for some whites and painful for many more. Historians recently have focused attention on what several see as generalized black unrest and conspiratorial activities in eighteenth-century New York. During the century's first decade, slaves in New York and New Jersey grew increasingly angry over new, harsher laws restricting their activities. In rural areas the result was an occasional murder of a slave owner, followed by the horrors of a slave execution; in the city, slave unrest was more likely to involve group activity. On April 6, 1712, some two dozen slaves led by a core of Akan-speaking, Gold-Coast Africans (identified by contemporary whites as "Coromantees") set fire to the outbuilding of a prominent New Yorker and then shot and stabbed whites who were coming to extinguish the flames, killing nine of them and wounding half a dozen others. Authorities eventually captured twenty-one conspirators and, after a quick trial, publicly executed eighteen of them in a variety of inhumane ways.

Other plots and conspiracies turned up in New York City in 1721 and 1734, but the grandest of all may have been one in 1741. The conditional is required here because historians have yet to agree on whether or not a bona fide, grand, and dangerous (to whites) plot truly existed. According to some, over the winter of 1740–41 a group of blacks, with support from poorer Irish, English, Dutch, and Spanish men and women who frequented some of New York's waterside taverns, joined to plan a rebellion with mighty potential. Graham Russell Hodges in *Root and Branch: African Americans in New York and East Jersey, 1613–1863* (1999) detects "a powerful proletarian republicanism" in the plot, the conspirators held together by the fact that (as one of the slaves involved was reported saying) "a great many people had too much, and others too little." Evidence turned up also of some of the conspirators being aware of a general black rebelliousness around the western Atlantic and many slaves being displeased that their Christianity held out little prospect for freedom. As before, arson was their favored tool. Over several weeks, fire destroyed New York's Fort George and several white homes before whites uncovered the plot, held a showy trial, and executed or sent away those found guilty. "Only the discovery of loose talk," Hodges writes, "kept the 1741 plot from becoming the worst racial uprising in colonial North America."

But it was not the worst racial uprising, even of its time or place, and more recently Jill Lepore in *New York Burning: Liberty, Slavery, and Conspiracy in Eighteenth-Century Manhattan* (2005) leaves one wondering if any "Great Negro Plot" truly existed, as some wondered at the time. Was it all a reflection of the generalized fears of Manhattan's 10,000 whites of the 2,000 slaves in their midst, or even more the sad result of the actions of a venal and racist judge on New York's Supreme Court, than an indication that a carefully planned slave (or underclass) uprising was in the works? Lepore casts doubt on the veracity of slaves' confessions and labels the state's primary witness, a sixteen-year-old indentured servant who received her freedom and a £100 reward for her testimony, "comically corrupt." Still, enough wealthy whites in New York believed that blacks were plotting to kill them, take over Manhattan, and install a king to bring mass arrests. Trials of the conspirators lasted through the summer of 1741 and the resultant executions of thirty-four persons were an almost daily occurrence for several weeks. (David Grim, who was four years old at the time, had the executions so etched in his mind that he included details of burning and gibbeted blacks on a map he drew of the Manhattan of his childhood seventy-two years later.) Yet, it seems certain that no matter how many accused black conspirators were publicly burned at the stake, no matter how many charred corpses were gibbeted about the city in the most public of places, African Americans continued to chafe at their bonds and join others in thoughts of rebellion along and around the lower Hudson.

But slave uprisings were not limited to northern cities. In fact, the largest and likely most serious of these in all of England's mainland colonies occurred in plantation sections of Virginia and South

Carolina within a decade of the New York conspiracy (lending credence to Aptheker's idea of waves of slave unrest). In the fall of 1730, possibly on the basis of a rumor that planters were blocking an edict by England's King George II to free all slaves who were Christians, and with the likelihood that a good proportion of recent slaves arriving in the Chesapeake were from the Kingdom of the Kongo, which had a Christian heritage, captive Africans and African Americans held meetings in several parts of Virginia. These apparently triggered work slowdowns on farms and plantations at harvest time of a particularly bountiful year. In October, several hundred blacks assembled in Norfolk and Princess Anne counties, chose officers to lead an "intended Insurrection," and ran off into the Dismal Swamp, from which they made forays into surrounding plantations, doing "a great deal of Mischief." Using Pasquotank Indians to locate and round up these rebels and others in neighboring counties—and sometimes to mete out their own justice on the spot—white authorities hastily put down the rebellion and then beefed up militia patrols and warned Virginia slaveholders to be more vigilant.

It was nine years after this, near the Stono River, within twenty miles of Charleston, South Carolina, that occurred what most historians consider the most serious slave uprising of the colonial period—in part because it triggered other rebellions and acts of resistance over several years. A core of newly arrived "Angolan" slaves—again, likely men who once were part of the Kingdom of Kongo north of the Congo River—apparently planned the Stono Rebellion. Since many of these people were Portuguese-speaking Catholics, and since Spanish East Florida offered freedom in a setting friendly to Catholicism, some at the time speculated that Spanish propaganda played a role in instigating the uprising. Under the leadership of a slave named Jemmy, twenty blacks on the morning of September 9, 1739, broke into a store, where they stole small arms and powder, killing the storekeepers and leaving their severed heads on the front steps. By daybreak, as they moved southward along the road toward Georgia, they had killed eight whites. Through the early afternoon they killed most of the whites they encountered—they spared the life of a white tavern keeper who was known for his kindness to his slaves—and burned houses. Around midday the group, whose ranks had swollen to fifty or sixty, met up with South Carolina's Lieutenant Governor, William Bull, returning to Charleston for the commencement of a new legislative session. Bull apparently had to ride hard to escape with his life.

After halting in an open field in mid-afternoon, the rebels, according to a contemporary "Account of the Negroe Insurrection," "set to dancing, Singing and beating Drums to draw more Negroes to them." Although before evening a force of mounted planters attacked and dispersed the gathering that at one time may have approached one hundred persons, it took nearly a week for a white militia company to catch and overcome the largest remnant of the group. The remaining core of fighters may have been individuals who had been soldiers in Africa, knew how to use firearms effectively, and relied on proven tactics to hold off their pursuers. Some were not apprehended for several months after the uprising began, and one leader remained at large for three years. Altogether, thirty whites and forty-four blacks died in the slaughter associated with the insurrection. Another thirty slaves, these apparently more-assimilated creoles rather than the "Saltwater" insurgents, received rewards for fighting against the insurgents. This uprising prompted South Carolina to lump together all blacks as dangerous to white society, whether "of a rebellious nature" or not, and systematically tighten restrictions (on free blacks as well as slaves) with the harshest penalties of any mainland colony.

Through the middle of the eighteenth century, newcomers from Africa seem to have been the ones most likely to join in rebellion. Thereafter, open rebellion was something plotted by the most highly assimilated slaves. Mullin in *Flight and Rebellion* explains the irony of slave rebellions being tied to the acculturation process. As slaves acculturated according to their masters' designs, they learned their roles on the farm or plantation, the house or factory, but they also learned strategies that would help them rise against their owners. Late in the colonial period the liberal influence of the American Revolution and the increased need for skilled slaves around cities led to a relaxing of restraints upon African Americans in urban areas. For a time, this may have served as a safety valve, permitting slaves who might otherwise have lashed out to visit a relative, go underground, or even just vent in a grog shop. But, eventually, freer to move about and meet meant more able to plan, and it was skilled, urban slaves who in 1800 organized "Gabriel's Rebellion," which Mullin considers "the most sophisticated and ambitious slave conspiracy" in American history. Acculturation, he concludes, "ultimately created slaves who were able to challenge the security of the society itself."

One final form of rebellion in which African Americans participated turned out to be more ambitious than any other. James Oliver Horton and Lois E. Horton in *In Hope of Liberty: Culture, Community and Protest Among Northern Free Blacks, 1700–1860* (1997) place northern blacks in a class grouping with Indians and poorer whites, who increasingly resisted what they perceived as gross injustice of their social and economic position. "Interracial ceremony and celebration, social interaction, and familial connection became the building blocks of their alliance," write the Hortons. "Arson, riot, and even armed insurrection became their political tools." As the century wore on and notions of liberty spread among persons living around the colonial Atlantic, groupings of the so-called "lower sorts," which included blacks, became more willing to take action on such ideals in the ways that worked best for them.

After 1763, the British government became a target for such rebellious action. African Americans in northern cities joined others in feeling the pinch that came with the economic downturn following the end of the Seven Years' War, and they were in the mobs that took to the streets in protest of the tightening British regulations that were only making things worse. Interracial gathering places—taverns and back-alley gaming spots—again became centers for this rebellious activity. It must have been with mixed feelings that white colonial elites and middle-class elements looked on, perhaps disliking England's tightening controls on the colonies more than they feared the public expression of the "lower elements." Many in Boston approved of the activities of the "saucy boys, negroes and mulattoes, Irish teagues and outlandish jack-tarrs," led by runaway slave Crispus Attucks, who on March 5, 1770, following an incident with a British soldier in a dockside tavern, taunted and harassed the guards at the Custom House until the Redcoats opened fire. The Boston Massacre was a spark for the fire of liberty that swept across the colonies soon afterward. African Americans in and out of slavery played no small part in the work of kindling that flame.

CHAPTER FOUR

The Revolutionary Era

*To contend for our own liberty and to deny that blessing
to others involves an inconsistency not to be excused.*

—JOHN JAY, 1785

For African Americans the American Revolution was full of contradictions. The clearest of these involved slavery and the ideology the Founding Fathers used to justify breaking with England. A third of the men who signed the document declaring their right to independent nationhood on the self-evident truth that all men are created equal owned other humans. In addition, the nation these men would create—one that would secure the blessings of liberty to themselves and their posterity—was one whose social and economic fabric was woven with the thread of black slavery, whose population included half a million African and African-American slaves, and whose wealthiest southerners would not consider joining a union of states without a clear recognition of their right to own black men, women, and children.

But the contradictions involved more than slavery and Revolutionary ideology. Among the results of the Revolution were paradoxical changes in African-American society and culture. The Revolution helped make it possible for some blacks to gain their freedom. It played an important role in the ending of slavery in the states north of Maryland and in considerable manumission in the Upper South, and it gave even more African Americans the idea that freedom was not merely something good to obtain, but something one had a right to expect. Yet, when one considers numbers, it becomes clear that the Revolutionary era did little to reduce the nation's reliance on slaves. Not 500,000 slaves lived on the British North American mainland in 1776; nearly 700,000 were counted in the first census of the new United States in 1790. Where emancipation did occur, in the North and Upper South, in almost every instance it came grudgingly, and in all areas white sons of the Revolution began circumscribing that freedom soon after more than a few blacks had gained it. North and South, white men in positions of authority cut away at African-American rights, privileges, and opportunities, so that the black men and women who no longer were slaves remained separated and ostracized from the rest of American society.

Also, for those thousands of Americans who remained in bondage and for the many thousands of Americans who would be slaves over the next four-score years, the Revolution made freedom more difficult to obtain. Following the break with England, slavery in the states south of Maryland grew in size and strength. Southern slave-holders became all the more convinced that the institution was necessary for their economic survival. And American independence entrenched slavery into the laws of the new land. Without mentioning the words *slave* or *slavery*, the Constitution made the institution legitimate and gave slaveholders greater means to protect and defend their human property. In legitimizing slavery and strengthening the hold of slave owners, founders of the new nation set the stage for the enormous expansion of slavery into what would become the Cotton South—the open and newly acquired lands to the south and west—beginning early in the nineteenth century.

Yet most important for blacks in the United States over the long term, and probably most ironic, the Revolution brought a broadening and strengthening of the hierarchical order to American race relations. Although most English colonists held strong feelings about race before the Revolution, they did not need to use race so centrally to justify enslaving other human beings. Once slaves made adaptations when they provided their own food. Most masters allowed a weekly ration of cornmeal—a peck (or about a pound) a day for each slave was standard—and pork, often salted and commonly the least desirable parts, in small amounts. There were regional additions. African Americans in the southern Low Country ate the rice that was broken in the cleaning process and thus unsalable, and also chickpeas, but they still consumed more corn than rice; those in the Chesapeake in later years had greater access to wheat flour, from which they baked biscuits, but they preferred corn and cornbread and their masters preferred giving it to them. Adult African Americans did not drink milk because of their genetic intolerance for lactose, and they ate little beef because it did not preserve well. Few slaves in colonial times supplemented their diets with peas, beans, sweet potatoes, or greens, as they may have done in the Cotton South of later times. Most masters allowed slaves to raise produce, poultry, and pigs, but many did so to barter for tobacco, alcohol, or better clothes rather than to improve their diets with fruits, vegetables, and more meat. The most popular (and dietarily useful) supplements were fish and game, the former easiest to get in the Low Country and around New England ports. Blacks in Gracia Real de Santa Teresa de Mose ate fish, shellfish, deer, rabbit, raccoon, and turtle.

Kenneth F. Kiple and Virginia Himmelsteib King in *Another Dimension of the Black Diaspora: Diet, Disease, and Racism* (1981) show that blacks had two major difficulties relating to diet and nutrition. Over centuries they had become adapted for survival in the African tropics, so once removed from that specialized environment they faced particular nutritional requirements that could not easily be satisfied in the British mainland colonies of North America. But regardless of their special needs, the diet they received in America, if sufficient in bulk, was not sufficient in balance. Under such circumstances, many blacks in colonial America lived a nutritional nightmare. The majority of slaves received insufficient protein of good quality and insufficient amounts of the vitamin B complex, vitamins C and D, and calcium and iron. Among the results were frighteningly high rates of infant and early-child mortality, at times and in places up to 60 percent. "The mortality of negro children," wrote one commentator, "is as two to one when compared to whites." Of course, mothers' rigorous work, up to the point of childbirth and soon again afterward, when added to the problems caused by inadequate diet, resulted in high rates of mothers' deaths in childbirth as well. Also related to poor nutrition were development of personality disorders and a host of debilitating and often fatal diseases in the slave population—what masters called "the Negro diseases"—that were largely foreign to whites: rickets, pica (referred to as "dirt-eating"), hookworm, and pellagra ("black tongue"). Malnutrition also made slaves more susceptible to common diseases and more vulnerable to secondary infections when wounded or suffering a common virus.

Diet was the largest factor in African-American children faring as poorly as they did. In fact, the old image of throngs of thinly-clad children playing gayly about the slave quarter must be laid to rest. The more one learns about slaves' diet, their disease environment, and work patterns of slave mothers and children—the elements most directly affecting infant and child mortality—the more one accepts Richard H. Steckel's statement that the experience of enslaved children was "dreadful." In "Women, Work, and Health under Plantation Slavery in the United States" in *More than Chattel: Black Women and Slavery in the Americas,* edited by David Barry Gaspar and Darlene Clark Hine (1996), Steckel summarizes data from just after colonial times that show the effects of diet, work demands, and disease on infant and child health as manifested in height. In a word, slave children were tiny. At age five the average height of enslaved blacks did not make it into the first percentile of modern height distribution. Steckel writes, "The slums of Lagos, Nigeria, and urban areas of Bangladesh provided environments for growth superior to those faced by slave children." Once they reached adolescence, mainland slaves largely caught up, height-wise, with their white peers, likely the result of increased protein from meat distribution that came with the onset of work.

Given the nature of medical treatment in colonial times, which included the letting of blood, application of leeches, administration of harsh purgatives, and lancing with unsterilized instruments, slaves who were unwell frequently were better off when masters did not summon professional medical advice. Blacks maintained their own medical system in the form of plantation or neighborhood "root doctors," men and women who combined knowledge of herbal remedies and ritual skills with a holistic approach to devise therapeutics for many ills. Actually, practitioners of folk medicine in Africa long had been adept at matching the medicinal properties of plants to the symptoms of diseases. Also, the psychological benefit of believing in the healer, as African Americans seemed to do in their "root doctors," may have been as important as the medication.

Closely tied to black medical practice was another group of activities important to black folk culture that included magic, sorcery, and witchcraft. Belief in individuals with special powers to manipulate the spiritual realm to effect good and evil was widespread in West Africa, where it moved beyond the religious and into the secular world. Africans brought such traditions to colonial America and melded them into a body of beliefs and practices sometimes called "voodoo" or slave magic. Most sizable groups of African Americans comprised one or more individuals, often called "conjurers" by whites, who worked their magic to help or harm people as requested. One of the most frequently used magical practices was the wearing of amulets or talismans to ward off illness or misfortune. Blacks visited conjurers to ascertain ways to get even with evil overseers or cruel masters, or to give "the mis'ries" to fellow slaves who had done misdeeds. Individuals in the African-American community practiced divining, which included discovering lost property and predicting the future. Belief in ghosts was also common. It is important to note that in colonial America such African-American folk beliefs were close to those of whites of the time and place. New England slaves feared witches nearly as much as whites did, and many a white Yankee visited a black medium for protection against ghosts or to be healed of some affliction.

Speaking to spirits was one thing; speaking to humans was another. To do this, African Americans learned and developed forms of English comprising, to varying degrees, elements of African languages. Colonial masters deemed arriving Africans slow learners of a usable language (which had to have a basis in English, since whites were not at all willing learners themselves). This varied with age, of course—younger immigrants finding language acquisition easier than older ones—and with the amount of contact the newcomers had with English speakers. Still, it was practically axiomatic in the colonial Low Country that almost no adult Africans having resided there for less than a year spoke any recognizable English, and that some of those who had "been above twenty years in this Province," lamented one white South Carolinian, "can hardly speak even common things, so as to be understood." The situation was slightly different farther north, where saltwater slaves had more contact with creoles and whites.

The linguistic challenge was indeed a difficult one. Because West Africans spoke many mutually unintelligible languages and because most slaves in mainland North America were sufficiently dispersed as to be rarely in close contact with same-language speakers, few newcomers could talk easily with other slaves. Thus, over several generations African Americans developed their own ways to communicate.

Across most of the mainland colonies, blacks held onto common elements of African languages—certain grammar, words, sounds, and tones—as they fashioned their own variants of English. This resulted in sharp local differences in earlier periods, followed by regional variation, with a language closer to standard English being spoken farther north and more of a creole tongue, lingering longer, farther south. Where African slaves were relatively isolated for a long time, they spoke what are often regarded as wholly different languages—"Gullah" in the Sea Islands off the Low Country and an African-French-Portuguese creole along the Lower Mississippi.

Voice was a factor in music, too. West Africans surrounded themselves with music that had a deep heritage, and music was always important in the lives of African Americans. African influence was evident in the forms that black music took. A host of stringed instruments, most notably the banjo, certain fiddles (though this style melded quickly with that of the European violin), tambourines, flutes, xylophones, and drums rested on African technology. Blacks played these instruments in times of joy and sorrow; they sang together while hoeing crops, grinding corn, or rowing boats; they sang relatives to the afterlife in funerals; and they joined together on moonlit nights to sing "sweet chants." African-based call-and-response forms of song served a variety of purposes. Finally, folk narratives merged with song to provide instruction to children while entertaining them. Storytelling ranged from the amusing to the raunchy, depending on the audience.

Though there is little evidence of the forms of African-American dance in the colonial period, it was clearly a major part of celebrating. On holidays, recalled New Englander Jane Shelton, groups of women "shuffled and tripped to the sound of the fiddle." African-style ring dances were popular, and some dances were raucous, noisy affairs that whites neither understood nor appreciated. Thomas Hazard seemed not to care for the dancing style of the Rhode Island slave Sam, "who had a way of his own of fetching a terrific screech like a catamount, and then dashing forward to the middle of the floor." Likewise, Pierre de Laussat wrote that slaves in South Carolina celebrated the Christmas holiday in dance by "distorting their frame in the most unnatural figures and emitting the most hideous noises." When African Americans persisted in gathering at William Grimes's "upper room" in New Bedford, Connecticut, dancing late into the night, Grimes's neighbors complained until his landlord revoked his lease.

African Americans knew how to enjoy a holiday or an evening away from work. Alcohol regularly had a place in relaxation and merriment. Low Country slaves enjoyed boat races; blacks in port towns from Charleston to Boston liked to drink and play dice, especially "paw paw," an African gambling game. A black/Indian/lower-class-white tavern culture existed in cities of any size. White authorities did not approve of much of what went on in and around the taverns—they were places where the poorer folk could fence stolen goods and, with boldness enhanced by spirits, plan acts of resistance—and neighbors disliked the noises that accompanied tavern revelry. As early as 1692 New York's Common Council ordered the sheriff to give twenty lashes to any slaves "making any hooting or disorderly noise in the Street on the Lords Day." Such efforts tended to be in vain, however. Among the biggest single celebrations in colonial African-American culture was Election Day in New England, when slaves took a holiday to elect their own "kings" and "governors" in a satire of white society. Free of normal restraints, slaves dressed elaborately and celebrated the day with parades and "inaugural" parties. The officers elected became important personages in the black community. In coastal slave communities, mainly in the Low Country, Christmas-time extravaganzas called John Canoe festivals (seemingly named after a mythical or historical figure from the West-African coast) served the same purpose. Some slaves attending these mixtures of African and Anglo-Saxon celebrations dressed in animal masks, others wore headdresses shaped like houses or ships, and music and dance prevailed everywhere.

Whites and Blacks, Men and Women, Humanity and Inhumanity

Of a work so grand in scope and stature as Morgan's *Slave Counterpoint,* it is probably inappropriate to highlight any one particular element. But among the things that set the book apart from many others is Morgan's illumination of the relationships between and among different groups of whites and blacks in colonial America. Morgan not only describes these relationships, but shows how they changed over time and how such changes affected African Americans. After all, blacks in a subordinate position in a society had to relate constantly with white people considered above them, and how they did so affected much about their existence. So too, of course, did the fact that some of those white people owned them, making them at once pieces of property, like farm implements, and human beings with souls and feelings and minds of their own.

Into the early eighteenth century, a social model of patriarchy was dominant in the minds of persons of power—and, they hoped, others—in British mainland North America. In a perceived social hierarchy, male father figures existed at the top, from which lofty position they protected the weak, demanding obedience and loyalty in return. Colonial planters, the patriarchs, regarded slaves as property, made decisions about them with profit in mind, and applied discipline impersonally and severely to exact work from their physically close but socially distant subordinates. Yet many of these same masters could not overcome the notion that it was their duty to look after the well-being—in the lights of that time and place—of their dependent underlings, who were part of the planter's household in its broadest sense.

After the middle of the eighteenth century, the more austere and less emotional patriarchal relationships began to change and become, on the surface at least, softer and gentler, less authoritarian. Morgan cites the rise of evangelicalism, romanticism, and humanitarianism, among other things, as reasons for this shift to a more "enlightened patriarchalism." Eventually, masters who had dealt with members of the same slave families for several generations developed closer relations with them, perhaps cared more for them as individuals, and treated them more humanely. Masters also grew increasingly concerned with their reputations for benevolence: some of them made efforts to ameliorate slave codes and to provide their bondspeople better food, clothing, and housing. Through all of this, whites expected loyalty from their slaves and grew to develop a false sense that the men and women they owned and worked were grateful to them and happy with their lot. It was as if persons of African descent, who earlier were regarded as unfortunate (and perhaps dangerous) beings of a lower order, became perpetual children. The change was not equal across colonial America. It came more slowly and to a lesser degree in the Low Country than in the Chesapeake; in such venues as North Carolina, where the slave system matured late and African imports rose after 1750, it hardly appeared at all. But by the end of the colonial period, master-slave relations were moving toward the out-and-out paternalism that would characterize black-white dealings through much of the nineteenth century.

Lower-class whites generally did not share these views, and in earlier times blacks and whites worked together and interacted considerably. The evidence of white servants running away with enslaved blacks in the seventeenth century is extensive, and on the fringes of plantation country and in the growing urban settings of eighteenth-century colonial America, blacks and whites worked together, drank together, prayed together, and produced offspring together outside the law. In time, however, forces worked to separate African Americans and lower-class whites. The economic condition and status of plain whites rose, if haltingly, and poorer whites began to see blacks more clearly as potential competitors in the economic sphere. At the same time, members of the white gentry, for a multitude of reasons that included the need for greater control in societies that contained a great many slaves, courted poorer whites to identify and align themselves with their wealthier and more powerful neighbors. The result was a steadily growing antipathy between black slaves and white laborers. "The eighteenth century was a crucible in which the deep and increasingly reciprocal contempt felt between lower-class whites and blacks was forged," writes Morgan. "The contempt had not emerged in fully polished form by 1800, but the essentials were in place."

There was never enough antipathy to keep blacks and whites entirely apart in sexual relations, however. The considerable number of persons of mixed black and white parentage is mute evidence of such activity. Sex between white men and black women, and black men and white women, was bound to occur in societies that had such thorough contact. Inter-racial sexual relations probably took place more—at least per capita—in earlier colonial times than later, because strictures against such activity—public condemnation and ridicule often the most effective—grew stronger with the heightened religiosity of the late eighteenth century and the movement toward creation of a common white identity. They also took place more frequently in some places—along the Lower Mississippi or around the Chesapeake, for instance, than in the Low Country. But colonial America was a place where men and women of both races were together frequently and alone sufficiently for sex to take place. And it did.

Black-white sexual relationships in the colonial period could indeed be caring and affectionate. Edward Ball found evidence that his eighteenth-century Low Country ancestor, the planter Elias Ball, had a long and seemingly caring relationship with his slave Dolly, thirty-six years his junior, which produced two children, Edward and Catherine, the only of his slaves to bear English forenames and the only ones to be granted their freedom. The elder Ball summoned a physician for a house call when Dolly took ill—a momentous occurrence indeed—and hired a cobbler to make her expensive shoes that were a far cry from the "Negro shoes" allotted to the rest of his slaves. Other evidence from various places shows white and black men and women living together as man and wife. A white woman in Northampton County, Virginia, paid a fine and served a six-month prison term in 1738 so she could marry a mulatto man.

Of course, a good portion of the inter-racial sexual activity must have been less caring. Sex for money was certainly known in colonial times, and as cities grew larger, toward the late eighteenth century, blacks and whites met in "disorderly houses" and did as they would, in spite of the law. Out on plantations, some masters and their male offspring could be downright predatory in nature toward female slaves. It is not clear how frequently these liaisons constituted violent rape, since such incidents did not come before the law.

But that some of the sexual unions between white men and black women were violent in nature should hardly be surprising, given that slave societies were based on violence. Wherever one turned and regardless with whom the slaves were dealing, the world of master and slave was one of violence. It was corporal punishment that coerced the African-American men and women to work for another's gain, and such punishment and the threat thereof maintained order in the larger slave societies. Plantation justice, meted out on the spot by a master or his agent to an offending slave, was the most common form of "correction." Often, this involved whipping, a punishment done in public for the deterrent effects of the display and one that brought the danger of infection with the slicing action and pain of the cowhide. More serious crimes invoked a greater number of lashes or escalated beyond whipping to dismembering. Perhaps it was only economic practicality—the wariness of losing a working hand—that kept plantation justice from resulting in larger numbers of deaths. Death-by-punishment is evident in the more formal court systems. Marvin L. Michael Kay and Lorin Lee Cary analyze criminal justice in North Carolina in *Slavery in North Carolina, 1748–1775* (1995) and leave no doubts about the barbarity of the system. All whites executed by order of North Carolina courts were hanged, but slaves, whose rate of execution exceeded that of whites by thirteen times, faced sadistic treatment before meeting a savage death. Half the slaves whose mode of execution is known in North Carolina between the mid-seventeenth century and the outbreak of the Revolution suffered clear brutality. "One was chained alive in a gibbet to die slowly and horribly," write Kay and Cary as they describe some of the executions: "Six were burned, two were castrated and then hanged, five were hanged and decapitated with their heads displayed on poles, one was hanged and burned . . . , two died as a result of castration, seven slaves . . . were shot or beaten to death when captured, and five outlawed runaways drowned themselves to avoid capture and sadistic treatment."

In populated areas from New York City to New Orleans, such executions often were prolonged and public. African-American men and women accused of plotting a rebellion might be burned alive—or, in the case of one person executed after the 1712 slave uprising in New York, slowly roasted to death over a low fire—or killed "at the wheel," a torturous medieval device that broke the person's limbs and left him or her outdoors to linger in pain before dying. For the purpose of teaching appropriate lessons, white authorities left bodies hanging in gibbets or severed heads atop poles, about town or at busy crossroads, until they decomposed.

Such brutality had to affect all elements of slave societies. One need not wonder where the men who wrote the United States Constitution in the 1780s came up with the idea for strictures against cruel and inhuman punishments.

Resistance, Escape, and Rebellion

A spirit of resistance and the potential for escape or rebellion ran deep in the colonial slave population. Masters who were honest with themselves never harbored any notion that the men and women they held in bondage were a contented lot. They lived in a world where African Americans were daily expressing rebellious disgust for their situations in dozens of little ways, and one where the potential for uprising was always present.

Proof of this is in the body of laws that existed to prevent such action. As slave populations grew, suspicion, distrust, and fear filled the minds of white colonists and became manifest in colonial statutes. Eighteenth-century slave codes limited the number of blacks who could meet in groups, forbade their carrying anything resembling weapons, kept blacks on the farm or plantation and off streets after dark, and even outlawed their possession of drums or horns, "which may give notice to one another of their wicked designs." Capital offenses included arson, poisoning, repeated theft, inciting insurrection, and resisting interrogation. Police kept a close eye on urban blacks, slave patrols guarded rural areas, and white colonists remained vigilant. Local justices could resort to the equivalent of medieval torture to keep the slave population docile, but it was masters and overseers who most frequently corrected slave misbehavior in the myriad ways the law allowed. Colonial statutes permitted branding, flogging, burning, amputation of limbs, hamstringing, and execution. Records of administration of these punishments are wondrously matter-of-fact. Middlesex County, Virginia, in the first twenty-five years of the eighteenth century was probably typical. During that period the government saw to the sale of eight blacks to the West Indies (with compensation for their owners) for "frequent disorderly meetings." A minister and two accomplices beat to death the clergyman's slave for running away. A vengeful slave owner castrated one slave for "running away, lying out and distroying peoples Stocks"; cut off the toes of another for "lying out and doing Severall Misdemeanors"; and pilloried and cut off the ears of a third for a second offense of stealing. Another Middlesex court executed a slave for treason, dismembering him and hanging one of his quarters in a public place.

In the face of such punishments, slaves were imminently practical. Forms of resistance ranged along a continuum from acts of forgetfulness (failure to remember critical parts of a message, for instance) or carelessness (which might result in breaking a tool, ruining a plant, harming a pig, or burning a stack of hay); to feigning illness or malingering; to mocking whites (masters in particular) in clever words, songs, and actions; to stealing; to running away; and ultimately to organized, armed rebellion. The particular form resisting slaves selected at any time or place depended on its chances for success, but the extent of slaves' acculturation and the kind of work they did had a bearing on how they resisted.

"Saltwater" slaves had a tendency on arrival to run away with others who spoke the same language—or even, sometimes, with shipmates. It did not take them long to grasp the reality of their situations, however. Africans not long in the colonies, lacking command of English and living an isolated existence with few other slaves, resisted in subtle ways. They ruined crops, broke tools, malingered and balked, feigned sickness or stupidity, or stole goods or animals to sell on the black market. Household slaves under closer supervision worked slowly, acted surly, or got drunk. Most blacks not fully acculturated who did run away were more truant than long absent. Their limited ability to exist unnoticed in white society made them "outliers," hiding in the woods, close to the people they knew.

But more often than people at the time wished to admit, African men and women headed for the near or more distant frontier and attempted to form settlements of runaways—called "maroon" settlements (from the Portuguese *cimarrón,* for runaway). It was harder to do this in the Chesapeake, given the African minority and a topography that did not lend itself to hiding, but the Low Country, with its black majority and a terrain difficult to cross, with more places to remove oneself and go unnoticed, was the scene of more maroon camps. Once Spanish authorities established the town of freed Carolina slaves at Gracia Real de Santa Teresa de Mose near St. Augustine in 1738, more Low Country slaves lit out southward to gain their freedom. Some, who chose not to attempt the difficult passage all the way to Florida, built their own settlements. A 1765 expedition against a maroon group up the Savanna River found the escapees inhabiting a small "town" surrounded by a swamp. Members of the force of whites sent to run off the residents, a group that included "two Negroes on a Scaffold one Beating a Drum and the other hoisting Colours," found "a square consisting of four Houses 17 feet long and 14 feet wide, that the kettles were upon the fire boiling rice and about 15 bushels of rough rice." White colonists were intent on rooting out these settlements and taking steps to prevent their further establishment. At the Savanna River town, they gathered up "Blanketts, Potts, Shoes, Axes, and many other tools all of which together with the Town they set fire to."

The more assimilated slaves became, the wiser they were to the ways of whites and thus the more capable of finding more subtle, but still satisfying, intellectual responses to their condition in bondage or, in more extreme cases, fleeing it. Runaway advertisements provide unintended evidence of African-American expressions of resistance and contempt for whites through such normal manifestations of feelings as body movements. Colonial masters described fugitives who, "when speaking looks you full in the face," or who possessed "a sneaking down look," a "sour countenance," or "a Swaggering Air with him in his Walk." Piersen in *Black Legacy* calls attention to "more civilized and more common forms of social pressure based on the African predisposition for wry humor and verbal cleverness" that blacks regularly used in mocking white figures of authority. One observer found whites in such a situation "good naturedly submitting to the hard hits leveled against themselves." Outside of Charleston, South Carolina, in 1772, a white man who sneaked a view of African Americans at a Saturday night country dance failed to find it so funny. "The entertainment was opened by the men copying (or taking off) the manners of their masters," he reported, "and the women those of their mistresses, and relating some highly curious anecdotes, to the inexpressible diversion of that company." Songs of colonial Louisiana slaves could be more biting still:

> Negro cannot walk, without corn in his pocket,
>   It is to steal chickens.
> Mulatto cannot walk without rope in his pocket,
>   It is to steal horses.
> White man cannot walk without money in his pockets,
>   It is to steal girls.

Perhaps it was those less clever with words and better with their hands who took to flight. Skilled artisans who were fully acculturated and moved freely between rural and urban environments were the ones most likely to try to escape from slavery altogether. Carpenters, "fishing Negroes," and boatmen were especially apt to run away for good. In the colonial era there was no northern bastion of freedom to run to, but these runaways often headed for towns where they could get lost among the handful of free blacks and lower-class whites that made up the substratum of society. The North Carolina piedmont, populated by nonslaveholding whites, was another haven for fugitives, as was Spanish Florida. Black artisans ran away alone, many to rejoin relatives, and they relied on their skills and savvy to get jobs and carry on new lives.

Outright rebellion occupied the extreme end of the resistance-rebellion spectrum. Herbert Aptheker in *American Negro Slave Revolts* (1943, rev. ed. 1969) notes that periods of widespread slave rebelliousness came in waves every generation or so, "as though anger accumulated and vented itself and then a period of rest and recuperation was needed before the next upsurge." There seem to have been waves of general slave unrest, which may have corre-sponded with slave rebelliousness in the Caribbean and the greater Atlantic world between 1710 and 1722, 1730 and 1740, 1765 and 1780, and 1790 and 1802. If full-scale rebellions did not occur regularly every few years, when they did occur they gained notice in colonial society out of proportion to their significance. Here, again, chance of success was a guiding principle. African Ameri-cans greatly outnumbered by whites thought better of joining insurrections. Because this was frequently the case in the main-land colonies—different from most other New World slave societ-ies, where slave rebellions were more common—incidents of open rebellion were relatively rare. Still, since colonial publications did not spread word of conspiracies and insurrections, more were prob-ably planned than most white colonists (and, subsequently, most historians) perceived. Evidence from such widely separated loca-tions as New York City, Charleston, and New Orleans suggests that Africans, or blacks who were able to create some real or artificial African identity with other slaves in this country, were involved in some of the largest conspiracies and rebellions. The urban setting, where enslaved men and women had greater freedom of movement and broader choice of their contacts—and where blacks met with all sorts of people in back-alley taverns where rum flowed freely, was particularly conducive to organized rebellion. Benjamin Franklin seems to have captured the general tone of some urban slaves when he described Philadelphia blacks as being of a "plotting Disposition."

Indeed, plotting that occurred in New York City and its environs bore fruit that was deadly for some whites and painful for many more. Historians recently have focused attention on what several see as generalized black unrest and conspiratorial activities in eighteenth-century New York. During the century's first decade, slaves in New York and New Jersey grew increasingly angry over new, harsher laws restricting their activities. In rural areas the result was an occasional murder of a slave owner, followed by the horrors of a slave execution; in the city, slave unrest was more likely to involve group activity. On April 6, 1712, some two dozen slaves led by a core of Akan-speaking, Gold-Coast Africans (identified by contemporary whites as "Coromantees") set fire to the outbuilding of a prominent New Yorker and then shot and stabbed whites who were coming to extinguish the flames, killing nine of them and wounding half a dozen others. Authorities eventually captured twenty-one conspirators and, after a quick trial, publicly executed eighteen of them in a variety of inhumane ways.

Other plots and conspiracies turned up in New York City in 1721 and 1734, but the grandest of all may have been one in 1741. The conditional is required here because historians have yet to agree on whether or not a bona fide, grand, and dangerous (to whites) plot truly existed. According to some, over the winter of 1740–41 a group of blacks, with support from poorer Irish, English, Dutch, and Spanish men and women who frequented some of New York's waterside taverns, joined to plan a rebellion with mighty potential. Graham Russell Hodges in *Root and Branch: African Americans in New York and East Jersey, 1613–1863* (1999) detects "a powerful proletarian republicanism" in the plot, the conspirators held together by the fact that (as one of the slaves involved was reported saying) "a great many people had too much, and others too little." Evidence turned up also of some of the conspirators being aware of a general black rebelliousness around the western Atlantic and many slaves being displeased that their Christianity held out little prospect for freedom. As before, arson was their favored tool. Over several weeks, fire destroyed New York's Fort George and several white homes before whites uncovered the plot, held a showy trial, and executed or sent away those found guilty. "Only the discovery of loose talk," Hodges writes, "kept the 1741 plot from becoming the worst racial uprising in colonial North America."

But it was not the worst racial uprising, even of its time or place, and more recently Jill Lepore in *New York Burning: Liberty, Slavery, and Conspiracy in Eighteenth-Century Manhattan* (2005) leaves one wondering if any "Great Negro Plot" truly existed, as some wondered at the time. Was it all a reflection of the generalized fears of Manhattan's 10,000 whites of the 2,000 slaves in their midst, or even more the sad result of the actions of a venal and racist judge on New York's Supreme Court, than an indication that a carefully planned slave (or underclass) uprising was in the works? Lepore casts doubt on the veracity of slaves' confessions and labels the state's primary witness, a sixteen-year-old indentured servant who received her freedom and a £100 reward for her testimony, "comically corrupt." Still, enough wealthy whites in New York believed that blacks were plotting to kill them, take over Manhattan, and install a king to bring mass arrests. Trials of the conspirators lasted through the summer of 1741 and the resultant executions of thirty-four persons were an almost daily occurrence for several weeks. (David Grim, who was four years old at the time, had the executions so etched in his mind that he included details of burning and gibbeted blacks on a map he drew of the Manhattan of his childhood seventy-two years later.) Yet, it seems certain that no matter how many accused black conspirators were publicly burned at the stake, no matter how many charred corpses were gibbeted about the city in the most public of places, African Americans continued to chafe at their bonds and join others in thoughts of rebellion along and around the lower Hudson.

But slave uprisings were not limited to northern cities. In fact, the largest and likely most serious of these in all of England's mainland colonies occurred in plantation sections of Virginia and South

Carolina within a decade of the New York conspiracy (lending credence to Aptheker's idea of waves of slave unrest). In the fall of 1730, possibly on the basis of a rumor that planters were blocking an edict by England's King George II to free all slaves who were Christians, and with the likelihood that a good proportion of recent slaves arriving in the Chesapeake were from the Kingdom of the Kongo, which had a Christian heritage, captive Africans and African Americans held meetings in several parts of Virginia. These apparently triggered work slowdowns on farms and plantations at harvest time of a particularly bountiful year. In October, several hundred blacks assembled in Norfolk and Princess Anne counties, chose officers to lead an "intended Insurrection," and ran off into the Dismal Swamp, from which they made forays into surrounding plantations, doing "a great deal of Mischief." Using Pasquotank Indians to locate and round up these rebels and others in neighboring counties—and sometimes to mete out their own justice on the spot—white authorities hastily put down the rebellion and then beefed up militia patrols and warned Virginia slaveholders to be more vigilant.

It was nine years after this, near the Stono River, within twenty miles of Charleston, South Carolina, that occurred what most historians consider the most serious slave uprising of the colonial period—in part because it triggered other rebellions and acts of resistance over several years. A core of newly arrived "Angolan" slaves—again, likely men who once were part of the Kingdom of Kongo north of the Congo River—apparently planned the Stono Rebellion. Since many of these people were Portuguese-speaking Catholics, and since Spanish East Florida offered freedom in a setting friendly to Catholicism, some at the time speculated that Spanish propaganda played a role in instigating the uprising. Under the leadership of a slave named Jemmy, twenty blacks on the morning of September 9, 1739, broke into a store, where they stole small arms and powder, killing the storekeepers and leaving their severed heads on the front steps. By daybreak, as they moved southward along the road toward Georgia, they had killed eight whites. Through the early afternoon they killed most of the whites they encountered—they spared the life of a white tavern keeper who was known for his kindness to his slaves—and burned houses. Around midday the group, whose ranks had swollen to fifty or sixty, met up with South Carolina's Lieutenant Governor, William Bull, returning to Charleston for the commencement of a new legislative session. Bull apparently had to ride hard to escape with his life.

After halting in an open field in mid-afternoon, the rebels, according to a contemporary "Account of the Negroe Insurrection," "set to dancing, Singing and beating Drums to draw more Negroes to them." Although before evening a force of mounted planters attacked and dispersed the gathering that at one time may have approached one hundred persons, it took nearly a week for a white militia company to catch and overcome the largest remnant of the group. The remaining core of fighters may have been individuals who had been soldiers in Africa, knew how to use firearms effectively, and relied on proven tactics to hold off their pursuers. Some were not apprehended for several months after the uprising began, and one leader remained at large for three years. Altogether, thirty whites and forty-four blacks died in the slaughter associated with the insurrection. Another thirty slaves, these apparently more-assimilated creoles rather than the "Saltwater" insurgents, received rewards for fighting against the insurgents. This uprising prompted South Carolina to lump together all blacks as dangerous to white society, whether "of a rebellious nature" or not, and systematically tighten restrictions (on free blacks as well as slaves) with the harshest penalties of any mainland colony.

Through the middle of the eighteenth century, newcomers from Africa seem to have been the ones most likely to join in rebellion. Thereafter, open rebellion was something plotted by the most highly assimilated slaves. Mullin in *Flight and Rebellion* explains the irony of slave rebellions being tied to the acculturation process. As slaves acculturated according to their masters' designs, they learned their roles on the farm or plantation, the house or factory, but they also learned strategies that would help them rise against their owners. Late in the colonial period the liberal influence of the American Revolution and the increased need for skilled slaves around cities led to a relaxing of restraints upon African Americans in urban areas. For a time, this may have served as a safety valve, permitting slaves who might otherwise have lashed out to visit a relative, go underground, or even just vent in a grog shop. But, eventually, freer to move about and meet meant more able to plan, and it was skilled, urban slaves who in 1800 organized "Gabriel's Rebellion," which Mullin considers "the most sophisticated and ambitious slave conspiracy" in American history. Acculturation, he concludes, "ultimately created slaves who were able to challenge the security of the society itself."

One final form of rebellion in which African Americans participated turned out to be more ambitious than any other. James Oliver Horton and Lois E. Horton in *In Hope of Liberty: Culture, Community and Protest Among Northern Free Blacks, 1700–1860* (1997) place northern blacks in a class grouping with Indians and poorer whites, who increasingly resisted what they perceived as gross injustice of their social and economic position. "Interracial ceremony and celebration, social interaction, and familial connection became the building blocks of their alliance," write the Hortons. "Arson, riot, and even armed insurrection became their political tools." As the century wore on and notions of liberty spread among persons living around the colonial Atlantic, groupings of the so-called "lower sorts," which included blacks, became more willing to take action on such ideals in the ways that worked best for them.

After 1763, the British government became a target for such rebellious action. African Americans in northern cities joined others in feeling the pinch that came with the economic downturn following the end of the Seven Years' War, and they were in the mobs that took to the streets in protest of the tightening British regulations that were only making things worse. Interracial gathering places—taverns and back-alley gaming spots—again became centers for this rebellious activity. It must have been with mixed feelings that white colonial elites and middle-class elements looked on, perhaps disliking England's tightening controls on the colonies more than they feared the public expression of the "lower elements." Many in Boston approved of the activities of the "saucy boys, negroes and mulattoes, Irish teagues and outlandish jack-tarrs," led by runaway slave Crispus Attucks, who on March 5, 1770, following an incident with a British soldier in a dockside tavern, taunted and harassed the guards at the Custom House until the Redcoats opened fire. The Boston Massacre was a spark for the fire of liberty that swept across the colonies soon afterward. African Americans in and out of slavery played no small part in the work of kindling that flame.

The Revolutionary Era

To contend for our own liberty and to deny that blessing
to others involves an inconsistency not to be excused.

—JOHN JAY, 1785

For African Americans the American Revolution was full of contradictions. The clearest of these involved slavery and the ideology the Founding Fathers used to justify breaking with England. A third of the men who signed the document declaring their right to independent nationhood on the self-evident truth that all men are created equal owned other humans. In addition, the nation these men would create—one that would secure the blessings of liberty to themselves and their posterity—was one whose social and economic fabric was woven with the thread of black slavery, whose population included half a million African and African-American slaves, and whose wealthiest southerners would not consider joining a union of states without a clear recognition of their right to own black men, women, and children.

But the contradictions involved more than slavery and Revolutionary ideology. Among the results of the Revolution were paradoxical changes in African-American society and culture. The Revolution helped make it possible for some blacks to gain their freedom. It played an important role in the ending of slavery in the states north of Maryland and in considerable manumission in the Upper South, and it gave even more African Americans the idea that freedom was not merely something good to obtain, but something one had a right to expect. Yet, when one considers numbers, it becomes clear that the Revolutionary era did little to reduce the nation's reliance on slaves. Not 500,000 slaves lived on the British North American mainland in 1776; nearly 700,000 were counted in the first census of the new United States in 1790. Where emancipation did occur, in the North and Upper South, in almost every instance it came grudgingly, and in all areas white sons of the Revolution began circumscribing that freedom soon after more than a few blacks had gained it. North and South, white men in positions of authority cut away at African-American rights, privileges, and opportunities, so that the black men and women who no longer were slaves remained separated and ostracized from the rest of American society.

Also, for those thousands of Americans who remained in bondage and for the many thousands of Americans who would be slaves over the next four-score years, the Revolution made freedom more difficult to obtain. Following the break with England, slavery in the states south of Maryland grew in size and strength. Southern slave-holders became all the more convinced that the institution was necessary for their economic survival. And American independence entrenched slavery into the laws of the new land. Without mentioning the words *slave* or *slavery*, the Constitution made the institution legitimate and gave slaveholders greater means to protect and defend their human property. In legitimizing slavery and strengthening the hold of slave owners, founders of the new nation set the stage for the enormous expansion of slavery into what would become the Cotton South—the open and newly acquired lands to the south and west—beginning early in the nineteenth century.

Yet most important for blacks in the United States over the long term, and probably most ironic, the Revolution brought a broadening and strengthening of the hierarchical order to American race relations. Although most English colonists held strong feelings about race before the Revolution, they did not need to use race so centrally to justify enslaving other human beings. Once

Revolutionary theory made all persons free and equal with God-given inalienable rights, many who spoke the new ideals had cause to further entrench their racist feelings. Now they could rationalize slavery only by recognizing African Americans as a lower order of persons, short on morals, long on muscle, quick to pilfer, slow to move, and hard to work. And they could remain above the new and rapidly growing body of free blacks they despised only by using the same rationale. This affected all Americans and laid the foundation for a stronger and more pervasive racist ideology that would plague the country from the time the Revolution had run its course until the present day.

Slavery and Ideology

Westerners had long been in conflict over the existence of slavery in their society. Within the eighteenth-century body of thought we know as the Enlightenment, strong intellectual forces emerged that worked against chattel slavery. Based initially on religious principles, and then bolstered by philanthropic tendencies accompanying the early growth of capitalism, antislavery sentiment arose in continental Europe and spread to England. By the time of the American Revolution, regardless of what else was going on, Western intellectuals and philosophers were reading and thinking and acting in a world that was debating slavery.

It was not as if there had been no opposition to slavery among British colonists on the North American mainland before 1750. To a few seventeenth-century Americans, human bondage had always been immoral and unchristian, and the number of opponents to slavery grew with the size of the slave population. A handful of New England Puritans and a few Scots and Salzburgers in Georgia spoke out against slavery in the eighteenth century, but those who took the lead in expressing antislavery sentiment were members of the Society of Friends—the Quakers. The Quakers were an anomaly because many of them made profits from the slave trade, owned slaves themselves, and harbored doubts about Africans' abilities. Not until the 1760s, when the supply of indentured servants increased and the supply of slaves decreased, did significant numbers of Philadelphia Quakers, for instance, begin following the antislavery principles they expressed formally in their yearly meetings. Nevertheless, as David Brion Davis writes in *The Problem of Slavery in Western Culture* (1966), "It would be difficult to exaggerate the central role Quakers played in initiating and sustaining the first antislavery movements."

Some of them had spoken out early. At a Friends meeting in Germantown, Pennsylvania, in 1688, a group of Quakers drafted a formal protest against slavery and "the traffic of men-body." In 1711 the Society of Friends in Rhode Island rid itself of a member who was mistreating a slave, and a year later a prosperous Philadelphia Quaker vainly petitioned the Pennsylvania Assembly to emancipate all slaves in the colony. By the middle of the eighteenth century the English-speaking world was becoming increasingly aware of the official Quaker antipathy for slavery. Under the leadership of such persons as Benjamin Lay, John Woolman, and Anthony Benezet, uncompromising Quakers were pressing for disowning members of the Society who continued to hold slaves. If, as Donald L. Robinson argues in *Slavery and the Struggle for American Politics, 1765–1820* (1971), the Quaker efforts were "like fireflies in the night," at least by the time of the Seven Years' War the nighttime horizon that framed the hills and valleys and village greens of the American colonies was aglow. By then, Quakers had launched a frontal attack on the slave trade and had brought the broader ideas of antislavery thinking before the educated public, where they were ripe for debate. The tensions that grew between England and its mainland colonies after the Seven Years' War thus raised arguments against and flushed out a rationalization for slavery, even as they prompted colonists to question existing mercantile practices and to dwell on ways in which their political and economic lives could be better.

Many of the men doing this questioning considered themselves scions of the Enlightenment. Their faith in Man's limitless creative intelligence and rational, benevolent behavior brought them to apply their minds to creating a new order: no more oppression from religious zealots or tyrannous monarchs, no more misery or deprivation for the people in their society. The new order would provide persons of all classes the freedom to seek happiness and unleash their talents on their natural circumstances to the benefit of all. The result would be what the rational, benevolent Creator intended. Of course, this was an ideology into which slavery did not fit, and the American patriots knew it. Like despotism, slavery was a vestige of old ways of the Old World, a violation of human rights. By being born human, individuals had inherent rights to freedom, to gain from their work, and to improve their lives as they wished. Skin color was not supposed to matter.

Early expression of such ideas came from some of the very men who are now considered the nation's Founding Fathers. Just a year after conclusion of the Seven Years' War, James Otis, Jr., the Massachusetts lawyer frequently associated with the statement, "Taxation without representation is tyranny," described slavery as a "vile and miserable. . . estate of man" and asked, "Does it follow that tis right to enslave a man because he is black?" Two years later, Benjamin Rush, en route to Edinburgh, Scotland, to study medicine, was outraged when he saw slaves massed in Liverpool harbor. On his return to his home in Philadelphia in 1773, Rush wrote a pamphlet assailing the slave trade and labeling slavery "so foreign to the human mind, that the moral faculties, as well as those of the understanding are debased, and rendered torpid by it."

Such thinking was about, then, and no doubt in the mind of young Thomas Jefferson when he wrote the document, which Rush and fifty-five others would sign in 1776, justifying the colonists' political break with England. Jefferson even blamed the English monarch for the slave trade in the first draft of the Declaration of Independence, though members of the Continental Congress excised those portions, recognizing the utility of the argument but fully aware of the absurdity of blaming George III for what Rhode Island merchants and Virginia planters had been getting rich from for scores of years. But the Declaration seemed to doom slavery nonetheless with its first paragraph. All men were created equal; their God-given, unalienable rights included life, liberty, and the pursuit of happiness; governments were created to secure these rights. Nowhere did it limit application of this heady language.

But the new republic did not end slavery. Instead, it perpetuated the institution for the better part of another century. Why this happened and how the signers of the Declaration and framers of the Constitution, which put ideals into policy, could justify slavery even as they asserted the inalienable right of freedom for all are questions with which historians still grapple.

Jefferson easily becomes a symbol of the Revolutionary paradox and thus the focus of much of the questioning. Because he penned the words of the Declaration of Independence and espoused most eloquently its ideals, he stands out among those "enlightened" men who waged the rebellion and put together the new nation. Jefferson spoke often of wanting to end slavery in the spirit of the French *philosophes* he admired. Many have asked why the framer of the Declaration, the future president, and the slave owner never put into action his libertarian ideals, even with his own slaves.[1] Answers have varied. One turns on the practical argument. In addition to being one of the most respected men in colonial America, Jefferson was first and foremost in his mind a member of the Virginia gentry. He lived among and socialized almost exclusively with his peers, members of an elite social class of slave-owning tobacco farmers. Jefferson himself owned over two hundred slaves. They were the men and women who built his beloved Monticello and made it run—at low cost. He never failed to recognize that his economic position and his status among his fellow gentry were tied to a slave system. And he knew that system was growing; demand for slaves was increasing steadily, values of human property were rising. Ending slavery would have meant social and economic, not to mention political, suicide for Jefferson and wealthy slave owners like him. Once he tried and failed to alter the ideas of his peers and supporters, argues Ronald L. Hatzenbuehler in *"I Tremble for my Country": Thomas Jefferson*

---

[1] Paul Finkelman in *Slavery and the Founders: Race and Liberty in the Age of Jefferson,* 2nd ed. (2001) argues that questions about Jefferson and slavery arise primarily because historians and biographers who treat Jefferson as "the most popular saint of American civil religion," have regularly "tried to fudge the evidence, or simply ignored it, to make Jefferson into something he was not. . . . Admirers of Jefferson would like him to be one of us—an opponent of slavery," Finkelman writes. "But he was not."

and the Virginia Gentry (2006), Jefferson gave up and put off the problem for future generations to deal with.

Another answer is based on Jefferson's professed, deep-seated feelings of dislike for blacks—his racism, in other words. It is difficult not to be startled by the strength and character of the racist feelings he wrote of in *Notes on the State of Virginia* (1785), which he intended for European intellectuals. Jefferson described blacks as "inferior to the whites in the endowments of body and mind." From "scientific observation" he wrote of blacks' laziness and slowness, their inability to reason, their lack of imagination, their "disagreeable odour," and their unsightly appearance compounded by "wooly hair" and an "ungainly" physique.[2] If Jefferson truly joined others of the Enlightenment in wanting to end chattel slavery, as he often wrote, his commitment to do so was only theoretical. He expressed strong dislike for African Americans and did not want to live with them as his equals in a free society. When he pondered abolition, it always involved sending the freed bondsmen back to Africa. Racial prejudice joined with economic necessity, as he saw it, to keep him from putting theory into practice.

A third answer goes beyond Jefferson and has to do with proslavery sentiment among whites in at least part of the British North American mainland. White Virginians seemed to have shared Jefferson's dislike for blacks, but not so many held his expressed concern for slaves as humans. After all, Jefferson was one of the most enlightened members of American society—schooled at William and Mary, thoroughly read in history and philosophy, and by

---

[2] We now are reasonably certain that neither "odour" nor "wooly" hair nor ungainliness stood in the way of Jefferson having a long-standing sexual relationship with one of his slaves, Sally Hemings, who bore six children by him. In 1998 DNA testing established a link that has since convinced most historians and a committee convened at Monticello by the Thomas Jefferson Foundation of Jefferson's paternity. What they remain unconvinced of is the nature of the relationship. In *The Hemingses of Monticello: An American Family* (2008), Annette Gordon-Reed argues that it must have been a long-term, romantic attachment, but in a review of the book (*The New York Times Book Review*, October 5, 2008) Eric Foner asks, "Was it rape, psychological coercion, a sexual bargain or a long-term loving connection?" That the relationship could have been characterized as any of these, or as different ones at different times, reveals something about the nature of slavery, race relations, and gender in the late-colonial period.

the age of thirty well versed in current libertarian ideas. Most of the rest of American society was different.

In 1784 and 1785 over twelve hundred people signed petitions to the Virginia General Assembly opposing a 1782 Virginia law that simply allowed masters to free their slaves without legislative approval. The signers based their proslavery arguments on scripture and the right to private property that the Revolution had affirmed—though this right apparently did not, in their minds, include authority to free their human property if they so chose—and they felt less of a necessity to rationalize their stance on slavery than did the man who wrote so eloquently about the "rights of man" in the Declaration of Independence.

For that matter, the long focus on Jefferson and slavery seems to have kept the microscope away from examination of other noteworthy Founders, making it easy to think of them as different in this regard and, from a post–civil-rights era perspective, better. After all, did not Benjamin Franklin become President of the Pennsylvania Society for the Abolition of Slavery at its founding in 1785, and did not George Washington resolve two years earlier never again to buy or sell another slave? These set the men apart from Jefferson and many other Americans on the issue. But scholarship of late has begun raising questions about these men, as well. David Waldstreicher in *Runaway America: Benjamin Franklin, Slavery, and the American Revolution* (2004) shows that Franklin, while opposing slavery on moral and practical grounds (finding it inefficient and dangerous), never acted to limit the institution, declining in 1787 to bring the matter of slavery before the Constitutional Convention when his abolition society requested he do so, and was largely behind the creation of America's "founding myth"—that being of a nation built and based on the labor of free men—when he knew otherwise. Washington is harder to criticize since he did, in his will in 1799, arrange for all of his slaves to be freed after the death of his wife, Martha (three years later). But Washington never took action as a public figure to limit slavery—beset by problems with runaway slaves himself, he signed the Fugitive Slave Act late in his first term as president—and, like Jefferson, profit was foremost on his mind as manager of his estate.

"The work ethic reigned supreme at Mount Vernon," writes Fritz Hirschfield in *George Washington and Slavery: A Documentary Portrayal* (1997), "while humanity ran a distant second."

In all of this reflection on individual thought and action, it is important to keep in mind the national issue: the fragile coalition of diverse economic and social groups that joined forces against England did so to wage a political, rather than a social, revolution. What held the coalition together was agreement on wanting to rid the colonies of tight English control. It was to justify independence that they agreed on the application of Enlightenment theory. But the small farmers and urban artisans, the northern capitalists and southern planters agreed on little else—indeed, the coalition broke apart before the newborn United States of America was past toddling—and they clearly did not agree on whether the new nation should proceed with or without slavery. Strong leadership might not have carried the day for abolition.

So, in spite of the lofty ideals held up to justify it, the Revolution failed to eradicate slavery from the nation that replaced British rule over the North American mainland. But in raising the issues of freedom and human dignity the Revolution did bring significant change to all parts of American society. For blacks in the northern states and for growing numbers of them in the Upper South, this change meant becoming free persons. For many in the Lower South it meant greater personal independence, albeit within a slave system that was growing and becoming more deeply entrenched. Finally, the arguments for freedom and the growing presence of free blacks in certain segments of society led toward a hardening of racial lines and movement toward a system in which all African Americans, slave or free, would be regarded as members of a despised lower caste.

Freedom for Some

The history of African Americans in the English North American mainland colonies for the century between 1670 and the outbreak of the American Revolution is a story of persons in bondage. In most places in North America there simply were no blacks who were not enslaved. Good population figures do not exist for the colonies, but it seems that before 1770 free blacks made up only about 5 percent of the colonial African-American population. Nearly all of these resided in the northern colonies, where they lived largely without influence in white society. Many of the free blacks in pre-Revolutionary America were children of black-white marriages. A few had physical disabilities or were simply too old to be useful slaves.

But the situation with free blacks changed during the time of the American Revolution. The 1770s and 1780s saw the beginning of the slow but steady eradication of slavery in the North and the startling growth of a free-black population in the Upper South. From the situation, it is natural to assume cause and effect: that the moral, intellectual, political, and military ferment of Revolutionary times prompted the colonies' white population to take action that resulted in slavery's demise in one section and its decline in another. But other factors besides the moral arguments of the rising libertarian ideology were important in the turn away from dependence on slavery in some locales. In particular, no end of resolute African Americans, mostly (though not entirely) those enslaved, forced the issue on a white public not altogether eager to end their advantaged and exploitative position with those in bondage and, as it turned out, not at all ready to provide opportunity for, or witness the social or economic advancement of, persons of African descent.

From the time of the codification of slavery a century earlier, whites steadily had reduced the liberties of those few free African Americans in their midst. In various places blacks' political rights did not exist, and African Americans were ostracized socially. Through most of the eighteenth century individual Virginians could manumit their slaves only with permission of the state assembly. Whites in southern colonies were especially blunt in expressing their views on free blacks. The governor of Virginia in 1723 asserted whites should place "a perpetual Brand upon Free-Negroes & Mulattos by excluding them from the great Priviledge of a Freeman," in order to "make the free Negroes sensible that a distinction ought to be made between their offspring and the

Descendants of an Englishman, with whom they never were to be Accounted Equal."

Neither Virginia's governor nor other southern whites—nor northern whites, for that matter—had cause to worry about free blacks before 1770, but the Revolution altered the situation for all. The slave system of the nonplantation North did not last in the milieu of Revolutionary America. By the middle of the eighteenth century it was already a weak institution in the rural areas. Land-holders were busy dividing large estates that slaves had worked into small farms. And those who owned more than a few slaves were having difficulty finding employment for their bondspeople through the winter months. Persons not fond of African Americans in the first place began questioning the necessity of slavery and, thus, of a black presence in the colonies. And after 1763, with large numbers of Germans and Scots-Irish eager to come to America and work off indentures or for low wages, the notion of getting along without forced black labor gained support.

Then came war. A few owners manumitted slaves on condition they enlist in colonial militia units, and some northern blacks participated in the war's early skirmishes. Benjamin Quarles in *The Negro in the American Revolution* (1961) names a dozen African Americans who fought with the other "minutemen" at Lexington and Concord, and he cites a December 1775 petition of fourteen Massachusetts officers to the General Court, stating "that a negro called Salem Poor, of Col. Frye's regiment, Capt. Ames' company, in the late battle at Charlestown [Bunker Hill], behaved like an experienced officer, as well as an excellent soldier."

Not so many slaves simply waited around for their masters to act, however. Once fighting began in earnest and armies were afoot in the land, foraging, stealing, occupying and then evacuating cities, and bringing general chaos to broad areas of the eastern seaboard, African-American men, and eventually women and children as well, took advantage of the situation and set out for the combat zones. Soon fugitive slaves were doing everything from scouting and foraging to cooking for the armies of both sides. Some served as camp prostitutes. Regardless of their personal skills, escaped slaves chose to ally themselves with the side offering them the easier route to freedom.

Southern whites' fears over the prospect of arming blacks led to prohibitions on black recruitment, but not for long. By 1777, when Congress fixed troop quotas for each state and legislatures began offering bounties for enlistment, free blacks and slaves sent to serve for their masters began filtering into recruitment stations. By 1781 several states were ready to grant freedom to the slave and a bounty to the master for the bondsman's three-year enlistment.

A good number of northern slaves ended their bondage by siding with the British. When British regulars and Hessian mercenaries swept across Long Island and moved into New Jersey over the summer and fall of 1776, slaves from all around the region fled their masters, and when the patriots pushed the British back into New York City, the fugitive blacks stayed with the Redcoats. In all of the coastal cities to which British forces clung tenaciously, blacks served as auxiliaries on the promise of freedom. They worked as teamsters, carried messages, prepared food, and collected rubbish in New York and Philadelphia. In the latter city, following its evacuation in 1778, a local newspaper admitted that a "great part of the slaves hereabouts, were enticed away by the British army." And rarely did those who joined the British ever return to their masters. At war's end British officers refused to turn over the former slaves who had joined them prior to 1782. When they evacuated New York in 1783 the British took with them three thousand African Americans. The remainder of the story of these bold Americans who went through years of ordeal in quest of their freedom is, in almost every case, not a good one. Douglas R. Egerton writes in *Death or Liberty: African Americans and Revolutionary America* (2009) that "British promises of freedom rarely translated into prosperity or political equality." Some of those who left with the British ended up in East Florida, Jamaica, or the Bahamas; others made it to London, where poverty forever nipped at their heels. Most, however, were taken to the cold, hard, rocky soils of Nova Scotia, where they tried and failed to make a go of farming, before moving again, this time to Britain's new Sierra Leone colony in West Africa.

The Revolution was a fertile medium for a growing moral opposition to slavery in some of the northern colonies. Antislavery forces had been active on the local level in New England since the 1750s. The Quaker campaign was strongest in Pennsylvania, and in Massachusetts and New Hampshire blacks' petitions for freedom and land of their own did not always appear before blind eyes. By the late 1770s these efforts paid off, as states began drafting constitutions that applied some of the Revolution's humanitarian ideals. Vermont was first to spell these out: "No male person ought to be holden by law to serve any person as a servant, slave, or apprentice after he arrives to the age of twenty-one years, nor female in like manner after she arrives to the age of eighteen years."

Meanwhile, in Massachusetts, in an atmosphere of rising religious moralism and growing debate about English oppression, the executions of two slaves, one for murder and one for rape, focused public questioning on the morality of human bondage. Test cases began pecking away at the institution's constitutionality. As they did, slaves began leaving their masters, convinced that courts would not support their forced return. One such fugitive was Quok Walker, who, during the Revolutionary War, left his master, Nathaniel Jennison, and took a job for wages with a neighbor barely a mile down the road in Barre, Massachusetts. In 1781 Jennison, with some of his white farmhands in tow, approached Walker at work in the neighbor's field, beat him soundly, and took him home. Whites in Barre reacted strongly and Walker quickly escaped again and sued. In 1783, Massachusetts's Supreme Judicial Court, in *Commonwealth v. Jennison*, found that the clause of the state's 1780 constitution declaring "all men are born free and equal" applied to Walker and indeed to all. According to T. H. Breen in "Making History: The Force of Public Opinion and the Last Years of Slavery in Revolutionary Massachusetts," in *Through a Glass Darkly: Reflections on Personal Identity in Early America,* edited by Ronald Hoffman, Mechal Sobel, and Fredrika J. Teute (1997), stories of the executions and of Walker's exploits "briefly influenced the course of public opinion, shaping it, driving it forward, exposing tensions, crystallizing doubts, so eroding the institution of slavery that, at some critical moment in the history of Massachusetts, emancipation became common sense."

Elsewhere in the North abolition moved more slowly. In *Many Thousands Gone,* Berlin writes that slavery's waning there "was propelled more by atrophy of the slave population—owing to high mortality, low fertility, the close of the transatlantic slave trade, and the southward exportation of slaves for profit—than by the growth of liberty among blacks," and Nash and Soderlund in *Freedom by Degrees* write of post-Revolutionary, non-Quaker slaveholders as having been "overwhelmingly oblivious to the antislavery message." Policies of gradual abolition that northern state legislatures drew up ensured the Revolutionary generation its labor supply and enabled whites to keep African Americans in service until they could replace them with inexpensive white workers. The Pennsylvania General Assembly passed a gradual abolition law in 1780, long regarded favorably because it was the first of its kind. But Nash and Soderlund argue that the Pennsylvania act was most remarkable for what it did not do: free a single slave. The act consigned to twenty-eight years of labor (at a time when the average life expectancy of African Americans was thirty-four years) every child born to a slave woman after March 1, 1780, meaning that Pennsylvanians would continue—legally—to have black slaves in their midst for another seventy years. Connecticut and Rhode Island passed similar, though less-restrictive, acts in 1784. New York and New Jersey, where Hudson River farmers dug in their heels on the issue, were slow to follow. In *Emancipating New York: The Politics of Slavery and Freedom, 1777–1827* (2006), David Gellman shows how persistent were forces seeking abolition in New York, in the face of clearly mounting proslavery sentiment, at inserting the issue of slavery in public debate over all sorts of foreign and domestic policy. Eventually, the persistence paid off. New York passed its own gradual abolition bill in 1799; New Jersey did the same in 1804; so slavery lingered in the two states for several decades longer. New York remained the last northern bastion of the institution—its slave population grew by 25 percent in the 1790s, putting the number of slaves in the state at nearly twenty thousand in 1800. These numbers declined through the next two decades, however, and for all practical purposes slavery ceased to exist in the northern states by the end of the first quarter of the nineteenth century.

In the end, two factors helped abolition spread in the North. One simply was African Americans' unstoppable propensity to run away. As many as three-quarters of all young slave men in Philadelphia escaped in the 1780s; those who were caught ran again. In time, some slave owners recognized the impossibility of continuing to own human beings who had a will for freedom, an element of assistance in society to escape, and places to hide. The other factor had to do with the economic conditions of the North. Basic to the issue was that the northern economy did not have to rely on slavery, especially with the increasing number of inexpensive white laborers entering the nation. Those who did not own slaves began to resent the advantages of those who did, and white workers grew angry over having to compete with slave labor. Both groups soon favored abolition. So it turned out to be easier to apply the humanitarian ideology of the Revolution to all people in places where universal freedom did not ravage the economy and even seemed to open the marketplace to fairer competition.

Freedom did not bloom in the same fashion in the states of the Deep South, however. South Carolina and Georgia masters prohibited enlistment of blacks in the militia and freed only a tiny number of slaves during Revolutionary times. In fact, fears of any hint of a conspiracy that would lead to emancipation caused southern whites to react, sometimes with little respect for the law or humanity. In the summer of 1775, Jeremiah, a fisherman and valuable free-black harbor pilot in Charleston, was accused, on thin and questionable evidence, of collecting guns and urging other blacks to ready themselves to fight against the patriots in South Carolina. The court retained him in the workhouse for two months as it sought further evidence and hoped for his confession. As neither came and fears heightened, the court brought him to trial ("if such a process deserves the name," admitted South Carolina Governor Lord William Campbell), convicted him, and sentenced him to be "hanged and afterwards burned."

After reviewing the trial transcripts, Campbell wrote, "my blood ran cold when I read on what grounds they have doomed a fellow creature to death."

Not even public dealing with episodes of such dubious disloyalty could keep slaves in the Lower South from seeking their freedom. The British-occupied islands off Charleston and Savannah became havens for runaways; patriot militias mounted raids on the islands to discourage this population's growth. But over time it became clear to Low Country slaves that British forces had no more inclination to serve as their liberators than did the patriots. "While the war for the low country raged," writes Robert Olwell in *Masters, Slaves, and Subjects: The Culture of Power in the South Carolina Low Country, 1740–1790* (1998), "neither the royalist nor the republican combatants expressed much interest in slaves' hearts and minds. Rather, they fought for control of slaves' bodies to use as labourers, soldiers, or merely as confiscated property." Black men and women fled to the British in Charleston, but to have the best shot at achieving freedom, Low Country slaves knew they had to escape the bounds of what would become the new nation. This meant heading west or south, toward Spanish Florida. In 1790, South Carolina had fewer than two thousand free blacks, mostly around Charleston. Georgia had four hundred. At the beginning of the nineteenth century the two states held only 7 percent of the free African-American population of the South.

Many of the forces that affected African Americans in other areas of the land during Revolutionary times seemed to have been magnified for blacks in the Chesapeake. Perhaps this was because the region was at once the heart of the mainland slave society and the seedbed of rebellion and revolutionary ideology. Talk of abolition and acts of manumission had greater implications for whites who were so dependent on a system of human bondage. For Chesapeake blacks, the lure of freedom, which seemed as close and real as anywhere on the mainland, prompted men and women to take bold action. Virginia planters were quick to recognize their vulnerable position. Late in 1774, not long before British naval officers in Norfolk Harbor began taking aboard runaway slaves, a young James Madison wrote to a friend in Philadelphia:

If America and Britain should come to a hostile rupture I am afraid an Insurrection among the slaves may and will be promoted. In one of our Counties lately a few of those unhappy wretches met together and chose a leader who was to conduct them when the English troops should arrive—which they foolishly thought would be very soon and that by revolting to them they should be rewarded with their freedom. Their intentions were soon discovered and the proper precautions taken to prevent the Infection. It is prudent such attempts should be concealed as well as suppressed.

Through the summer of 1775, slaves weighed their options and made whites wary of their armed revolt in every southern colony. Then, as Madison feared, in November Virginia's British governor, John Murray, fourth Earl of Dunmore, who was fighting the provisional government for control of the colony, offered freedom to slaves and servants who would join the British and bear arms against the rebellious colonists. In less than a year a thousand slaves made off to Dunmore's vessels in Chesapeake Bay. He would likely have gotten more had not a smallpox epidemic among the refugees discouraged others who thought of following. The governor was able to use some fugitives in the December 1775 British defeat at Great Bridge; then over part of the next year he sent small bands of armed blacks on boats and barges to forage and plunder tidewater plantations, luring or forcing away more slaves.

After Dunmore's expulsion from a land base, British armies and privateers struck from the water at the plantation district between the James and York rivers, stealing livestock, tobacco, and slaves. When heavier fighting came to the region, royal armies in Virginia and North Carolina took in runaways. Members of the Virginia Convention reacted by instituting measures to keep their labor force intact. They authorized summary punishment of runaways, sanctioned transportation and sale of recaptives to the West Indies, and sentenced others to incarceration with the hardest labor. Still, the African Americans fled. Hanover County, Virginia, physician Robert Honyman wrote in his diary in 1781 that local planters had lost "20, 30, 40, 50, 60, or 70 Negroes"; twenty-three enslaved men and women from Jefferson's Monticello absconded. Over the course of the fighting five thousand Chesapeake men and women in bondage found their way to the British forces. Many more learned of the promise of freedom, and their lives would never again be the same.

Unfortunately for the runaways, as was the case elsewhere, once cast with the British their lot seldom improved. Neither Dunmore, who never freed his own slaves, nor British army officers in Charleston or Savannah, nor privateers were advocates of emancipation. The British army was interested in undermining the patriots' economic base and getting military laborers for its campaigns in North America or recruits for service in the West Indies. Black "spoils of war" ended up victims of army priorities. The poorly fed, clothed, and quartered African Americans worked long hours in hot weather constructing earthworks, digging and filling latrines, burying garbage, and generally doing labor no one else cared to perform (to save British soldiers for battle, officers argued). Bouts of dysentery swept through their ranks, and because officers ordered the inoculation of white troops only, smallpox epidemics hit blacks frequently, and they died at alarming rates. Those who survived faced transport to East Florida, the British West Indies, or Nova Scotia, where life in slavery or freedom would be hard.

But fleeing to join the British was not the only way African Americans in the Upper South gained freedom. In the years immediately following the fighting, the existence of a new group of free blacks became apparent to residents of Maryland and Virginia. These free African Americans were darker skinned than the small handful of prewar free blacks in the two colonies, and their numbers soon were substantial. Fighting on the side of the patriots, especially as substitutes for their masters, brought freedom to some slaves in the Upper South. Wartime chaos helped slaves run away too, and some fugitives found their way to Maryland or Virginia cities and simply blended into the lowest urban class. Then, throughout the 1770s and 1780s, abolition sentiment, abetted by a sense of egalitarianism from the evangelical revival movement that continued to sweep the South, grew teeth. As Methodist and Baptist ministers chastised their congregations over the evils of slaveholding, some guilt-ridden masters began freeing slaves or letting them accumulate enough personal property to purchase their freedom. Around Baltimore, masters with less religious motivation acted out of awareness that the promise of freedom was the best incentive to get unmotivated slaves to work, knowing they could always buy replacements for those they eventually freed. In this milieu, some laws barring manumission fell to repeal.

With public acts of manumission occurring and talk of freedom in the air at war's end, more African Americans began taking individual action to join the ranks of the free. Black fugitives began heading north toward freedom, sometimes with assistance but largely unaided, beginning a trend that would continue and grow over the next seventy-five years. Although slave patrols increased, flight from slavery was easier now. With more free blacks in circulation and with light skin no longer a determinant of free status, runaways of all shades of skin could avoid detection once in the free African-American society. This was especially true in urban areas of the Upper South.

And once secure in their freedom, blacks worked to free their relatives. Some with good jobs saved for years to purchase kinsmen. In New Bern, North Carolina, black farmer and barber John C. Stanley had extraordinary success following his freedom in 1798. Between 1805 and 1818 Stanley purchased and freed his wife and two children, his wife's brother, and nineteen other African Americans in slavery. Some free blacks, unable to buy their loved ones, took other action. Enough free blacks assisted kinsmen in running away that wise masters kept tabs on their slaves' free relatives and thus knew where to look first for their fugitives.

It was in northern Virginia and Maryland where the ranks of free blacks swelled most steadily and dramatically. By 1790 there were twenty-five thousand African Americans living in freedom in the Upper South—nearly the same number as existed in the northern states—and over the next decade that number would double. The presence of such a sizeable body of African Americans outside the controls of the slave system would cause white society anxiety and consequently be a factor in bringing change to the Chesapeake's black society.

Changing African-American Society

Up and down the Atlantic Coast and inland toward the newly opening backcountry, the Revolution altered the lives of African Americans. North of Maryland, blacks naturally experienced greater
personal freedom as slavery there died its slow death. In South
Carolina and Georgia, slaves achieved greater independence, but it
was an independence within a slave system that was growing and
becoming even more entrenched in white society. Blacks in the
Chesapeake enjoyed greater freedom, too, with the rapid appearance and growth of the free-black population and with more liberties for those within slavery, but this occurred against a backdrop
of growing commitment to slavery through the southern parts of
the region. And the geographical parameters of black life in bondage were spreading through the period, for out on the Virginia and
Carolina frontiers a new slave society was forming, with implications for further expansion.

So through the last decades of the eighteenth century, black
society continued to evolve differently in various sections of the
country. There was even growing diversity within regions. But,
as the group of essays in *Slavery and Freedom in the Age of the
American Revolution,* edited by Ronald Hoffman and Ira Berlin
(1983), shows, across the variety of black living conditions and
lifestyles one can detect, at least in retrospect, the beginnings of a
single, broad, distinctly African-American society.

The transition from servitude to freedom in the North was
surprisingly difficult. The timing of manumission, which varied
by decades among the northern states, affected how the individual
made the transition. So did regional demographic patterns, economic conditions, and white attitudes.

The popular image of African Americans learning of their
freedom, usually through a statement from a sad master, and immediately casting off toward new and better lives appeals to romantic
notions, but for most cases is inaccurate. Ties to "home," however
connected with bondage home may have been, were strong, and
there were practical considerations before one could hie for the
city or even the farm down the road. First was livelihood. Freed

slaves had to find a way to care for themselves, which usually meant they had to enter into arrangements of wage labor. Many went to work right away where they lived, and extrication from the master's household turned out to be a slow process. Between one-half and two-thirds of the men and women freed in the North were able to leave their masters' estates within a few years of abolition, but for a third or more ties were firm, the security was real, and leaving for good took longer.

Still, even those African Americans who remained in or around the master's residence with the end of slavery quickly gained a clear sense of being different people, no longer bound by the personalities or rules of their masters. Studies of slave naming patterns in northern states show how African-American men and women broke with their past almost immediately upon becoming free by ceasing to use the old, derisive first names their masters had given them—the classical Pompey or Caesar, the African day names of Cuffee or Quash, or such place names as York or Jamaica. They moved away also from the surnames of their masters. The names they chose, however, with many biblical first names and more English first and last names, suggest how far acculturation had come.

Blacks in northern rural districts, with little chance to obtain land and the wherewithal to gain true economic independence, quickly experienced the bite of poverty. Their lot resembled that of the sharecropping families of the Deep South a century later, with every family member working from youth to old adult, with children often bound out to apprenticeship, with men frequently hitting the road or seeking better times at sea, and with women left to hold the family together as the heads of house, often as they worked in white people's homes for next to nothing. In such circumstances, it is hardly surprising that many newly freed blacks tended to move toward the greater opportunities offered in the northern coastal cities. African-American populations of Boston, New York, and Philadelphia fairly soared with the ending of the war. New York's population of free blacks lagged behind that of the other two cities because of the continuing existence of a large slave population in the area. Philadelphia attracted newly freed blacks and runaways from Maryland and Virginia to the extent that between 1780 and 1800, while the city's white population doubled, its African-American population increased sixfold.

If the urban setting offered little room for true economic advancement, it still held the possibility of sustaining oneself on a low level. More African-American women moved to the city than men because jobs there as domestics were always plentiful, if not lucrative. Meanwhile skilled urban black men began losing their positions, finding discrimination in apprenticeships once open to them as slaves and realizing that whites would now hire free blacks for only the most menial labor. Some free men took to the sea, figuring that work on vessels provided the greatest economic opportunity, but most free African-American men remained in the city and worked as day laborers or servants. So even in their new status, it was black men and women who ended up doing much of a city's dirty work.

What the city did offer free blacks was the advantage of living with others of their culture. Blacks living in small numbers in the northern countryside were isolated and thus targets for white hostility, which rose with the ending of slavery. But in the city, African Americans in good numbers lived near one another and soon black community institutions came into existence that provided some level of security. It was in the city that men and women could more easily find marriage partners and begin families; it was there they could join in worship, combine resources to educate their young, and come together for camaraderie and mutual support.

All of this movement associated with freedom, however, was hard on African-American families. By 1770 the family was the cornerstone of most of black society in America. Becoming free and moving away from the master's household disturbed family stability. In addition to normal problems associated with poverty, especially husbands and wives being too poor to live together, many black families experienced the unsettling circumstances of wholesale relocation. It would take time to recreate a stable family life in a new setting. Once extricated from white residences but not yet able to form their own nuclear households, poor blacks often combined with relatives or friends to establish separate residences. Having two or more nuclear families in a single household or taking in boarders helped pay expenses. Transition to a pattern of two-parent households took time following abolition. Yet far from being the unstable, matrilocal institution that social scientists long portrayed, the post-abolition African-American family in the North became stable and autonomous about a generation after it appeared. Both parents lived at home and played important roles in the maintenance of the household. What is more, the black family broadened its boundaries and tended to include everyone who was part of the household, from boarders to members of other families. Thus it quickly resembled the extended family of the African village, with faux "uncles" and "aunties" abounding, more than it did any similar American institution.

In rural areas black residence patterns remained separate and varied, but in northern cities one could see by the 1780s the beginnings of a pattern of residential clustering and the formation of small but integral neighborhoods. Separate black churches appeared, initially as refuges from discrimination in white churches and as places where blacks could worship in the emotional fashion they preferred. Churches provided burial grounds, centers for common activities, and seedbeds for benevolent and fraternal organizations. Congregations pooled their resources and started "African" schools for training their young. Pulpits of the early black churches in the North were the springboards of the leaders of the new free-black community. From unimpressive beginnings, usually in small church buildings with minimal facilities, came recognition of blacks as individuals with a common culture as well as common problems. Along with this recognition came some of the earliest efforts to improve the lot of those persons in America who began thinking of themselves as "free Africans."

Gary B. Nash in "Forging Freedom: The Emancipation Experience in the Northern Seaport Cities, 1775–1820" in *Slavery and Freedom in the Age of the American Revolution* shows how the continued existence of slavery delayed development of community institutions in northern cities. Obtaining freedom required the resources of those who were free. Then, once free, a generation passed before African Americans were able to relocate and become part of a neighborhood where people had a community of interests. But by the end of the Revolutionary era, the basis had been laid for the growth of black social and community institutions that, by the early nineteenth century, would be the envy of poor whites in similar situations.

If the Revolution prompted questioning, and then the demise, of slavery in the North, it generally failed to cause whites in the country's southern extreme to reflect seriously on the rectitude of slave society. In fact, slavery in South Carolina and Georgia began a period of entrenchment and expansion just as the institution began to die in the northern states. The result by the time of the new nation's beginning would be the existence of a more powerful and viable southern institution, with prominent whites sure of slavery's necessity and, therefore, adamant about their right to own and forcibly work other humans. For the slaves, ironically, the same period brought still greater autonomy on the plantation and, with the start of a new wave of importation of Africans, a reinvigoration of a subculture that became more "African" than any other on the mainland.

Philip D. Morgan in "Black Society in the Low Country, 1760–1810" in *Slavery and Freedom in the Age of the American Revolution* argues that demographic and economic changes of the last half of the eighteenth century had considerable effect on the lives of African Americans and on the institution of slavery in South Carolina and Georgia. The natural increase of the slave population from about 1750; the growing size of Low Country plantations, with increasing specialization of slave duties; the movement of rice cultivation to tidewater lands, which changed the kinds and amount of work black people performed; and the gradual opening of the backcountry to slavery, with overland importation of slaves, brought greater change to the lives of blacks in the Lower South than did the Revolution.

For the half-century Morgan covers this may be so, but for about a decade following 1775, when South Carolina and Georgia either were prime theaters of the Revolutionary conflict or recovering from the effects thereof, one can hardly imagine anything more disruptive. The British military presence was stronger, for a longer period, in South Carolina and Georgia than anywhere else, and loyalists knew well which issues were most likely to set off patriot alarms. Before beginning the critical South Carolina campaign in the summer of 1779, General Henry Clinton, British commander in chief, issued his "Phillipsburg Proclamation" (from his headquarters in Phillipsburg, New York), similar to Dunmore's earlier edict, promising sale into slavery of every black serving the patriot forces but "to every Negro who shall desert the Rebel Standard, full security to follow within these lines, any Occupation which he shall think proper." Some African Americans heeded the call, but more hunkered down in their plantation existence, waiting to see where their best options might lie. Alarmed white patriots reacted in a variety of ways. Sylvia Frey in *Water from the Rock: Black Resistance in a Revolutionary Age* (1991) argues that the Phillipsburg Proclamation was critical to the southern theatre of the war because it galvanized Low Country planters, ever fearful of a slave uprising as well as the loss of their laboring force, "and turned a potentially loyal area [to the British] into a hostile countryside." At least part of what made South Carolina the site of "the most savage civil war fought in America during the Revolution," she contends, was Clinton's raising "the specter of emancipation" and the planters' decision to fight ferociously to keep intact the heart of their social and economic system.

Nowhere was the revolutionary warfare more fierce and pervasive than in South Carolina and Georgia. British armies occupied Charleston and Savannah; marauding groups of soldiers from both sides marched back and forth across Low Country lands, foraging, plundering, and killing. Some planters hustled their human property off, ahead of one or another army. Others just took care of themselves. Out of the disturbance came real hardship for many blacks on the one hand, but the opportunity to flee on the other. As in Virginia, African Americans in South Carolina were the victims of kidnapping and plundering, and epidemics swept off many more than usual. A good number, of course, and more women than usually was the case, simply made off and sought their fortunes wherever promise might lead them—to the backlands to join bandit or maroon groups, to Indian settlements, or off toward Florida.

Eventually, a throng of slave refugees was moving around the Low Country in the wake of the royal army, looting whatever grand estates they came upon. Royalist William Bull had to watch as his "plantation at Ashley Hall . . . [was] plundered and greatly damaged by the irregular and great swarm of Negroes that followed . . . [the British] Army." That the refugees did not distinguish between rebel and loyalist plantation owners, writes Olwell in *Masters, Slaves, and Subjects,* indicates "that their war was against slavery itself."

Boston King, a slave of patriot Richard Waring living near Charleston through the late 1770s, tells in his memoirs of the difficulties the Revolution brought and the kind of opportunities for a new life it provided. When the British captured Charleston in May 1780, King "determined to go to Charles-Town, and throw myself into the hands of the English." So many others did so at the same time that the British troops were nearly overwhelmed. King recalled feeling "the happiness of liberty, of which I knew nothing before, altho' I was much grieved at first, to be obliged to leave my friends, and reside among strangers."

King's happiness soon was tempered, however, as he fell victim to the smallpox epidemic then sweeping through the ranks of the African Americans in the city. He spent miserable days at a camp where the British army attempted to quarantine the sick fugitives. "We lay sometimes a whole day without any thing to eat or drink," he remembered, "but Providence sent a man, who belonged to the York volunteers whom I was acquainted with, to my relief. He brought me such things as I stood in need of; and by the blessing of the Lord I began to recover." Eventually, soldiers hauled him in a cart with twenty-five other invalids to a cottage, near a British hospital, where slowly he regained his health.

King then marched off with the army of General Cornwallis, serving as an orderly to a succession of British and loyalist officers. Somehow, he found himself with a unit of 250 British soldiers who were surrounded by a force of 1,600 patriots. On promise of a reward, King stole through the patriot lines and traveled twenty-four miles to a larger British force, taking word of his unit's plight. His reward turned out to be a few shillings. Soon back in Charleston, King joined the crew of a British man-of-war and sailed to New York. He was one of the three thousand blacks evacuated from New York in 1783 and taken to Nova Scotia.

By war's end, countless African Americans in South Carolina had died, disappeared, or gained their freedom. The colony's black population had been reduced by about one-quarter—twenty-five thousand men and women. A larger proportion of Georgia slaves actually escaped during the period, two-thirds by some accounts, as many as 7,000 to a haven behind British lines and untold numbers to Spanish lands or Indian territory to the south and west.

For the blacks who remained, the war had long-term effects. British occupation and the unsettled conditions in the countryside left a void in control. South Carolina slaves did not run away in the enormous numbers owners feared because of continual, more careful patrolling and because both sides in the war discouraged runaways. South Carolina's white leaders "received with horror" a Continental Congress proposal in 1779 to recruit slave soldiers, paying them nothing but offering them emancipation when they turned in their arms at war's end. In spite of surprise support for the proposal by South Carolina planter, politician, and businessman (actually slave trader) Henry Laurens, the South Carolina legislators voted against the proposal 100 to 12. As for British forces in the area, they were hardly armies of liberation, the Phillipsburg Proclamation notwithstanding. Without resources to handle large numbers of dependents, and never having much desire to liberate enslaved African Americans anyway (since many loyalists were slave owners), the British army rationalized that the slaves were "ungovernable" and saw to it that they stayed put. British officers published names of runaways picked up in Charleston so their loyalist masters might reclaim them, and sometimes they even gave captured runaways to soldiers as bounties for their enlistment.

Out in the countryside, those slaves who stuck it out on the plantation often found themselves entirely on their own. With masters off fighting or seeking safety away from possible military action, these African Americans were in a position to carve out new, more liberal bounds for their activities. Black slave drivers, already powerful with the frequent absence of owners, became more involved in plantation planning and management. Their authority reached new levels, and as the war made it nearly impossible to export rice or indigo, some blacks took it upon themselves to begin growing crops they could eat or make into clothing. Other slaves shouldered greater responsibilities, accumulated more property, and participated more in inter-plantation commerce and regional trade. Black women in particular became fixtures at crossroads markets, hawking vegetables, poultry, and clothing. Once the English left and the planters returned, it was practically impossible to return to the old, more restrictive ways of Low Country plantation life, and some whites were not convinced they should, since women and men active in the black underground economy purchased imports from whites without offering competition in the regular marketplace.

Urban slaves expanded their parameters in the Lower South, too. By 1770 many Charleston slaves had grown up in the open urban environment and were typical of city populations everywhere—more autonomous, more highly skilled, more ready to take advantage of opportunities, especially in trade. Between periods of loyalist and patriot control, African Americans assumed larger roles in supplying each side with provisions. They also marketed their skills to the highest bidders. Slaves worked for both armies as spies, informants, and couriers. One Savannah slave, Quamino Dolley, guided British forces through a maze of swamps to surprise colonial forces from the rear, helping ensure British capture of the city. Blacks from the region were especially adept at foraging, as they knew the plantations with the best livestock and other provisions.

When the British evacuated Charleston and Savannah in late 1782 and early 1783, they took with them more than fifteen thousand African Americans, and they removed six thousand from St. Augustine. Unfortunately, freedom for those readying to leave the plantation South was not assured. The British allowed masters to reclaim some of the African Americans to whom they had promised freedom, and some others they sold into slavery in the British West Indies, Louisiana, or West Florida. Others had to try to scratch out an existence in Nova Scotia.

The greater independence of the blacks who remained in South Carolina and Georgia allowed them to strengthen family ties and broaden their already strong, hybrid subculture. After the Revolution, more African-American men and women on plantations were able to live with their families, which now extended over several generations, and owners showed more respect for the family units of their slaves. African-American culture remained divided, as before the Revolution, with urban slaves more acculturated and rural blacks clinging to African customs. The small but growing number of free blacks in Charleston and Savannah, many of them children of white-black relationships, remained close in identity and proximity to the white master class. Taking advantage of their positions in the skilled trades and marketing, and perhaps recognizing that they were better off economically than most other blacks in the country, these men and women of the southernmost cities looked down all the more on the Lower South's black majority. Some even became slave owners themselves, and though unable to associate socially with whites, they formed institutions—like the Brown Fellowship Society of 1790 Charleston—to advance and protect their unique place in the social and economic hierarchy.

But out on the plantations, things would soon move in the opposite direction. The reinstitution of the Atlantic slave trade after the war, with much of the captive cargo now carried in American vessels, brought an additional influx of Africans into the rural Low Country and ensured that its society would continue to have strong African influences and be, as Morgan puts it, "in many ways disengaged from the white world." On the other side, the end of the Revolutionary years saw Low Country landowners believing more strongly than ever in the efficacy of the slave system and more willing and able to perpetuate it. Rachel N. Klein in *Unification of a Slave State: The Rise of the Planter Class in the South Carolina Backcountry, 1790–1808* (1990), identifies in South Carolina's piedmont region as early as the mid-1760s a "fledgling elite," a sizeable body of "inland entrepreneurs [who] were the core of what would later become a backcountry planter class . . . oriented toward slave acquisition and commercial agriculture." The South Carolina Regulator Movement of the late 1760s was an effort on the part of the backcountry white elite to ensure their rights to property, including especially slave property, and to stifle any threats to their hierarchical dominance over slaves. Klein shows that "an emerging planter class had already [by 1770] begun to mold the frontier in its own image." Thus, the idea that acquiring slaves was the way to prosperity never dimmed among white elites south of Pennsylvania, and nowhere in the new country was it more current than in South Carolina and Georgia.

Soon after the end of hostilities, the economy of these states boomed as rice exporting made a steady comeback, helped along by the final rush among planters to incorporate the labor-saving tidal techniques into rice production. Georgia first and then South Carolina reopened the Atlantic trade and rapidly imported enough Africans to replace losses from the war. They kept their ports open to Atlantic slaving so that whites moving into the opening backcountry could take laborers with them. The power and wealth of southern landowners began to increase as the system of slave labor expanded to include the growing of new crops. With the loss of the English market in the war years and competition from Louisiana, the market for Low Country indigo disappeared, but planters began growing a new crop, cotton, which started spreading slowly inland after 1790. By 1800 slavery in South Carolina and Georgia had new life. Planters would be in good positions to take advantage of opportunities the expanding economy would offer.

As had happened in the Lower South, fighting associated with the Revolution loosened planter controls in the Lower Mississippi. Patriot forces were involved in only one major British foray into the region in 1778, but Spanish authorities in Louisiana, seeing Britain preoccupied with the Revolution, decided the time was right to enlarge their holdings. For four years, from 1779 to 1783, troops from Spanish Louisiana that included elements of the free-black militia waged war east of the Mississippi until they succeeded in winning all of British West Florida. When the fighting was nearby, slaves on British and Spanish plantations ran for their freedom, many ending up in already established maroon settlements along the Lower Mississippi's bayous and backwaters. Some of these settlements south of New Orleans grew to the size of small towns. Maroons traded with, and sometimes protected, slaves from nearby plantations, and their very existence served as a symbol of the freedom that Louisiana planters were denying their slaves.

Revolutionary times provided enhanced opportunities for freedom in Lower Mississippi towns as well. In control of Louisiana since the 1760s, Spanish authorities had established relatively liberal policies for slaves' self-purchase and Spanish masters had frequently seen fit to manumit favored men and women from the plantation labor force. When manumission declined in the Revolutionary years and afterward, self-purchase increased, bringing significant growth to the existing free-black populations of New Orleans, Mobile, and Pensacola. Instrumental in this were members of the expanded free-black militia, who used government rewards for their vital services in fighting the British and maintaining order at home to purchase kinsmen. Also involved were urban artisans and market women, who used money made in a postwar building and commercial boom for similar purposes. New Orleans's free-black population nearly doubled over the decade following 1777; it numbered 850 in 1791 and stood as the nucleus of what would become one of the largest and most significant, independent, and successful groups of free African Americans in the United States. By 1810 free blacks made up nearly one-third of the New Orleans population and nearly the same proportion of the urban populations of Mobile and Pensacola. For a variety of reasons, which included tendencies of masters to manumit their slave wives, mistresses, and mulatto children, and of black family members to purchase from slavery their women kinsmen and thus ensure the freedom of their offspring, the free-black population of the Lower Mississippi was disproportionately female and light-skinned.

As with free blacks in Charleston and Savannah, many of those in the Gulf port cities lived, worked, and identified closely with whites. Many kept and bore proudly the family names of their former masters; nearly all performed the sacraments of the Catholic Church. As their economic situation continued to improve, their desire for status as well as wealth increased, bringing some to own and work slaves just as did white associates.

But if prospects for free blacks looked reasonably bright through the time of the writing of the United States Constitution and the beginning of the new nation, they appeared considerably less so, at least in hindsight, for those remaining as slaves on Lower Mississippi plantations. Spain had wanted an economic boom for Louisiana and thus had taken measures to ensure a stable labor force for its planters, tightening the laws regulating slavery and opening ports to African slaves. During the Revolution, some planters had moved their slaves out along the mainland's eastern seaboard to the Lower Mississippi, where they found an open market for tobacco or indigo. Following the war, a few slave owners in northern states, where slavery's end was in sight, sold bondspeople into the region. Then, as the Chesapeake economy continued to evolve and the slave population appeared to some to be larger than needed, masters began selling off "surplus" slaves whose destination, perhaps after many months, would be Louisiana or West Florida.

Given the enormity of postwar activity in the slave societies of the new country's eastern seaboard, including the reopening of the Atlantic trade, the reinvigorating of the slave-based economy of the southernmost states, and the movement of planters with their slaves into the South Carolina and Virginia backcountry, few had cause to pay attention to this virtual trickle of slaves. Yet, this movement—this domestic trading of slaves off to areas of expanding potential to the south and west in the 1780s—held ominous portent. During the next decade, Spanish planters would introduce sugar production in the region around New Orleans and their American counterparts in Natchez, with newly invented "engines" to speed the previously slow seeding operation, would begin growing cotton for export. The plantation revolution that would follow, made possible primarily by importation of Africans at first, but then by an enormous expansion of the domestic slave trade, would turn the Lower Mississippi into one of the country's harshest slave societies and significantly alter the lives of slaves and free blacks through the first half of the nineteenth century.

In Virginia and Maryland the Revolution brought even greater dislocation and change. Blacks and whites appeared on the move everywhere through the years of war and beyond, and to some the movement seemed to be turning society about. In Virginia there was westward movement toward the Blue Ridge—and eventually beyond. Some slave owners took their bondspeople out of reach of the fighting; others merely saw advantage in establishing upland farms on fertile new lands. Those who stayed recognized that the heavily creole slave population would grow rapidly through natural increase. Already there were plenty of slaves—George Washington believed he had "more working Negros by a full moiety, than can be employed to any advantage in the farming system"—and land was available. As the market for tobacco fell with the war, Chesapeake planters turned still more to mixed farming and livestock raising. Although the tidewater soils had lost fertility over the generations of tobacco growing, planters relied on manure from the growing herds and increasing numbers of black workers to squeeze profits from the land.

Farmers in the Upper Chesapeake did not have the same outlet of a western frontier. Planters in Maryland already had turned to producing cereals, which thrived on small farms with free labor, so slavery did not grow and expand as it did in the central and southern parts of Virginia. Now slave prices fell in Maryland. So while the numbers of persons in bondage grew in the Upper Chesapeake for two decades after the war, the Revolution marked the beginning of the splitting of Chesapeake slave society. In Maryland and northernmost Virginia slavery would be less important for the economy and there would be a movement toward greater freedom. In the central and southern Virginia tidewater and piedmont the trend would be in the opposite direction. Slavery there became more entrenched, the number of white slaveholders increased, and the African-American population grew rapidly by natural increase as the nineteenth century approached.

As in the North, the number of free African Americans and their proportion to slaves skyrocketed during the Revolutionary era. Free blacks in the Chesapeake went through changes similar to those in the North. They found jobs, took new residences, changed names, reconstructed families or made new ones, and slowly developed the community institutions—schools, churches, benevolent societies—that helped ease the social transition, prepared people for life's problems, and provided individuals a communal identity.

It was common for some blacks in the Upper South to experience a decline in occupational status with freedom. Because white artisans feared competition from free blacks, they were hostile to African Americans trying to practice trades. Furthermore, free blacks seldom had resources to purchase or even rent land, and even when they did, whites were reluctant to sell or rent to them. Small numbers of free blacks overcame these obstacles and became successful farmers, professionals, shopkeepers, artisans, and showmen. They formed the seedbed of the southern African-American elite that would appear in the first decades of the nineteenth century.

Those who were not so fortunate still found benefits in the southern economy, which was changing in America's early years. With tobacco declining and cereal production increasing, whites were leaving the tidewater for opportunities in the newly opened lands to the west. Landowners needed to replace white tenants, and poor blacks saw farm tenancy as a step toward accumulating resources to buy land. Thus, with the exception of those in Baltimore or Fredericksburg, free African Americans in late-eighteenth-century Maryland and northern Virginia tended to live a rather isolated existence in the country, renting land or working as hired laborers at grain farming.

Slavery certainly remained the dominant economic and social institution in southern Virginia, with all of its tight controls over the activities of black men and women, but the area was one of several in the country that had new, rapidly growing cities where free blacks and slaves could find heightened opportunity. Richmond was one such place—it had only 500 residents in 1775, but in 1779 it became Virginia's capital and by 1790 its population was 3,700. African Americans did some of the building in the urban boom, worked in the tobacco factories and grain mills, and performed a share of the skilled and unskilled work that was ancillary to all the new economic activity. Black women gained their first opportunities in the region to participate in urban marketing; seamstresses, cooks, and washerwomen by weekday could be sellers of vegetables, breads, and fish at weekend markets. All of this infused an element of freedom of movement in the Upper-South urban scene that saw free blacks mixing formally and informally with slaves and both groups rubbing elbows at work and in backstreet taverns with white laborers in what James Sidbury in *Ploughshares into Swords* terms "intricate webs of alliance and contention." The increased autonomy urban blacks experienced and their broadening social contacts would bring some of them to form a culture that Sidbury calls "oppositional" to the slave society and lead to widespread unrest and in some places rebellions.

Unrest among blacks and whites that related to liberty was not limited to Virginia cities over the quarter century following the ending of the Revolutionary War. The libertarian rhetoric of the Revolution and the temporary weakening of planter authority made it difficult for many blacks to accept their servile status. Even before ideas from Revolutionary France began spreading among blacks and whites in the new American nation, even before black rebels in Saint Domingue fought successfully for the notion that those ideas of liberty, equality, and fraternity applied to them as well, African Americans still in slavery were seething, plotting, and rebelling. Lesser-known organized black uprisings occurred in such widely separated places as Boston; Ulster County, New York; Perth Amboy, New Jersey; the Tar River valley of North Carolina; and St. Andrews Parish, South Carolina. And it was the atmosphere in and around Richmond in the 1780s and 1790s, where talk of natural rights and liberty ran high, that nurtured Gabriel and his fellow conspirators for what may have been the most elaborately planned slave uprising in United States history, foiled the night before it began in the summer of 1800.

In addition to the culture of opposition, Sidbury shows how complex were black society and identity by late-Revolutionary times. The split between whites and blacks that one assumes always existed was not evident everywhere in the new republic. Outside of the urban centers and sometimes within them, the Revolutionary generation of free blacks in the Upper South did not try immediately to separate themselves from whites and their institutions. This is evident in black participation in white-dominated evangelical churches and, less commonly, in their joining with whites to establish integrated schools. Some evangelical ministers welcomed all who accepted the Gospel, and their emotional, participatory services appealed to many blacks, who flocked to the revivals, if not so fast to church membership. By the 1790s congregations of black and white Methodists and Baptists, although normally segregated, on occasion listened together to exhortations of African-American preachers.

By late in the century, however, a tendency of Chesapeake blacks to identify more broadly with other African Americans, regardless of their status as slave or free, and a related movement to separate institutions was underway. Barred from some white churches and never full members of others, free blacks began taking control of their religious lives by forming "African" churches. J. Gordon Melton in *A Will to Choose: The Origins of African American Methodism* (2007) shows that these churches had broad and deep roots. African-American Methodism brought together strains of influence from both sides of the Atlantic, including Moravians in the Caribbean, and was spread by a remarkable group of preachers on farms and plantations as well as in the growing urban regions of the Atlantic coast; like Catholicism in New Orleans, it quickly found "a new force in church life" in African American women. These black churches spawned fraternal organizations and benevolent societies, and they often developed auxiliary institutions for educating their young.

Still the best known example of this process was in the city that beckoned so many former slaves and fugitives from the Chesapeake—Philadelphia. It involved the work of Richard Allen in forming the Bethel African Methodist Episcopal Church. Allen had been a slave in Delaware until 1777, when he purchased his freedom and, almost simultaneously, was converted to Methodism. He was already a successful preacher when he moved to Philadelphia in 1786 and became a leader of prayer meetings for fellow African Americans. He attended and sometimes preached at the integrated St. George Methodist Church until white officials spoke of segregating blacks who came to hear Allen's exhortations.

When a church trustee interrupted Allen and several companions in prayer, pulling one from his knees and sending the group to the rear of the gallery to assume their "proper" place to pray, Allen led his flock elsewhere. Within a few years he would establish what would become the Bethel AME Church, and by 1799 Allen would be the church's first deacon.

Ministers like Allen were the focus of activity in the free African-American community. They preached on Sundays, led social and religious gatherings on weeknights, and during the day served as schoolmasters. Their churches grew rapidly to become the heart of the free-black society. The ministers became the community's leaders, and from their institutional bases they guided the long evolution of independent African-American culture through the nineteenth century.

Neither the growing independence on the plantation nor the development of the free-black community held the greatest implications for southern African Americans in 1790, however. It was the opening of new lands, the westward movement of slaves, and the early formation of expanded slave societies in new areas that would most effectively change their lives over the long run.

Once the fighting of the Revolution had ended, Americans quickly pushed Indians out of lands on the western frontier. Availability of these lands to white settlers brought adventuresome men in the 1780s and 1790s to migrate into Kentucky, Tennessee, and western parts of Georgia and South Carolina. To perform the difficult process of clearing land for farms, they brought along slaves. There were surplus slaves enough in the Chesapeake to meet the demands of the western migrants, but not nearly so in South Carolina and Georgia, where slave agriculture was booming and where many African Americans had run away or died during the war. Once Spain ceded much of modern Mississippi and Alabama to the United States in the Pinckney Treaty of 1795 and thus opened new lands to settlement, the southern states needed still more enslaved workers. As a consequence, South Carolina and Georgia insisted on keeping the Atlantic slave trade open for another two decades. Between 1788 and 1808 these two states imported Africans at a greater rate than ever before. Nearly one hundred thousand

Africans entered Charleston, Savannah, and smaller ports along the Low-Country coast before Congress ended the traffic in human beings on January 1, 1808.

Western migration disrupted the already settled African-American communities and slowed acculturation. In many cases such movement forcibly separated slaves from their families, relocating them permanently to different parts of the country to perform new and more grueling kinds of work. The proportion of southern slaves who had to face this separation grew steadily. In the Chesapeake it was one in twelve in the 1790s, one in ten in the 1800s, and as cotton production became increasingly important and Chesapeake slaves moved south and west, one in five in the 1810s. Africans arriving in the Low Country around the turn of the century, fresh from the middle passage, were likely to experience rapid sale and movement westward, where they mixed with native-born slaves and began to acculturate out on the frontier. Here, black communities would have to form all over again, and this would take time. In Kentucky and Tennessee slaves had difficulty finding new marriage partners in spite of a balanced sex ratio. Living in groups of fewer than four slaves on small farms, these workers did not enjoy the contact with large numbers of fellow blacks that made the formation of community possible. Farther south, slaves lived on larger units, but the creole-African split kept them separated for a generation. Back in the Chesapeake, African-American families had to weather the disruption. Those who remained rebuilt networks of kinship and camaraderie. Now, however, they were keenly aware of the enhanced threat of forced removal and of what would be a continuing struggle to maintain family and community ties.

By the end of the Revolution, ironic circumstances appeared in African-American society. On the one hand there was the new, clear division between free blacks and those enslaved that was similar in many ways to the old split between Africans and creoles. But on the other was the first indication of broad unity across the breadth of all African-American society. As always, regional variants of black society continued to evolve in their own fashion, and there remained obvious differences in black ways of life. No doubt it was difficult to recognize social commonalities between African

Americans living in Philadelphia, for example, and Gullah slaves on Low-Country plantations. Also, the waning social and cultural split between Africans and slaves born in America lingered in the South Carolina and Georgia backcountry.

But beyond these divisions was a hint of the emergence of the broad-based African-American cultural unity that would eventually prevail. Hardening racial attitudes of whites and their growing inclinations to separate and treat in discriminating fashion everyone of African descent, regardless of servile status, brought African Americans to recognize what they all had in common. In addition to their African heritage and such unifying manifestations of culture as religious practice, close kinship ties, and general folkways, free blacks were not so long out of slavery and not welcome enough in white society to lose contact and identity with their cultural counterparts in bondage. Thus, as African-American society continued to evolve—indeed, as free blacks in the North and Upper South proceeded to grasp what advantages they could find while southern blacks were becoming involved in a slave system of expanding scope and importance—it soon would become increasingly evident that their lots were cast together. By 1800, African Americans were part of a single American society. Over the long run of the nineteenth century, what befell one group would come to affect the other.

The Foundations of Caste

The debate over the origin of racism in America comes alive again with examination of the Revolutionary era. As noted, racism certainly existed prior to that time among English settlers of the North American mainland. Their ancestors had held strong feelings about Africans; racism was important in the establishment of black slavery in the colonies; and the existence of slavery, with the required brutal punishments to make black men and women work as hard as their masters demanded, reinforced and strengthened the racist sentiments and beliefs of white colonists. Still, on the eve of the Revolution, race was not of overriding importance in the day-to-day workings of English-colonial society—perhaps only because it did not need to be. The bodies of laws that governed slavery reflected the racial prejudices of the lawmakers, but few questioned society's right to design laws to regulate its lowest class of laborers. One did not have to justify slave codes with arguments of black inferiority. And through the middle of the eighteenth century, African Americans and white Americans continued to mix and share their values, their customs, and many aspects of their lives.

Developments that occurred in the 1760s and 1770s changed all this. The existing debate over slavery on moral and religious grounds took on new meaning when colonists began discussing the position of slavery in their new, democratic society. If the country's existence rested on the doctrine of people having individual freedom, how did slavery fit? More convinced than ever of the necessity of slavery for their economic well-being and their elevated social status, southerners were on the spot. How could they simultaneously subscribe to American principles and defend slave society? In devising answers to this question they looked to racist assumptions that focused on the "nature and character" of blacks.

Southern white racism thus descended into the depths of the evil and absurd. Blacks could not live in a free society as equals of white men because of their racial inferiority, white southerners argued. They were naturally of lower intelligence and lazy, making it impossible for them to compete in a free society; they were inclined toward crime, excessive drink, and boisterous behavior; and they had no compunction against lying. Most serious, southerners insisted, blacks were sexually depraved, the women promiscuous and the men rapists at heart. They argued that such people were dangerous in a free state and thus needed careful watch and close control. Keeping them in slavery, they conveniently reasoned, was the best way to do so.

As so often happens in instances of perceived economic necessity, southern whites took note of evidence that sustained them in their beliefs and ignored things that did not support their racist notions. Some of what was happening in urban centers, where a free African-American society was getting on its feet, seemed to support their thinking. Newly freed blacks in American cities were having expected difficulties that placed them in jail or made them wards of the community out of proportion to their numbers. But few southern whites considered the lingering effects of slavery or of life's struggles in poverty when pointing out these social ills. They likewise ignored the high incidence of crime among poor, urban whites of the same time, as well as the existence of highly skilled slaves all around them, so they could believe the problem was African Americans' base nature and general inability. Such were the workings of the racist mind.

Providing "scientific" justification for their arguments was some of the crude social inquiry of Western intellectuals of the time. A common belief was that humans stood at the top of a long "chain of being," with whites on a higher link than blacks. Linnaeus's *Systema Naturae*, tenth edition (1758–59), a standard reference for educated persons of the late eighteenth century, identified variants of *Homo sapiens* in physical and cultural terms. *Europaeus* was white, sanguine, and muscular with long, flowing hair and blue eyes; gentle, acute, and inventive, it was covered with close vestments and governed by laws. *Afer,* located below *Europaeus* on Linnaeus's vertical chart, was black, phlegmatic, and relaxed, with black, frizzled hair, silky skin, flat nose, and "tumid" lips. Black women were, in Linnaeus's view, "without shame"; their "Mammae lactate profusely." *Afer* was also crafty, indolent, and negligent; self-anointed with grease; and governed "by caprice." Those believing in human brotherhood had only Christian doctrine or the recently espoused Revolutionary principles on which to base their beliefs. It was difficult to argue against the vehement southern slaveholders when they held up "scientific evidence" to support their position.

With antislavery agitation spreading and with increasing numbers of free blacks circulating in their presence, southern whites thus began, as Winthrop Jordan asserts in *White Over Black,* "hardening and polishing the structure of slavery." In parts of Virginia, proslavery petitions abounded. One, signed by 161 freeholders of the state's southside Lunenburg County, showed the animosity that fear wrought, as it predicted that general emancipation would result in

Want, Poverty, Distress & Ruin to the free Citizens; the Horrors of all the Rapes, Robberies, Murders, and Outrages, which an innumerable Host of unprincipled, unpropertied, vindictive, and remorseless Banditti are capable of perpetrating; Neglect, Famine and Death to the abandoned black infant and superannuated Parent; inevitable Bankruptcy to the Revenue; Desperation and revolt to the disappointed, oppressed Citizen; and sure and final ruin to this happy, free and flourishing Country.

Now the Southern states began to curb the practice of hiring out slaves, according to a Maryland act, "to prevent the inconvenience arising from slaves being permitted to act as free." Steadily, they made private manumission more difficult to accomplish, and they moved even more in the direction of establishing slavery as the tightly guarded and restricted institution it would become in the Antebellum South.

The early manifestations of hardening racist ideas fell most directly not on slaves but on free blacks. For a short time after the war, when their numbers were small, free African Americans basked in the Revolution's limelight. Even southern states wrote constitutions guaranteeing basic rights to all, and there was little thought of barring any free citizens from these rights. But as the number of free blacks in the Upper South grew, and as it came to include many who were not easily identified as such by their lighter skin tones, southern whites began to fear and loathe African Americans not in bondage. Some considered them dangerous to the institution of slavery in their capacity, and perhaps inclination, to promote slave unrest and aid runaways. Others recognized how free blacks succeeding at the same kinds of endeavors whites might undertake undermined the racist arguments of black incapacity that justified race-based slavery in the era of "rights of man." In such circumstances, whites could no longer allow free blacks a hint of equal treatment. Controlling the size of the free African-American community became a priority for state legislatures. In the 1790s states began limiting and then banning African American immigration. Southern states encouraged free blacks to emigrate to middle and northern states, prompting some of the latter to enact laws prohibiting blacks entering for purposes of residence.

When states could not purge themselves of free blacks, they set about expropriating the new liberties their Revolutionary constitutions provided them. African Americans had to register with state governments and in some cases provide security, by posting a sizeable bond, for good behavior. Authorities presumed blacks to be slaves until they proved otherwise; restrictions on free blacks waxed stringent the farther south one went. States limited inter-county mobility and authorized the binding over of young, free African Americans to white guardianship. Some free blacks soon found themselves required to register with city governments and wear notification of their status on their clothing—in North Carolina it was a shoulder patch inscribed "FREE." In places they were required to pay special taxes, refused enlistment in militias, and deprived of their rights to vote and bear arms.

Before the eighteenth century was over, a clear tendency to separate the races was becoming evident. This was neither necessary nor possible on plantations and smaller farms, but in cities throughout the country, whites moved to exclude all African Americans, free or slave, from social activities in which whites were involved. In public facilities African Americans received separate, and inferior, accommodations. White churches either proscribed blacks or treated them as second-class members. Restaurants and taverns removed blacks to separate sections; clubs, fraternal organizations, and trade unions simply refused to admit blacks to membership. And African Americans were not welcome in white schools or, in many cases, in white cemeteries. Such patterns of segregation seldom needed to be written into law. They merely entered into custom and became society's norms. The issue was no longer slavery. It was race.

Securing the Blessings of Liberty

It was in this context of a growing racist rationale for enslaving blacks that the states sent representatives to Philadelphia to agree on a Constitution setting up a stronger union. Northern states were beginning to dismantle slavery, and some of their delegates thought abolition should be a natural, if gradually instituted result of the Revolution. But delegates from the Lower South blocked the road. Increasingly as convinced of their racist beliefs as they were of the necessity of slavery for their economic survival, southern statesmen let it be known they would not join a union that would not guarantee slave interests. The greatest split among state delegates at the Constitutional Convention was between those from the North and from the South, or, as James Madison put it, in the important debates at the convention, "the institution of slavery and its implications formed the line of discrimination."

The Constitution that resulted rested on compromises between slaveholders and nonslaveholders, and it was particularly remarkable for the words it left out. Delegates from South Carolina and Georgia made known their opposition to any government that might immediately restrict their ability to import slaves or ignore human property in counting population for representation. They found northern delegates willing to compromise on these issues for the sake of union—and for southern concessions to federal authority in regulation of interstate and foreign trade.[3] So the final draft of the Constitution showed agreement on prohibiting Congress from interfering with the importing of slaves before 1808 and on counting three-fifths of all slaves for apportioning taxes and representatives. The Northwest Ordinance of 1787, while prohibiting slavery in states to be formed north of the Ohio River, already had tacitly allowed the institution to be part of life in new states south

---

[3] Gary B. Nash is one who believes the northern delegates did not need to give in on slavery to preserve unity. "The argument that slavery could not have been abolished," he writes in *The Forgotten Fifth* (2006), "reeks of the dangerous, indeed odious, concept of historical inevitability, almost always in historical writing a concept advanced by those eager to excuse mistakes and almost never by those writing on behalf of victims of the mistakes." In the 1780s and 1790s, he argues, the sentiment to rid the new nation of slavery on the basis of the principle of universal rights was at its peak, fitting in with opinion in England and France; the states of the Lower South most adamantly opposing abolition, South Carolina and Georgia, were too vulnerable to risk not uniting with the others; and there was money to compensate slaveowners from sale of western lands. He adds that "historians have seldom considered that a national plan for abolishing slavery might have been an integrative rather than a devisive mechanism," helping to create "a genuinely national society out of semi-separate, fractious regions."

of there. Delegates came to terms more easily on a clause requiring states to return fugitive slaves.

Nowhere in its finished state did the Constitution specifically authorize the holding of humans in bondage or so much as use the words *slave* or *slavery*. In curiously vague references, it forbade Congress to prohibit importation of "such persons as the several states shall think proper to admit"; it added to the whole number of free persons "three-fifths of all other persons" for representation and taxation; and it required a state to deliver up on claim a "person held to service or labour" in another state. But in final analysis, the document did not need to sanction slavery or even refer to it by name to solidify the institution in southern society because it guaranteed individual rights to property above all else. As such it accommodated slavery, for slaves were the property that, next to land, was most important to white southerners. Providing this tacit recognition of slavery, the Constitution left to the individual states the authority to determine the institution's fate, and it provided the power of the federal government to enforce the law generally and keep order. In so doing, it strengthened the hold slaveholders had on their bondspeople, and it made possible the steady extension of slavery across newly opened southern and western lands as the nineteenth century unfolded.

This was a way "to secure the blessings of liberty to ourselves and our posterity," as written in the Constitution's preamble," only if African Americans were not included among "we, the people" and considered part of "all men." Historians for a long while were reluctant to criticize members of the nation's founding generation for the fact of slavery's continuance and racism's growth, however. They preferred instead to emphasize how the founders were instrumental in overturning the hierarchical world that they, and so many of their time, inhabited. Gordon Wood in *The Radicalism of the American Revolution* (1991), for instance, writes of how the Revolution "transformed American society. . . . , [bringing] respectability and even dominance to ordinary people long held in contempt and [giving] dignity to their menial labor in a manner unprecedented in history and to a degree not equaled elsewhere in the world." But more recently, the founders have come under attack. Douglas R. Egerton is one who includes African Americans among the country's "ordinary people" and thus looks differently upon the Revolution and its drivers. In *Death or Liberty* he suggests that if we judge the Revolution by what it meant to the black men and women who struggled through it with their white countrymen for their mutual freedom, we would, as they did, find it "sadly wanting and white Patriots deeply hypocritical." The Republic that the founders created, Egerton believes, was "crippled by its inability to live up to its own Revolutionary ideals, and half free at best."

Larry E. Tise is even more broadly critical. The founders started backsliding from their stated ideals about liberty and human freedom soon after the war's end, he argues in *American Counterrevolution: A Retreat from Liberty, 1783–1800* (1998). African Americans "quickly understood the drift of white Americans away from the stated principles of the American Revolution." (Interestingly, the Patriots' fabled French ally, The Marquis de Lafayette, recognized this and understood its significance as well: "I would never have drawn my sword in the cause of America," Lafayette wrote to George Washington in 1786, "if I could have conceived thereby I was founding a land of slavery.") The overriding reason Tise offers for the founders' abandoning their stated principle of universal liberty in the 1780s and 1790s is the same one Edmund Morgan identified as behind the move to race-based slavery in Virginia a century earlier: whites' concerns over order. "The implications of calls to order," Tise writes, "of a new constitution vague on the question of black citizenship and the future of slavery; of laws permitting the naturalization of only free white residents; of laws regulating the movement of blacks from state to state and forbidding their testimony in courts of law were thoroughly counterrevolutionary." These elements brought persons in authority to move away from the ideals of liberty and freedom they had championed through the years preceding, and through the fighting of, the Revolutionary War.

Those who suffered greatest from the retreat from Revolutionary ideology were the African Americans who lived on in the United States of America after the founding generation had finished its work.

EPILOGUE

For African Americans there was nothing magic about the ending of the Revolution and the beginning of the new nation. In most of the states that ratified the Constitution, slavery proceeded unchecked. Its death in the North would be a slow one, and in the South the institution was not many years away from gaining new vitality. As the first Congress was working on constitutional guarantees of what Representative James Madison called the "great rights of mankind," which included the Fifth Amendment assurance that no person was to "be deprived of life, liberty, or property without due process of law," South Carolina and New England merchants were beginning again to bring captive Africans into southern ports. Also at that time, southern planters were experimenting with varieties of cotton they could produce to meet the demand of the expanding English textile industry. It would be only a few years before invention of a device to separate cotton seeds from the lint would make feasible the widespread growing of a short-staple variety of the plant. Cotton production was then quick to spread in the new country's fertile soils. Once it began doing so, even such momentous events as the successful slave revolution on Saint Domingue in 1791 in the Caribbean or the prohibition on the importation of slaves into the United States, after January 1, 1808, could not check slavery's expansion in those southern states where cotton might grow.

What was important for African Americans about the ending of the colonial period, however, was that by then the major institutions and forces that would affect their lives and those of their descendants over the next two centuries were established or well in motion. By the time the United States of America came into existence, the South's economy and society were so thoroughly bound up in slavery that its most prominent citizens opposed entering a union that threatened their right to own human beings. Adventuresome southern whites, who knew the way to get ahead was to obtain land and make it produce with slave labor, already were beginning to move westward with the African-American men, women, and children they held in bondage, anticipating the movement of the cotton boom a generation later. To help recover from the Revolution and to service the expanding economy, southerners imported over one hundred thousand more African slaves between 1790 and 1808.

Yet by 1790, the sectional split among states that would lead to the Civil War and slavery's end was also evident. The libertarian ideals of the Revolution and the egalitarian spirit of the Great Awakening had served as catalysts for antislavery sentiment, and a movement toward abolition, although weak, was alive in the country. The Northwest Ordinance of 1787 already marked lands north of the Ohio River as free states for the union's future. Most of the arguments for and against slavery (and its extension into new territories) that statesmen would debate so vigorously in the 1840s and 1850s had been aired by the time the Founding Fathers signed the Constitution.

By the end of the eighteenth century, black individuals had established their own modes of resistance to the institution that bound their lives, and they would continue to make fun, malinger, hide out, steal, escape, or rebel as their situation made possible until slavery ended. Even afterward, when free blacks in the South found themselves bound to tenant farms on the same land their ancestors tilled as slaves, they would use some of the same means to resist their oppressors. On into the twentieth century, running away—after 1910 it occurred so frequently that it was thought of as "migration" out of the South, to northern and western cities—remained a popular black reaction to onerous conditions.

Moreover, the long period of black Americans' social and cultural evolution brought into existence by 1790 a stable, identifiable African-American culture that encompassed the societies of free blacks as well as slaves. This black culture was anchored in the expanded family and a community that had found the means to survive under difficult circumstances. Variants of the culture existed in different parts of the new country, to be sure, but the church was a focal point for African Americans, who shared religious beliefs as well as unique folkways and traditions. A handful of African-American writers were even beginning to encompass an intellectual and emotional identity with Africans and others of African descent around the Atlantic. After 1790, when African Americans moved, their culture moved with them. Thus, a variation would constitute the culture of slaves in the Antebellum South. As Genovese shows in *Roll, Jordan, Roll,* this culture, which continued to grow and change and move with American blacks from its earlier foundation, formed the basis for African-American identity in a hostile world.

Late colonial demographic trends among African Americans even show the beginnings of population movements and settlement patterns characteristic of free blacks before the Civil War and of all persons of African descent for the century thereafter. A vague and gradual, but still noticeable, northward movement of black people began in the Revolutionary era, at least out of the Upper South toward the Middle states. As the body of free blacks increased in size, individuals and groups began moving toward urban areas, where jobs were more numerous and existing African-American communities offered more comfortable settings and group support. In the largest northern cities, Philadelphia and New York in particular, the seeds that would grow much later into African-

American neighborhoods, then black ghettos, were already in the soil by the close of the colonial period.

Nor does one have to look deeply into the American society of 1790 to see the roots of the racism that has since plagued the nation. Rigid, unreasonable racial prejudice was evident and spreading, and it was more than a southern phenomenon. Already by 1786 New Jersey had prohibited free blacks from entering the state. Other states would follow suit. Within two decades northern states began disfranchising blacks—President Jefferson signed a bill in 1802 excluding African Americans from voting in the nation's new capital—and as soon as blacks threatened to take white jobs, whites moved to deny skilled African Americans opportunities to practice their trades. Across the growing country, from bases where whites and blacks lived together, spread customary racial separation and along with it the discrimination, social ostracism, and exploitation that would persist and continue to evolve.

Thus, the truly formative years of the black experience in America were the earliest ones. By the beginning of the nineteenth century major forces already were in motion that would affect the way African Americans would live over the long period to follow.

BIBLIOGRAPHICAL ESSAY

New circumstances require new methods. When I wrote the first edition of this book in 1989, the literature on African Americans in the colonial era was less substantial and I could treat it in an essay of reasonable length, even with mention of journal articles and short essays on narrow topics. The outpouring of historical literature on this subject over the last two decades has changed my ability to be so inclusive. Now, in an effort to keep this discussion of the most useful, relevant published scholarship on the subject to essay length, I include only those much older books that at the time were pivotal in the direction of the field, that offered for the first time arguments or interpretations that still help guide our thinking, or that remain the only good study on a particular topic. Also, I include only the most important and useful of earlier articles and chapters in collected works, and only the most recent ones of these that provide useful summaries, offer especially clear understandings, or point toward new directions for research. If a book makes the same general point as an article, I note the former and not the latter. I also exclude books that are primarily compilations of documents designed for classroom use. Readers wanting more can look to the bibliographical essays in this book's earlier editions, which went back further in greater detail and included more articles on narrower topics.

Until recently, study of the experience of African Americans from their African origins through the American Revolution necessitated working in two distinct bodies of historical literature. To examine the African background and the slave trade one had to consult work done largely by specialists in Africa or the South Atlantic zone, but to study the institution of slavery in the British mainland colonies one needed to rely on the work of American historians who considered their study as part of a larger body comprising a history of the United States. Today that is much less the case because of the growing number of persons who focus more specifically on "Atlantic history." Such studies tend to show greater awareness of the economic, cultural, and intellectual relationships of peoples on all four continents bordering the Atlantic. We have begun erasing the artificial lines that separated early American history from its Atlantic context, which has allowed heightened recognition of the importance of Africa, trans-atlantic slaving, and slave-based production for a foreign market in our (collective) colonial past. Americans historians in particular are increasingly aware that Africa and Africans are important parts of the American heritage. A number of the new books noted in this essay reflect this awareness. Our understanding of all American history, not simply early African-American history, is better for it.

In different ways, Douglas R. Egerton et al., *The Atlantic World: A History, 1400–1888* (2007) and *Atlantic History: A Critical Appraisal,* ed. by Jack D. Greene and Philip D. Morgan (2009), serve as the best introductions to the Atlantic context for the experiences of African Americans in the colonial era. The former is a narrative written by experts on different aspects of Atlantic history, the latter an introduction and assessment of the utility of an Atlantic perspective by noted authorities, with notes on recent findings. A concise overview of the wider context for Britain's empire in the Americas is John E. Crowley's "A Visual Empire: Seeing the British Atlantic World from a Global British Perspective" in *The Creation of the British Atlantic World,* ed. by Elizabeth Mancke and Carole Shammas (2005). Michael A Gomez's *Reversing Sail: A History of the African Diaspora* (2004) deals with the Atlantic slave trade and slavery in the Americas in the context of the still wider historical spreading of Africans from the continent and the eventual return.

David Brion Davis's *Inhuman Bondage: The Rise and Fall of Slavery in the New World* (2006) is an insightful examination of the broad contexts of colonial American slavery by an acknowledged expert. Kenneth Morgan's *Slavery and the British Empire: From Africa to America* (2008) places English slaving in its Atlantic imperial context. Though it covers a period of only two decades, Carla Gardina Pestana's *The English Atlantic in the Age of Revolution, 1640–1661* (2004) treats the topic through a formative time for the North American mainland colonies and those who would labor there.

Useful surveys of African Americans in the colonial era are Betty Wood's *Slavery in Colonial America, 1619–1776* (2005); Peter H. Wood's concise *Strange New Land: Africans in Colonial America* (2003); William D. Piersen's *From Africa to America: African American History from the Colonial Era to the Early Republic, 1526–1790* (1996); the first half of Peter Kolchin's *American Slavery, 1619–1877,* rev. ed. (2003); and Gary B. Nash's *Red, White, and Black: The Peoples of Early North America,* 5th ed. (2005). The Piersen, Kolchin, and Nash books have useful bibliographical essays. *Slavery and Slaving in World History: A Bibliography,* ed. by Joseph C. Miller, 2 vols. (1998), is good for that topic. One wanting to see how far scholarship on African Americans in the colonial era has come since the 1970s can compare the essay presented here with Peter H. Wood's "'I did the Best I Could for My Day': The Study of Early Black History During the Second Reconstruction, 1960 to 1976," *William and Mary Quarterly,* 3rd series, 35 (1978).

Atlantic Origins

The best exposition of the Atlantic slave trade for readers of this book, partly because it focuses on English participation in the Atlantic commercial system, is David Eltis's *The Rise of African*

Slavery in the Americas (2000). Herbert S. Klein's *The Atlantic Slave Trade* (1999) is also useful. Eltis and Klein are long-time students of the subject. Robin Blackburn's *The Making of New World Slavery, from the Baroque to the Modern, 1492–1800* (1997), has more of a British-Caribbean focus. Hugh Thomas's *The Slave Trade* (1997) is a popularly written 800-page compendium that, while not flawless, is grounded in solid scholarship. James A. Rawley's *The Transatlantic Slave Trade: A History* is in a new edition (2005) with Stephen D. Behrendt.

Several books examine the Atlantic trade and focus on its effects on Africans. A work by the British Africanist Basil Davidson, *Black Mother: The Years of the Atlantic Slave Trade* (1961), was the first to draw attention to the destructive nature of the trade for African societies. Two studies by Walter P. Rodney, *A History of the Upper Guinea Coast to 1816* (1968) and *West Africa and the Atlantic Slave Trade* (1967), broaden and advance Davidson's argument. Anthony G. Hopkins in *An Economic History of West Africa* (1973) takes issue with the focus on destructive effects. Patrick Manning's *Slavery and African Life: Occidental, Oriental, and Atlantic Slave Trades* (1990) places the Atlantic trade in its widest perspective and suggests that Atlantic slaving caused demographic problems for specific regions of Africa in particular periods. Manning's "Migration of Africans to the Americas: The Impact on Africans, Africa, and the New World," in *Slave Trades, 1500–1800: Globalization of Forced Labor* (1996), ed. by Manning, is also useful in this regard.

To understand why there was a trade of slaves from Africa to the mainland colonies of British North America, one must examine the context, looking into reasons for the existence of a grand Atlantic economic system. David Brion Davis does this in concise fashion in the first chapter of *Challenging the Boundaries of Slavery* (2003), as does Kenneth Morgan in *Slavery and the British Empire: From Africa to America* (2007). Philip D. Curtin's *The Rise and Fall of the Plantation Complex: Essays in Atlantic History,* 2nd ed. (1999) places American slavery in its spatial and historical context, as does William D. Phillips, Jr.'s "The Old World Back-ground of Slavery in the Americas" in *Slavery and the Rise of the Atlantic System* (1991), ed. by Barbara L. Solow. Johannes Postma's *The Dutch in the Atlantic Slave Trade, 1600–1815* (1990) highlights that country's critical contributions to expansion of the plantation system. In "White Atlantic? The Choice of African Slave Labor in the Plantation Americas," in *Slavery in the Development of the Americas*, ed. by David Eltis, Frank D. Lewis, and Kenneth L. Sokoloff (2004), Seymour Drescher highlights reasons Europeans did not enslave other Europeans. James Walvin's *Questioning Slavery* (1996) focuses on the broad parameters of slavery in the English Americas. Articles in Paul Lovejoy and Nicholas Rogers, eds., *Unfree Labor in the Development of the Atlantic World* (1994) are insightful.

For understanding of the wider, Atlantic-centered economic realm of the mainland colonies, see chapters in *Tropical Babylons: Sugar and the Making of the Atlantic World, 1450–1680*, ed. by Stuart J. Schwartz (2004). David Hancock's *Citizens of the World: London Merchants and the Integration of the British Atlantic Community, 1735–1785* (1997) treats wider issues at a time when slaves began pouring into the mainland from Africa. David W. Galenson's *Traders, Planters, and Slaves: Market Behavior in Early English America* (2002), although focused on the English Royal African Company and its trading in the Caribbean, provides insight into the workings of the late-seventeenth and early-eighteenth-century slave trade. Older, still useful studies include Michael Craton's *Sinews of Empire: A Short History of British Slavery* (1974); James Walvin's *Black Ivory: A History of British Slavery*, 2nd ed. (2001); and Richard S. Dunn's *Sugar and Slaves: The Rise of the Planter Class in the English West Indies, 1624–1715* (1972).

It is not easy to understand what West and West-Central African societies were like before the heavy flow of slaves to the Americas. Even if the Atlantic trade had not altered those societies, Africans did not leave many written records and in many places oral history has fallen short of its promise as a tool for reconstructing the precolonial African past. In spite of this, John Thornton has done a good job describing ways of life among societies of Africa's Atlantic zone at some time in the past and relating those societies to the Atlantic trade in *Africa and Africans in the*

Making of the Atlantic World, 1400–1800, 2nd ed. (1998). Thornton's "The African Background to American Colonization" in *The Cambridge Economic History of the United States, Volume I: The Colonial Era,* ed. by Stanley L. Engerman and Robert E. Gallman (1996), is a fine, much briefer survey of the topic. In "The Gulf of Guinea and the Atlantic World," in *The Atlantic World and Virginia, 1550–1624,* ed. by Peter C. Mancall (2007), David Northrop shows how sophisticated and developed were some West African economies before contact with Europeans.

Studies of slavery in Africa are valuable for understanding how the institution differed from American chattel slavery and the role it played in the development of slave trading in Africa. The best single accounts in this regard are Paul E. Lovejoy's *Transformations in Slavery: A History of Slavery in Africa,* 2nd ed. (2000) and Claude Meillassoux's *The Anthropology of Slavery: The Womb of Iron and Gold,* translated by Alide Dasnois (1986). *Essays in Slavery in Africa: Historical and Anthropological Perspectives* (1977), ed. by Suzanne Miers and Igor Kopytoff, add useful insight. John Wright's thorough *The Trans-Saharan Slave Trade* (2007) offers valuable background and numbers for comparison to the Atlantic trade.

Discussion of numbers of slaves traded across the Atlantic begins with Philip D. Curtin's pioneering *The Atlantic Slave Trade: A Census* (1969). Before publication of this book, careful historians offered a "rounded off" figure of 15–20 million for the total of African slave exports. Others spoke of much higher numbers—up to 100 million. Curtin spent years corralling existing data and arrived at a tentative estimate of 9,566,100 for slave imports into the Americas between 1451 and 1870. He regarded his book as a "point of departure" and challenged others to produce data revising his figures.

What followed was a forceful attack on Curtin's accuracy and methodology. A persistent leader of this criticism, suggesting Curtin seriously underestimated the volume of slave exports, was J. E. Inikori. A summary of his critique is in the introduction to *Forced Migration: The Impact of the Export Trade on African Societies,* which he edited (1982). Other scholars worked to revise Curtin's figures, as Curtin did himself. Paul E. Lovejoy sorted through the first decade of this controversy in "The Volume of the Atlantic Slave Trade: A Synthesis," *Journal of African History,* 23 (1982), showing that Curtin's original estimates were indeed low, but not so far off the mark.

In the late 1980s, a project was launched that, in time, would end the wrangling. Under sponsorship of the W. E. B. Du Bois Institute of Harvard University, several scholars began work on bringing together existing data on Atlantic slave voyages from separate, published and unpublished compilations. In 1999 the data set from their work was made available as *The Transatlantic Slave Trade, 1562–1867: A Database CD-ROM,* ed. by David Eltis and David Richardson. It contained information of 27,233 slave voyages, 70 percent of all those undertaken. Then, between 2001 and 2005, more data were included covering underrepresented voyages to Latin America, and in 2006 Emory University received funding to provide public access to the continually expanding dataset: http://www.slavevoyages.org. At last count, it contains records of 34, 941 vessels that left Africa bound for the Americas with slaves, an estimated 81 percent of all such voyages that occurred between 1514 and 1866. *Extending the Frontiers: Essays on the New Trans-Atlantic Slave Trade Database,* ed. by David Eltis and David Richardson (2008), contains information on the data set with summaries of recent findings. Gregory E. O'Malley helps complete the picture by revising upward, to 15 percent of the total, the number of mainland North American slave imports that came from one of the Caribbean islands in "Beyond the Middle Passage: Slave Migration from the Caribbean to North America, 1619–1807," *William and Mary Quarterly,* 3rd series, 66 (2009).

No work on the slave trade to the British colonies on the North American mainland should begin elsewhere than with Elizabeth Donnan's four-volume *Documents Illustrative of the History of the Slave Trade to America* (1930–35). Donnan introduces the documents and supports them with full annotations.

Studies of European aspects of the trade often focus on one country or colony. Works dealing with aspects of British and colonial American participation include David Richardson, Suzanne

Schwarz, and Anthony Tibbles, eds., *Liverpool and Transatlantic Slavery* (2007), Walter E. Minchinton's *The Trade of Bristol in the Eighteenth Century* (1966); Jay Coughtry's *The Notorious Triangle: Rhode Island and the Atlantic Slave Trade* (1981); and Charles Rappleye's *Sons of Providence: The Brown Brothers, the Slave Trade, and the American Revolution* (2006). K. G. Davies's *The Royal African Company* (1957) remains the standard for British operations on the African coast in the time of seventeenth-century monopolies. William A. Pettigrew's "Free to Enslave: Politics and the Escalation of Britain's Transatlantic Slave Trade, 1688–1714," *William and Mary Quarterly*, 3rd series, 65 (2007), shows how the Royal African Company lost its monopoly in part because it lost its political backing at home. Though it deals with a French vessel on a voyage taking slaves to Martinique in 1731–32, Robert Harms's *The Diligent: A Voyage Through the Worlds of the Slave Trade* (2002) deserves special mention. Harms located a journal kept by the first lieutenant on the vessel and he uses the document and his extensive knowledge of African and Atlantic history to take the reader on a slaving voyage, which, as he emphasizes, passes through different worlds. Refutation of the claims made in the Nation of Islam's supposedly scholarly *The Secret Relationship between Blacks and Jews* (1991) that Jews played an important role in the slave trade and slavery in the Americas is in Eli Faber's *Jews, Slaves, and the Slave Trade: Setting the Record Straight* (1998).

Those interested in the material basis for the European side of the trade can refer to Stanley B. Alpern's "What Africans Got for Their Slaves: A Master List of European Trade Goods," *History in Africa: A Journal of Method,* 22 (1995), which treats the reasonable nature of African demand and includes detail on the products.

Knowledge of how the slave trade operated along various sections of the African coast has advanced in recent years with a group of specialized, regional studies. Among the best for different parts of the coast and related inland areas are, moving generally from north to south, James L. A. Webb's *Desert Frontier: Ecological and Economic Change along the Western Sahel,*

1600–1850 (1995); James F. Searing's, *West African Slavery and Atlantic Commerce: The Senegal River Valley, 1700–1860* (1993); Boubacar Barry's *Senegambia and the Atlantic Slave Trade* (1998); Philip D. Curtin's *Economic Change in Pre-colonial Africa: Senegambia in the Era of the Slave Trade* (1975); Donald R. Wright's *The World and a Very Small Place in Africa: A History of Globalization in Niumi, The Gambia*, 2nd ed. (2004, 3rd ed. forthcoming 2010); Walter Hawthorne's *Planting Rice, Harvesting Slaves: Transformations along the Guinea Coast, 1400–1900* (2003); Edda Fields-Black's *Deep Roots: Rice Farmers in West Africa and the Atlantic Diaspora* (2008); Kwame Y. Daaku's *Trade and Politics on the Gold Coast, 1600–1720: A Study of the African Reaction to European Trade* (1970); Ray A. Kea's *Settlements, Trade, and Politics in the Seventeenth-Century Gold Coast* (1982); William St Clair's *The Door of No Return: The History of Cape Coast Castle and the Atlantic Slave Trade* (2007); Patrick Manning's *Slavery, Colonialism, and Economic Growth in Dahomey, 1640–1960* (1982); and Robin Law's *The Slave Coast of West Africa, 1550–1750: The Impact of the Atlantic Slave Trade on an African Society* (1991).

For the Niger Delta and below, see K. O. Dike's pioneering *Trade and Politics in the Niger Delta* (1956); early chapters of Alexander X. Byrd's *Captives and Voyagers: Black Migrants Across the Eighteenth-Century British Atlantic World* (2008); David Northrup's *Trade Without Rulers: Pre-Colonial Economic Development in South-Eastern Nigeria* (1978); A. J. H. Latham's *Old Calabar, 1600–1891: The Impact of the International Economy upon a Traditional Society* (1973); Randy Sparks's *Two Princes of Calabar: An Eighteenth-Century Atlantic Odyssey* (2004), which shows as well as any study how thoroughly creolized were both Africans and Europeans, enmeshed in local dealings wherever necessary around the Atlantic in pursuit of commerce; Phyllis Martin's *The External Trade of the Loango Coast* (1972); and two works by Joseph C. Miller, his monumental *Way of Death: Merchant Capitalism and the Angola Slave Trade, 1780–1830* (1988), and his broader treatment, "Central Africa During the Era of the Slave Trade, c. 1490s–1850s," in *Central Africans and Cultural*

Transformations in the American Diaspora (2002), ed. by Linda M. Heywood.

Paul E. Lovejoy's *Caravans of Kola: The Hausa Kola Trade, 1700–1900* (1980) is good for organization of caravans in the Central Sudan. Philip D. Curtin's *Cross-Cultural Trade in World History* (1984) has chapters on trading communities and such topics as landlords, brokers, and caravan leaders in West Africa.

Archaeological study of slave trading along Africa's Atlantic coast has advanced in recent years. Christopher R. DeCorse is behind part of this. See his *An Archaeology of Elmina: Africans and Europeans on the Gold Coast, 1400–1900* (2000) and his ed. volume, *West Africa during the Atlantic Slave Trade: Archaeological Perspectives* (2001). Another good collection is *Archaeology of Atlantic Africa and the African Diaspora,* ed. by Akinwumi Ogundiran and Toyin Falola (2007). Cheryl Finley is critical of how some of the sites on West Africa's Atlantic coast are presented in "Authenticating Dungeons, Whitewashing Castles: The Former Sites of the Slave Trade on the Ghanaian Coast" in *Architecture and Tourism: Perception, Performance and Place,* ed. by D. Medina Lasansky and Brian McLaren (2004).

Recently, historians have begun taking into consideration African perspectives on the African side of the slave trade, dealing with how the slave trade is remembered today. Anne C. Bailey's *African Voices of the Atlantic Slave Trade: Beyond the Sadness and the Shame* (2006) is such a work, discussing oral versions of a story involving an Anlo Ewe chief of the southern Gold Coast: was he victim or collaborator? Akosua Adoma Perbi's *A History of Indigenous Slavery in Ghana* (2004) supplements this, and in *Lose Your Mother: A Journey Along the Atlantic Slave Route* (2007) Saidiya Hartman travels a path once taken by captured slaves in the Gold Coast, paying attention to the ways Africans and African Americans deal with this complex, shared history.

For a number of years, study of the middle passage rested on contemporary accounts, some of which were published. The best examples are John Newton's *The Journal of a Slave Trader, 1750–1754* (1962), ed. by Bernard Martin and Mark Spurrell, and Alexander Falconbridge's *An Account of the Slave Trade on the Coast of Africa* (1788). The historical validity of such tracts has always been open to question, given that some were written by former slave traders who had seen the immorality of their ways through religion—Newton wrote the famous hymn "Amazing Grace" after his years of involvement in the inhuman traffic—and others were published to support abolition of the trade. Publication of the Atlantic Slave Trade database allowed for statistical assessment of the subject, evident most recently in articles in *Extending the Frontiers,* noted above. Two new studies bring together the prior work and do more, so that we now have detailed, sensitive treatments of the experiences of the African captives during the middle passage in Markus Rediker's *The Slave Ship: a Human History* (2007), which focuses on the English trade to North America and demonstrates how violence was the underpinning of human relations on board these ships, and Stephanie E. Smallwood's *Saltwater Slavery: A Middle Passage from Africa to American Diaspora* (2007). Emma Christopher adds details on the interactions of slave-ship crewman with the captives on board in *Slave Ship Sailors and Their Captive Cargoes, 1730–1807* (2006). Smallwood's article in the *William and Mary Quarterly,* 65 (2007), "African Guardians, European Slave Ships, and the Changing Dynamics of Power in the Early Modern Atlantic," brings to light slavers' use of African guardians, which highlights again the complexity of individual and group circumstances on the slave ships. Eric Robert Taylor studies slave uprisings at sea, 400 of them in the eighteenth century, in *If We Must Die: Shipboard Insurrections in the Era of the Atlantic Slave Trade* (2006), arguing they were not a rare occurrence and, more contentiously, that costs required to guard against insurrections were an important factor behind the ending of the slave trade.

A study of disease environments, epidemics, and medical practices as they relate to the middle passage is Richard B. Sheridan's *Doctors and Slaves: A Medical and Demographic History of Slavery in the British West Indies, 1680–1834* (1985). David Eltis and Stanley Engerman offer explanations of why the middle passage carried twice as many men as women in "Was the Slave Trade Dominated by Men?" *Journal of Interdisciplinary History,*

23 (1992) and "Fluctuations in Sex and Age Ratios in the Transatlantic Slave Trade, 1663–1864," *Economic History Review,* 46 (1993). *The Atlantic Slave Trade: Effects on Economies, Societies, and Peoples in Africa, the Americas, and Europe* (1992), ed. by Joseph E. Inikori and Stanley L. Engerman, consists of papers presented at a 1988 University of Rochester conference, several of which deal with issues relevant to transporting slaves to the New World.

Among the rare, first-hand accounts of African slaves are those of two kidnapping victims and one person captured by an enemy army, all from the eighteenth century. These are *Olaudah Equiano's Interesting Narrative of the Life of Olaudah Equiano, or Gustavus Vassa, the African, Written by Himself* (1789), ed. by Paul Edwards (1967); Ayuba Suleiman Diallo's *Some Memories of the Life of Job, the Son of Solomon the High Priest of Boonda in Africa* (1734), treated in Douglas Grant, *The Fortunate Slave: An Illustration of African Slavery in the Eighteenth Century* (1968); and Venture Smith, *A Narrative of the Life and Adventures of Venture, A Native of Africa but Resident about Sixty Years in the United States of America* (1798), dealt with recently in *Making Freedom: The Extraordinary Life of Venture Smith*, by Chandler B. Saint, George A. Krimsky, and James O. Horton (2009). Equiano's account should be read with Vincent Carreta's *Equiano the African: Biography of a Self-Made Man* (2005), since Carretta casts doubt on the author's veracity. Terry Alford's *Prince Among Slaves*, 30th anniversary edition (2007), is the remarkable story of Abd Rahman Ibrahima, who was captured in West Africa in 1788, brought to the Lower Mississippi, and sold as a slave.

Control of economic power and resources in the English mainland colonies affected sale of slaves there. Thus, the clearest discussions of sale and transportation of slaves on their initial arrival in the mainland colonies are in studies that deal with colonial society and slavery, discussed below. A good overview is Steven Deyle, "'By Far the Most Profitable Trade': Slave Trading in British Colonial North America," *Slavery and Abolition,* 10 (1989). Studies of particular colonial ports and importing regions are useful. For Charleston, where more slaves entered the mainland than any other port, compare W. Robert Higgins's "Charleston: Terminus and Entrepôt of the Colonial Slave Trade" in *The African Diaspora* with Daniel C. Littlefield's, "Charleston and Internal Slave Redistribution," *South Carolina Historical Magazine* (1986). For other areas see Darold D. Wax's "Africans on the Delaware: The Pennsylvania Slave Trade," *Pennsylvania History,* 50 (1983); and James G. Lyndon's "New York and the Slave Trade, 1700–1774," *William and Mary Quarterly,* 3rd series, 35 (1978).

Development of Slavery in Mainland North America

Ira Berlin's *Many Thousands Gone: The First Two Centuries of Slavery in North America* (1998) is a masterful synthesis of slavery's origin and development in lands that would become the United States. Berlin trims and updates these arguments in *Generations of Captivity: A History of African-American Slaves* (2003). These books complete the removal of the focus of American slavery on the Antebellum period, broaden understanding of the issues, and connect the development of slavery to the Atlantic economy on the one hand, and to African-American ways of life and black culture on the other. Against Berlin's work, future studies of the subject will be measured.

Because slavery on the North American mainland was so thoroughly involved with the situation of the colonies in the Atlantic economy, those wanting to study the origins of slavery and racism in America might turn to Elizabeth Mancke and Carole Shammas's *The Creation of the British Atlantic World* (2005) or Peter C. Mancall, ed., *Envisioning America: Plans for the Colonization of North America, 1580–1640* (1995). Alison Games points out in *Web of Empire: English Cosmopolitans in an Age of Expansion, 1560–1660* (2008) that English experience from beyond the Atlantic—from the Mediterranean and Indian Ocean—was a factor in decisions about labor and other matters in early colonial Virginia.

There is much, good, recent study of the economic setting for early English mainland settlement. *The Economy of British America, 1607–1789* (1985) by John J. McCusker and Russell R. Menard, a pathbreaking book in its day, reflects Menard's long-standing interest in, and deep knowledge of, early slavery in the colonies. *The Economy of Early America: Historical Perspectives and New Directions* (2006), ed. by Cathy Matson, surveys the field since McCusker and Menard's book, though Matson's "early America" extends to 1840. Matson's essay, "A House of Many Mansions: Some Thoughts on the Field of Economic History," shows how complex were early relationships of labor and production. James Horn's *Adapting to a New World: English Society in the Seventeenth-Century Chesapeake* (1994) describes landscapes, the economic situation, and the English "social web," excellent background for understanding how slavery grew around the Chesapeake. Also useful are articles in *Envisioning an English Empire: Jamestown and the Making of the North Atlantic World,* ed. by Robert Appelbaum and John Wood Sweet (2005). Early chapters of Lynn A. Nelson's *Pharsalia: An Environmental Biography of a Southern Plantation, 1780–1880* (2007) provide further understanding of the lives of African Americans in slavery with study of agroecology.

Modern studies of the origin of slavery in the English mainland colonies trace their roots to an article by Oscar and Mary Handlin, "Origins of the Southern Labor System," *William and Mary Quarterly,* 3rd series, 7 (1950). The authors argue that black slavery evolved over the seventeenth century because of labor needs that the colonists could not otherwise meet. According to the Handlins, black and white servants in the colonies received similar treatment and were unconcerned with people's color. Racial prejudice came after, and as a result of, enslavement. This argument appeared at a fortunate time for interest in black American history. Kenneth Stampp made the Handlins' interpretation popular in his widely read *The Peculiar Institution: Slaves in the Ante-Bellum South* (1956).

Soon, however, a counterargument appeared. In "Slavery and the Genesis of American Race Prejudice," *Comparative Studies of History and Society,* 2 (1959), Carl N. Degler suggests that racist ideologies preceded and played a major role in bringing about slavery in the English North American colonies. As the legal system of slavery evolved in the Chesapeake, Degler writes, "it reflected and included as part of its essence, the same discrimination which white men had practiced against the Negro all along." Thomas F. Gossett strengthened Degler's arguments in *Race: A History of an Idea in America* (1963). It remained for Winthrop D. Jordan to attempt resolution of the debate in *White Over Black: American Attitudes Toward the Negro, 1550–1812* (1968). Jordan calls the move to black slavery an "unthinking decision" and suggests "cause and effect" for the relationship between slavery and racism. Betty Wood in *The Origins of American Slavery: Freedom and Bondage in the English Colonies* (1997) reinforces Jordan's theme. "The economic argument must loom large," writes Wood, but "from the outset American slavery was characterized by an awareness of ethnic difference that over the course of a century hardened into . . . a racial contempt and hatred that was deliberately cultivated by those who stood to gain financially from the employment of enslaved Africans." Joyce E. Chaplin calls attention to Europeans being latecomers to the Americas, "aware of existing Iberian practices toward Africans and Indians," in a chapter on "Race" in *The British Atlantic World, 1500–1800,* ed. by David Armitage and Michael J. Braddick, 2nd ed. (2009). "In relation to Africans," she writes, "the English were *imitators* of Iberian theory and practice, especially in their adoption of enslaved African laborers for plantation regions."

National attention on civil rights toward the end of the 1960s stimulated further investigation into colonial slavery and the early development of the institution. Many studies focused naturally on the Chesapeake, where slavery first appeared and became established. Thad W. Tate's "The Seventeenth-Century Chesapeake and Its Modern Historians" in *The Chesapeake in the Seventeenth Century: Essays on Anglo-American Society* (1979), ed. by Thad W. Tate and David L. Ammerman, surveys this literature; Anita H. Rutman in "Still Planting the Seeds of Hope: The Recent Literature of the Early Chesapeake Region," *The Virginia Magazine of History and Biography,* 95 (1987) examines more current work. Tim Hashaw's *The Birth of Black America: The First African Americans and the Pursuit of Freedom at Jamestown* (2007) tells the story of the first Africans in Virginia from their origins in Angola through individual lives in seventeenth-century Virginia. In *Central Africans, Atlantic Creoles, and the Foundation of the Americas, 1585–1660* (2007), Linda M. Heywood and John K. Thornton show that many of the slaves who arrived in British and Dutch settlements in mainland North America before 1660 came from just above the Congo River in the north to just below the Kwanza River in the south. Many of these persons were Christians, knew some European language, and had adopted aspects of European material culture.

Opportunity available to these early Africans in the Chesapeake did not last. Why it did not, and why black slavery became the dominant form of labor in colonial Virginia, are subjects taken up by Edmund S. Morgan in *American Slavery, American Freedom: The Ordeal of Colonial Virginia* (1975). Morgan regards as especially important planters' perceived need in the last third of the seventeenth century for control of unruly, armed, freed white servants. Slaves could never be freed, could be more carefully controlled, and were thus preferable. Russell R. Menard takes issue with Morgan in "From Servants to Slaves: The Transformation of the Chesapeake Labor System," *Southern Studies,* 16 (1977) and a broader work, *Economy and Society in Early Colonial Maryland* (1985). He argues that the rise of black slavery was due principally to the change in white servant migration patterns after 1660 and the high cost of servants in comparison with the low cost of slaves. "Chesapeake planters did not abandon indentured servitude," Menard writes in summary. "It abandoned them." Farley Grubb and Tony Stitt support Menard's statement in "The Liverpool Emigrant Servant Trade and the Transition to Slave Labor in the Chesapeake, 1697–1707," *Explorations in Economic History,* 31 (1994), arguing that "the large and protracted wars of King William III (1688–1697) and of Queen Anne (1702–1713) produced dramatic declines in servant supplies which explain the exact timing of the transition from servants to slaves in the Chesapeake."

In pointing out the extent of communication and trade among English colonies in the seventeenth-century Americas, April Lee Hatfield, in *Atlantic Virginia: Intercolonial Relations in the Seventeenth Century* (2004), shows how the existence of African slavery in the English Caribbean, especially Barbados, was important not only for the coming into existence of the institution in Virginia, but for the form it would take. Kathleen M. Brown's *Good Wives, Nasty Wenches, and Anxious Patriarchs: Gender, Race, and Power in Colonial Virginia* (1996) adds patriarchy and gender to these arguments, pointing out that as Virginia males moved toward greater control of black slaves following Bacon's Rebellion, they removed women from labor in the field and relegated them to more subordinate positions. Anthony S. Parent, Jr., focuses on patriarchy, too, if down the road and with broader ends, in *Foul Means: The Formation of a Slave Society in Virginia, 1660–1740* (2003). Parent credits Virginia's "great-planter class" with "organizing land, labor, and trade to serve their interests" and then, in the face of threats from small planters, English merchants, the English crown, and their own slaves, with creation of a mythical patriarchy—"an ideal of hierarchical responsibility and obedience to deal with the contradictions ever present in slavery"—in a successful effort "to assert their authority and bolster their legitimacy."

Viewed as a group, the studies pointing out different reasons for the turn to African slavery in the colonial Chesapeake attest to the clarity of Jordan's insight that the decision was "unthinking." The concept of black slavery, writes Jordan, "was neither borrowed from foreigners, nor extracted from books, nor invented out of whole cloth, nor extrapolated from servitude, nor generated by English reactions to Negroes as such, nor necessitated by the exigencies of the New World. Not any one of these made the Negro a slave, but all."

A number of works that add evidence for standard arguments about slavery's beginnings in America also include study of black society and slave culture in the Chesapeake. Gloria L. Main supports the idea that opting for slavery was a rational economic choice in *Tobacco Colony: Life in Early Maryland, 1650–1720* (1982). Main documents the social life and material culture of all classes of early Marylanders with probate records, showing that slavery's institutionalization hastened permanent inequality. This last point is one Allan Kulikoff makes in *Tobacco and Slaves: The Development of Southern Culture in the Chesapeake, 1680–1800*

(1986). Guided by interest in class formation, Kulikoff focuses on the rise of a Chesapeake gentry and its co-optation of a yeoman class to solidify white control over economy, society, and government. Once whites united under leadership of the gentry, Kulikoff argues, the status of blacks as a permanent underclass, with slavery as its outward manifestation, was established as the basis of southern culture.

Other studies use some of the same kinds of sources to reach different conclusions. T. H. Breen and Stephen Innes's *'Myne Owne Ground': Race and Freedom on Virginia's Eastern Shore, 1640–1676* (1980) focuses on successful free blacks and their broad social and economic relations. The authors conclude that the loss of property rights moved blacks swiftly toward a more permanent position of slavery. J. Douglas Deal's *Race and Class in Colonial Virginia: Indians, Englishmen, and Africans on the Eastern Shore during the Seventeenth Century* (1993) takes a broader look at the same topic. Paul G. E. Clemens's *Atlantic Economy and Colonial Maryland's Eastern Shore: From Tobacco to Grain* (1980) considers the effect of wheat production after 1713 on the changing social order. Darrett B. Rutman and Anita H. Rutman's *A Place in Time: Middlesex County, Virginia, 1650–1750* (1984) analyzes everything from child-naming patterns to literacy and slaves' living conditions in a single Virginia population. For the beginnings of slavery the Rutmans conclude that, on the local level, individual choice and good or bad fortune played surprisingly important roles. Most recently and particularly insightfully, Lorena S. Walsh, in "Mercantile Strategies, Credit Networks, and Labor Supply in the Colonial Chesapeake in trans-Atlantic Perspective," in Eltis, Lewis, and Sokoloff, eds., *Slavery in the Development of the Americas*, shows how practical considerations of shippers, merchants, planters, and smaller farmers, with the goal of accumulating the greatest wealth over the longest period at their base, determined which areas of the Chesapeake would have what sorts of laborers, from where, and when.

Marvin L. Michael Kay and Lorin Lee Cary's *Slavery in North Carolina, 1748–1775* (1995) shows how different slavery was in this colony because of its late-maturing, slave-based economy and the diversity of its exports. Because a relatively large proportion of North Carolina slaves were Africans (as opposed to creoles) so late in the colonial period (two-thirds in 1750), the authors argue that these men and women relied more than others at the time on tools and ideas that stemmed from their African heritage to comprehend, react to, and cope with their situation.

The beginnings and early years of slavery in the Chesapeake held historians' attention for a while, but studies of the subject in South Carolina and the Georgia Low Country caught up fast. Peter H. Wood set high standards thirty-five years ago with *Black Majority: Negroes in Colonial South Carolina, from 1670 through the Stono Rebellion* (1974) and Daniel Littlefield in *Rice and Slaves: Ethnicity and the Slave Trade in Colonial South Carolina* (1981) followed with a narrower examination of rice production in particular and the African ethnic mix that provided much to white South Carolina as it formed a basis for blacks' own, separate subculture. Both Wood and Littlefield emphasize the role West African slaves played in bringing the skills and technologies that planters used to turn the Low Country swamps into lucrative plantations. This argument about African and African-American slaves' agency Judith A. Carney broadens (to the Americas) and deepens (with knowledge of West African rice production and emphasis on women's roles) in *Black Rice: The African Origins of Rice Cultivation in the Americas* (2001). More recently, however, while Carney has turned to examining the many seeds and plants that Africans brought to the Americas and began cultivating between the sixteenth and nineteenth centuries in *Seeds of Memory: Africa's Botanical Legacy in the Atlantic World* (2009), David Eltis, Philip Morgan, and David Richardson have questioned her emphasis on African slaves at the expense of European planters in the development and growth of Low-Country rice production in "Agency and Diaspora in Atlantic History: Reassessing the African Contribution to Rice Cultivation in the Americas, *American Historical Review,* 112 (2007). These authors argue that "[t]he rice regime owed much to improvisation; it was a hybrid, synthetic rather than European or African in character."

Other books treating the earliest years of slavery in South Carolina include Peter Coclanis's *The Shadow of a Dream: Economic Life and Death in the South Carolina Low Country, 1670–1920* (1989); Timothy Silver's *A New Face on the Countryside: Indians, Colonists, and Slaves in South Atlantic Forests, 1500–1800* (1990); Converse D. Clowse's *Economic Beginnings in Colonial South Carolina, 1670–1730* (1971); and Edward Ball's *Slaves in the Family* (1998), the latter the story of Ball's efforts to trace his ancestors, white and black, through slavery and freedom on the family's rice plantations in South Carolina. Ball shows that the lives of men and women in and out of slavery were woven together in just about every way. Robert Olwell's *Masters, Slaves, and Subjects: The Culture of Power in the South Carolina Low Country, 1740–1790* (1998) describes the circumstances surrounding the lives of Low Country slaves. As James Horn does for the Chesapeake in *Adapting to a New World,* Olwell shows how so much of what became the slave society of the Low Country had a basis in English legal and social precedent. Essays in *Money, Trade, and Power: The Evolution of South Carolina's Plantation Society,* ed. by Jack P. Greene, Rosemary Brana-Schute, and Randy J. Sparks (2001) treat separate, related topics.

Now, perhaps, properly regarded as a culmination of this long line of scholarship, is S. Max Edelson's *Plantation Enterprise in Colonial South Carolina* (2006). Edelson believes that the origins and development of the unique, Low Country plantation system were the result of English landowners being particularly open to innovation in order to make a profit in the face of an interesting variety of factors: a strange, new environment; a surging Atlantic economy with the Low Country on the periphery; and cultural and technological input from Europe, Africa, and the Americas.

The movement of planters with slaves to the South Carolina backcountry has gained interest in recent years. Works dealing with this include Rachel N. Klein's *Unification of a Slave State: The Rise of the Planter Class in the South Carolina Backcountry, 1760–1808* (1990); Alan Gallay's *The Formation of a Planter Elite: Jonathan Bryant and the Southern Colonial Frontier*

(1988); George Lloyd Johnson, Jr.'s *The Frontier in the Colonial South: South Carolina Backcountry, 1736–1800* (1997); and Joyce E. Chaplin's *An Anxious Pursuit: Agricultural Innovation and Modernity in the Lower South, 1730–1815* (1993), in which she argues that Lower South planters were always innovators and "overtly commercial," making them eager to borrow new technology and plantation models that promised improvement of their slave-based production system. Peter N. Moore in *World of Toil and Strife: Community Transformation in Backcountry South Carolina, 1750–1805* (2007) describes the marginal position of slaves in the household exchange economy of one South Carolina backcountry region, which brought them to inhabit an "ambiguous place," a "kind of social limbo."

Two studies dominate work on blacks in colonial Georgia. Betty Wood's *Slavery in Colonial Georgia, 1730–1770* (1984) is especially good for the period of the colony's social experiment, when planter pressures brought about the demise of the ideal colony. Wood devotes the second half of the book to the form of slavery that came to exist in Georgia up to the time of the Revolution, with chapters on the public and private lives of slaves. Julia Floyd Smith's *Slavery and Rice Culture in Low Country Georgia, 1750–1860* (1985) is interesting for its perspective. Smith believes slavery on Georgia rice plantations was different from other manifestations of the institution in America. Rice production had its own requirements for labor, in particular a task system for fieldwork. This setting, Smith argues, enabled Low Country blacks to develop a culture with more African elements in the mix and to enjoy a physical well-being and treatment that was better than slaves experienced elsewhere.

Study of blacks in Spanish East Florida is detailed in Jane Landers's *Black Society in Spanish Florida* (1999). Leslie B. Rout, Jr.'s *The African Experience in Spanish America: 1502 to the Present Day* (1976) places the Florida experience in its broader Spanish perspective, and Landers examines some of the earliest Africans on the mainland in "Africans in the Land of Ayllón: The Exploration and Settlement of the Southeast" in *Columbus in the Land of Ayllón*, ed. by Jeannine Cook (1992).

The 1990s witnessed a relative explosion of works on African Americans in the Lower Mississippi Valley during colonial times, which add detail and interpretation to Joe Gray Taylor's *Negro Slavery in Louisiana* (1963). Each of the recent books has a different focus. Daniel H. Usner, Jr.'s *Indians, Settlers, and Slaves in a Frontier Exchange Economy: The Lower Mississippi Valley Before 1783* (1992) highlights how blacks had economic and social relations across race and class lines in the fluid setting of Louisiana and West Florida; Gwendolyn Midlo Hall's *Africans in Colonial Louisiana: The Development of Afro-Creole Culture in the Eighteenth Century* (1992) emphasizes that Africans in general, and Bambara slaves from Senegambia in particular, played a major role in shaping Louisiana creole culture; Thomas N. Ingersoll's *Mammon and Manon in Early New Orleans: The First Slave Society in the Deep South* (1999) argues that the development of slavery in the region's major city was not so different from other North American mainland slave societies; and Kimberly S. Hanger's *Bounded Lives, Bounded Places: Free Black Society in Colonial New Orleans, 1769–1803* (1997) shows how the period of Spanish control of New Orleans expanded opportunities for free African Americans, the basis of the city's more noted nineteenth-century creole population. David J. Libby's *Slavery and Frontier Mississippi, 1720–1835* (2004) deals with Natchez and West Florida. A chapter by Virginia Meacham Gould on Afro-Creole women in early New Orleans and one by David Wheat on cultural exchange in eighteenth-century Mobile in *Coastal Encounters: The Transformation of the Gulf South in the Eighteenth Century,* ed. by Richmond F. Brown (2007), are good introductions to those subjects.

Because of the relatively small number of blacks in New England and the Middle Colonies, and because states in the region terminated slavery around the time cotton production began to boom in the Deep South, historians in the field of slave studies prior to recent times tended to pay less attention to the area. A solid, general treatment of the topic is Edgar J. McManus's *Black Bondage in the North* (1973), which follows the story past Emancipation. Lorenzo J. Greene's *The Negro in Colonial New England* (1942) remains useful with its massive bibliography and appendices with population figures for each colony. William D. Piersen's *Black Yankees: The Development of an Afro-American Subculture in Eighteenth-Century New England* (1988) focuses less on the institution of slavery and more on "what it was like to be an African immigrant in colonial New England." Piersen examines African-American religion, rituals, arts and crafts, folklore, social mores, and daily behavior, concluding that in spite of being "engulfed in a pervasive, narrow-minded Euro-American society that had no interest in fostering Afro-American autonomy," blacks in New England created a viable folk culture that maintained African values and gave blacks a positive identity. More recently, Joanne Pope Melish in *Disowning Slavery: Gradual Emancipation and "Race" in New England, 1770–1860* (1998) argues that New England slavery held economic importance beyond its numbers because it was concentrated among influential white elites and because having slaves in the household freed masters to participate in lucrative mercantile activities.

The early pages of James O. Horton's and Lois E. Horton's *Black Bostonians: Family Life and Community Struggle in the Antebellum North,* rev. ed. (1999) discuss the colonial background for that population, and in "Slave-for-Sale Advertisements and slavery in Massachusetts, 1704–1781," *William and Mary Quarterly,* 3rd series, 59 (2002), Robert E. Desroches, Jr., provides considerable information about slavery and slave buying and selling. Elise Lemire's *Black Walden: Slavery and Its Aftermath in Concord, Massachusetts* (2009) is an insightful, new study. For New Hampshire, Connecticut, and Rhode Island, see Mark J. Simmons and Valerie Cunningham's *Black Portsmouth* (2004); Bernard Steiner's *History of Slavery in Connecticut* (1893); and Robert K. Fitts's *Inventing New England's Slave Paradise: Master/Slave Relations in Eighteenth-Century Narragansett, Rhode Island* (1998), the latter documenting how historians created a myth of "the comparatively mild and favorable conditions of Negro slavery, as it formerly prevailed in New England."

Scholarly study of slavery in the Middle Colonies has taken on new life over the last decade. Edgar J. McManus's *A History of*

Negro Slavery in New York (1960) and Roi Ottley's *The Negro in New York* (1967) remained authoritative on that topic until 1999, when Graham Russell Hodges published *Root and Branch: African Americans in New York and East Jersey, 1613–1863* (1999). This was followed in short order by Leslie M. Harris's *In the Shadow of Slavery: African Americans in New York City, 1626–1863* (2003) and Thelma Wills Foote's *Black and White Manhattan: The History of Racial formation in Colonial New York City* (2004), both carefully researched and deep with detail. Still more recently, chapters by Christopher Moore, Jill Lepore, Graham Hodges, and Patrick Rael in *Slavery in New York,* ed. by Ira Berlin and Leslie M. Harris (2005), offer concise summaries through Dutch, English, and American control of New Amsterdam and New York.

Cathy Matson's *Merchants & Empire: Trading in Colonial New York* (1998) provides the broad economic background for New Amsterdam and New York slavery. Shane White's *Somewhat More Independent: The End of Slavery in New York City, 1770–1810* (1991) treats the last decades of slavery in the city, as does David Gellman's *Emancipating New York: The Politics of Slavery and Freedom, 1777–1827* (2006); Joyce D. Goodfriend's *Before the Melting Pot: Society and Culture in Colonial New York City, 1664–1730* (1992) has a section on African-American culture; and Richard Shannon Moss's *Slavery on Long Island: A Study in Local Institutional and Early African-American Communal Life* (1993) treats a small portion of New York's slave population.

Similarly, for slavery in colonial Pennsylvania, one formerly had to rely on two dated books, Edward J. Turner's *The Negro in Pennsylvania: Slavery—Servitude—Freedom* (1911) and Thomas E. Drake's *Quakers and Slavery in America* (1950), and a few good articles. This situation was relieved by the publication of books by Jean R. Soderlund and Gary B. Nash: Soderlund's *Quakers and Slavery: A Divided Spirit* (1985) and Nash's *Forging Freedom: The Formation of Philadelphia's Black Community, 1720–1840* (1988). Then the two authors combined to write *Freedom by Degrees: Emancipation in Pennsylvania and Its Aftermath* (1991). All three works show that even the presence of abolitionist sentiment among some Quakers and others in the city had little effect when Philadelphia residents wanted slave labor.

For New Jersey, Graham Russell Hodges's *Slavery and Freedom in the Rural North: African Americans in Monmouth County, New Jersey, 1665–1865* (1997) supersedes Henry S. Cooley's *A Study of Slavery in New Jersey* (1896). Delaware did not fit many schematics in regard to slavery. Two solid studies of the topic are Patience Essah's *A House Divided: Slavery and Emancipation in Delaware, 1638–1865* (1996) and William H. Williams's *Slavery and Freedom in Delaware, 1639–1865* (1996).

Study of the legal basis of American slavery as it developed in the colonial period surged forward with publication of two books by A. Leon Higginbotham, *In the Matter of Color: Race and the American Legal Process, I: The Colonial Period* (1978), and *Shades of Freedom: Racial Politics and Presumptions of the American Legal Process, II: Race and the American Legal Process* (1996), the latter of which traces in American law the "precept" to "presume, preserve, protect, and defend the ideal of the superiority of whites and the inferiority of blacks." Thomas D. Morris's *Southern Slavery and the Law, 1619–1860* (1996) places greater emphasis on the antebellum era. Two books by Philip J. Schwarz focus on the legal basis of slavery in Virginia: *Twice Condemned: Slaves and the Criminal Laws of Virginia, 1705–1865* (1988), which examines trials of slaves to prove how conflict and brutality were so much at the heart of the relationship between white and black, and *Slave Laws in Virginia* (1996). Enforcement of slave laws is the topic, and violence the running theme, of Sally E. Hadden's *Slave Patrols: Law and Violence in Virginia and the Carolinas* (2001).

African-American Culture

Philip D. Morgan's massive, detailed *Slave Counterpoint: Black Culture in the Eighteenth-Century Chesapeake and Lowcountry* (1998) is the best study of African-American culture in the regions where slavery dominated. One finishes Morgan's book with an appreciation for how complex the situations were for Africans in America and how African-American life differed according to time and place. This corresponds with the theme of Berlin's *Many Thousands Gone* (which echoes a point he made earlier in

"Time, Space, and the Evolution of Afro-American Society on British Mainland North America," *American Historical Review,* 85 (1980). In emphasizing the importance of place and an evolutionary process in African acculturation, Morgan and Berlin complete the dislodging of historians from any idea that colonial black culture was mostly uniform and static. Shorter, and with a broader focus, is Morgan's "The Poor: Slaves in Early America" in Eltis, Lewis, and Sokoloff, eds., *Slavery in the Development of the Americas.* Jack P. Greene's *Pursuits of Happiness: The Social Development of Early Modern British Colonies and the Formation of American Culture* (1988) is a good introduction to the culture change that took place on the North American mainland. Morgan, in "British Encounters with Africans and African-Americans, circa 1600–1780" in *Strangers within the Realm: Cultural Margins of the First British Empire,* ed. by Bernard Bailyn and Morgan (1991), emphasizes that "[r]ace relations tended to be more flexible in slaveowning than in slave societies."

Some of the best studies of African-American acculturation in the New World have been anthropological works focusing on slave societies in the Caribbean. What they say about the process is instructive for colonial America. Melville Herskovits's *The Myth of the Negro Past* (1941) is the classic study of "creolization." Sidney W. Mintz and Richard Price's 's *Caribbean Transformations* (1974); Mintz and Price's *An Anthropological Approach to the Afro-American Past: A Caribbean Perspective* (1976); and the same two authors' *The Birth of African-American Culture: An Anthropological Perspective* (1992) offer valuable ideas about the joining of cultures. Joseph E. Holloway summarizes issues pertaining to "The Origins of African American Culture" and "What Africa Has Given America" in *Africanisms in American Culture,* ed. by Holloway, 2nd ed. (2005). Lorena S. Walsh's *From Calabar to Carter's Grove: The History of a Virginia Slave Community* (1997) follows generations of slaves from their African origins to the Virginia tidewater and piedmont, showing that even where large numbers of slaves shared the same African regional heritage, their ways changed rapidly in America and their culture was indeed something new. Walsh notes the kinds of things one can tell about individuals and about group culture in such things as names in "A 'Place in Time' Regained: A Fuller History of Colonial Chesapeake Slavery through Group Biography" in *Working Toward Freedom: Slave Society and the Domestic Economy in the American South* (1994), ed. by Larry E. Hudson, Jr.

Although most books on slave community and culture focus on the antebellum period, a good introduction to the topic is in the early chapters of Peter Kolchin's *American Slavery, 1619–1877* (1993). Relevant books that have references to colonial times include Lawrence W. Levine's *Black Culture and Black Consciousness: Afro-American Folk Thought from Slavery to Freedom* (1977); Eugene D. Genovese's *Roll, Jordan, Roll: The World the Slaves Made* (1972); and John W. Blassingame's *The Slave Community: Plantation Life in the Antebellum South,* rev. ed. (1977). The studies of blacks in specific regions of colonial America noted above—particularly those by Gloria Main, Allan Kulikoff, Darrett and Anita Rutman, Peter Wood, Daniel Littlefield, Betty Wood, Julia Floyd Smith, Lorenzo Green, and William Piersen—have useful parts on black community and culture. Kulikoff's book emphasizes the role demographics played in black family and community formation and shows how these institutions were the prerequisites for stable black culture in the Chesapeake. Jean Butendoff Lee's "The Problem of Slave Community in the Eighteenth-Century Chesapeake," *William and Mary Quarterly,* 3rd series, 43 (1986) questions assumptions about the existence of a stable African-American community by the time of the Revolutionary era. She recognizes the broad attempts of slaves to achieve communal lives, but emphasizes that these efforts were more difficult and often less successful than many historians believe.

A handful of books bring refreshing perspective to one or another aspect of colonial black culture. James Sidbury's *Ploughshares into Swords: Race, Rebellion, and Identity in Gabriel's Virginia, 1730–1810* (1997) traces African-American culture formation in eighteenth-century Virginia before emphasizing how many forces and experiences came to bear on individual and group identity—and thus cultural formation—in Richmond at the end of the century. Sidbury follows this with *Becoming African in*

America: Race and Nation in the Early Black Atlantic (2007), tracing the earliest expression of an "African" identity among diasporic Africans to a small number of African Americans and African British during the second half of the eighteenth century. Timothy James Lockley details "the fundamental multiplicity of lowcountry social relations" in *Lines in the Sand: Race and Class in Lowcountry Georgia, 1750–1860* (2001), and Jeffery R. Young's *Domesticating Slavery: The Master Class in Georgia and South Carolina, 1670–1837* (1999) shows the development of the thinking of the slaveholder through colonial times and after. Douglas R. Egerton's *Gabriel's Rebellion: The Virginia Slave Conspiracies of 1800 and 1802* (1993) places blacks in the context of Richmond's late-eighteenth-century working class and shows how such individuals were buffeted by the political and social winds of the times. W. Jeffrey Bolster's *Black Jacks: African American Seamen in the Age of Sail* (1997) shows the African roots of black seafaring in America and, more generally, how from the 1740s "seafaring men of color stirred black society and shaped Atlantic maritime culture." Mart A. Stewart's *"What Nature Suffers to Groe": Life, Labor, and Landscape on the Georgia Coast, 1680–1920* (1996) is a fascinating examination of the ecosystem of the Georgia Low Country and the effects it had on African-American lives—and vice versa, a theme touched on earlier in Timothy Silver's *A New Face on the Countryside: Indians, Colonists, and Slaves in South Atlantic Forests, 1500–1800* (1990), and later in Ras Michael Brown's "'Walk in the Feenda': West-Central Africans and the Forest in the South Carolina–Georgia Lowcountry" in Heywood, ed., *Central Africans and Cultural Transformations*. Mark M. Smith's *Mastered by the Clock: Time, Slavery, and Freedom in the American South* (1997) contains discussion of African concepts of time and shows that slaves' and masters' ideas about time were not so far apart through the colonial period. In *The World They Made Together: Black and White Values in Eighteenth-Century Virginia* (1987), Mechal Sobel examines religious and secular worlds and finds that black and white values and perceptions had considerable effect on one another's group culture. Sobel ventures into the fascinating realm of black and white concepts of space, time, home, the afterlife, and more to suggest that neither group developed its culture alone, but that indeed they made their worlds together. Piersen's *Black Yankees* makes a similar argument, concluding that blacks helped "mellow those rather puritanical" white Yankees, and his *Black Legacy: America's Hidden Heritage* (1993) makes the broadest case yet for southern white culture having "strong African blood-lines."

When considering influences of particular African groups on African-American and American culture, some authors contend that a limited number of African "nations" or "cultural units" dominated the Atlantic trade to specific regions of the Americas and thus were able to maintain many of their largely unified ways and affect American culture in those particular ways far more, and for a longer time, than previously considered. Thornton in *Africa and Africans in the Making of the Atlantic World* and Hall in *Africans in Colonial Louisiana* make such arguments, and Hall broadens the idea in *Slavery and African Ethnicities in the Americas: Restoring the Links* (2005). The most ambitious of such studies pertaining more strictly to mainland North America is Michael A. Gomez's *Exchanging Our Country Marks: The Transformation of African Identities in the Colonial and Antebellum South* (1998), which advances arguments about how particular West and West-Central African cultures affected African-American ways into the nineteenth century. More recently, Douglas B. Chambers highlights the "diasporic Igbo base" of a slave community in eighteenth-century Piedmont Virginia in *Murder at Montpelier: Igbo Africans in Virginia* (2005).

Philip D. Morgan counters the African-cultural-continuity thesis in "The Cultural Implications of the Atlantic Slave Trade: African Regional Origins, American Destinations and New World Development," in *Routes to Slavery,* and more recently (with James Horn) in "Settlers and Slaves: European and African Migrations to Early Modern America" in Mancke and Shammas, eds., *Creation of the British Atlantic World.* In the latter essay, the authors stress the cultural and linguistic diversity among captives that came from the same African region and argue that "New identities emerged in the Americas out of disparate African elements, but they did not follow any straightforward national form." Peter Caron's "'Of a nation which the others do not Understand': Bambara Slaves and African Ethnicity in Colonial Louisiana, 1718–60," in *Routes to Slavery,* supports the heterogeneity model and argues against Hall's emphasis on the existence of powerful, ethnic Bambara influences in eighteenth-century Louisiana. Gregory E. O'Malley in "Beyond the Middle Passage" points out that "Colonies that relied extensively on transshipments for their slaves also received a more polyglot assortment of African peoples . . . [which] affected the ability of such people to sustain cultural practices and languages brought with them from Africa." Most recently, James H. Sweet urges scholars to "break free from the 'straightjacket' of creolization versus survivals" and chart "fluid identities" of diasporic Africans in "Mistaken Identities? Olaudah Equiano, Domingos Álvares, and the Methodological Challenges of Studying the African Diaspora," *American Historical Review,* 114 (2009). Useful to read in this context is William S. Pollitzer's study of those African Americans, on the Sea Islands off South Carolina and Georgia, who retained African elements in their language and culture as long as any: *The Gullah People and Their African Heritage* (1999).

If work dominated the daily lives of African Americans in the colonial period, blacks dominated the colonial American world of work—for whites as well as blacks. One gets this strong impression from reading a number of studies noted earlier, none more so than Sobel's *The World They Made Together.* From reading Rhys Isaac's *Landon Carter's Uneasy Kingdom: Revolution and Rebellion on a Virginia Plantation* (2004) one recognizes that how to extract the most work out of his 401 slaves filled Carter's thought processes—and much of his thorough diary. Separate articles in *Cultivation and Culture: Labor and the Shaping of Slave Life in the Americas,* ed. by Ira Berlin and Philip D. Morgan (1993) deal with the various forms of slave labor and its effect on how people lived in different parts of the New World. Studies of specific kinds of African-American workers include David S. Cecelski's *The Waterman's Song: Slavery and Freedom in Maritime North Carolina* (2001), a book that emphasizes the labor of slaves on the water and on land—canal digging being the worst—and gives one a feel for the importance of the sea in the lives of eighteenth-century African Americans; Philip D. Morgan's "Black Life in Eighteenth-Century Charleston," *Perspectives in American History,* new series, 1 (1984), a detailed description of living and working conditions of urban slaves; Thad W. Tate's *The Negro in Eighteenth-Century Williamsburg* (1965), for a glimpse at the lives of, and kinds of work performed by, African Americans in the town setting; Sarah S. Hughes's, "Slaves for Hire: The Allocation of Black Labor in Elizabeth City County, Virginia, 1787–1810," *William and Mary Quarterly,* 3rd series, 35 (1978); and Ronald L. Lewis's *Coal, Iron, and Slaves: Industrial Slavery in Maryland and Virginia, 1715–1865* (1979).

That black women slaves had especially full lives of hard work is evident in Joan Rezner Gundersen's "The Double Bonds of Race and Sex: Black and White Women in a Colonial Virginia Parish," *Journal of Southern History,* 52 (1986). Gundersen reminds readers that black women on small farms often had to do their own domestic work after having finished the fieldwork. She shows also that in part of Virginia women were hired out more frequently than were men. Two collections, *Discovering the Women in Slavery: Emancipating Perspectives on the American Past,* ed. by Patricia Morton (1996) and *More Than Chattel: Black Women and Slavery in the Americas,* ed. by David Barry Gaspar and Darlene Clark Hine (1996), have articles on women in the colonial period. In the latter book, Cheryll Ann Cody points out in "Cycles of Work and Childbearing: Seasonality in Women's Lives on Low Country Plantations" that on some plantations women tended to have the most children during times of heaviest labor demand, and Richard Steckel summarizes his findings on "Women, Work, and Health under Plantation Slavery in the United States." Deborah Gray White's *Ar'n't I a Woman? Female Slaves in the Plantation South* (1985) contains a description of the mythology of female slavery as well as select information on black women in the colonial period. Other studies of women in slavery focus heavily on the antebellum South, but see Angela Davis's "Reflections on the Black Woman's Role in the Community of Slaves," *The Black Scholar,* 3 (1971) for a theoretical approach; Catherine Clinton's *The Plantation*

Mistress: Woman's World in the Old South (1982), which is good for "the sexual dynamics of slavery"; and Suzanne Lebsock's *The Free Women of Petersburg: Status and Culture in a Southern Town, 1784–1860* (1984) for the chapter on "Free Women of Color."

E. Franklin Frazier's *The Negro Family in the United States* (1939), which emphasizes the damage slavery did to the black family, was a standard work on the subject. However, Herbert G. Gutman's *The Black Family in Slavery and Freedom, 1750–1925* (1976) altered ideas that slavery brought disorganization and instability to black families. Gutman draws attention to the remarkable adaptive capacities of African Americans and credits the black family with preserving cultural traditions and the double-headed household. Most of Gutman's evidence is from the antebellum period and after, but a chapter on the family in the eighteenth century deals with African-American marriage and broadening kinship ties. Allan Kulikoff's "The Beginnings of the Afro-American Family in Maryland" in *Law, Society, and Politics in Early Maryland: Essays in Honor of Morris Leon Radoff,* ed. by Aubrey C. Land, Lois Green Carr, and Edward C. Papenfuse (1976), summarizes his thoughts on demographic considerations and the formation of colonial black families. Mary Beth Norton, Herbert G. Gutman, and Ira Berlin in "The Afro-American Family in the Age of Revolution" in *Slavery and Freedom in the Age of the American Revolution,* ed. by Berlin and Ronald Hoffman (1983), examine the workings of slave families in the Chesapeake and the Carolinas in a more mature African-American society.

Because many agree with Michael R. Bradley's assessment in "The Role of the Black Church in Colonial Slave Society," *Louisiana Studies,* 14 (1975), "that the formation of the Negro church is the key to the beginning of Afro-American community and culture," a number of studies have focused on the early years of black religion in America. Several noted historians have written on African-American religion. These include Carter G. Woodson's *History of the Negro Church* (1921); Benjamin E. Mays and Joseph W. Nicholson's *The Negro's Church* (1933); and E. Franklin Frazier's shorter *The Negro Church in America* (1963). Lester B. Scherer's *Slavery and the Churches in Early America, 1619–1819* (1975) treats the colonial period more thoroughly; Allan Dwight Calla-han's *The Talking Book: African Americans and the Bible* (2006) summarizes eighteenth-century slave conversion by white evan-gelicals before stressing the Bible's centrality in slave accultura-tion. Sylvia R. Frey and Betty Wood in *Come Shouting to Zion: African American Protestantism in the American South and Brit-ish Caribbean to 1830* (1998) argue that through most of the colo-nial period American blacks rejected Christianity because it was not adaptable to their African worldview and social customs, and that only with the more flexible push of the Baptist and Methodist faiths did blacks begin converting in large numbers—in the 1780s, but still more after 1800. Jason R. Young's *Rituals of Resistance: African Atlantic Religion in Kongo and the Lowcountry South in the Era of Slavery* (2007) is a trans-Atlantic comparison that shows how slaves in the Americas created "new and vibrant cul-tures informed by memories of Africa." Various essays in *African-American Religion: Interpretive Essays in History and Culture*, ed. by Timothy E. Fulop and Albert J. Raboteau (1996), pertain to early slave religion.

Works that deal with particular denominations and blacks in early America include T. Erskine Clark, "An Experiment in Pater-nalism: Presbyterians and Slaves in Charleston, South Carolina," *Journal of Presbyterian History,* 53 (1975); and Denzil T. Clifton, "Anglicanism and Negro Slavery in Colonial America," *Historical Magazine of the Protestant Episcopal Church,* 39 (1970). Carol V. R. George treats Richard Allen and the birth of the Bethel Afri-can Methodist Episcopal Church in *Segregated Sabbaths: Richard Allen and the Emergence of Independent Black Churches* (1973), but J. Gordon Melton in *A Will to Choose: The Origins of African American Methodism* (2007) traces African-American Method-ism's roots further back and more broadly, to rural as well as urban areas, to Moravians in the Caribbean as well as African-American preachers on the mainland, and to women as well as men. Har-old E. Davis's *The Fledgling Province: Social and Cultural Life in Colonial Georgia, 1733–1776* (1976) argues that Quakers and Moravians wanted their slaves to become literate so they could experience Christianity more fully. Davis maintains that churches in colonial Georgia were more integrated than previously believed. Jon F. Sensbach's *A Separate Canaan: The Making of an Afro-Moravian World in North Carolina, 1763–1840* (1998) shows how even Moravians, who believed in the universality of salvation and included slaves in biracial worship, moved toward separate services as race became increasingly important in North Carolina's slave society. Mechal Sobel's *Travelin' On: The Slave Journey to an Afro-Baptist Faith* (1979) includes ideas on acculturation as they pertain to the formation of African-American religions. Sobel's is the most thorough treatment of the "African Sacred Cosmos" and of how such African concepts as spiritual force, visions, travels to meet the Lord, and rebirth entered into the African-American Christian worldview. Leonard Barrett's *Soul Force: African Heritage in Afro-American Religion* (1974) shows how other Africanisms mingled with European Christianity in the formative years of black religion in America.

Thomas S. Kidd's *The Great Awakening: The Roots of Evangelical Christianity in Colonial America* (2007) is a valuable new survey countering arguments, first expressed by John Butler in "Enthusiasm Described and Decried: The Great Awakening as Interpretive Fiction," *Journal of American History,* 69 (1982) that such a phenomenon did not occur and treating its effects on slave communities. Callahan in *The Talking Book* reinforces Kidd, arguing that "[s]laves in significant numbers came under the influence of Christianity in the British colonies . . . through the mass Evangelicalism of the Great Awakening of the 1740s," and so does Alan Gallay with emphasis on slave societies in South Carolina and Georgia in "Planters and Slaves in the Great Awakening" in *Masters and Slaves in the House of the Lord: Race and Religion in the American South, 1740–1870,* ed. by John B. Boles (1988). In *Evangelism and Resistance in the Black Atlantic, 1760–1835* (2008), Cedric May credits several African-American writers with spreading religious principles that aided in black community formation and organizing for resistance. Jon F. Sensbach's *Rebecca's Revival: Creating Black Christianity in the Atlantic World* (2005) puts the eighteenth-century religious change that affected North-American slaves in a broader, Atlantic perspective. Emily Clark and Virginia Mecham Gould show how enslaved African women and their largely female, creole offspring took to Catholicism and over several generations created and sustained Afro-Catholicism in New Orleans in "The Feminine Face of Afro-Catholicism in New Orleans, 1727–1852," *William and Mary Quarterly,* 3rd series, 59 (2002).

Herbert Aptheker's *American Negro Slave Revolts,* rev. ed. (1969) remains the most thorough compilation of information on the subject. Peter H. Wood surveys the topic from a more recent perspective in "Slave Resistance" in Volume 2 of the *Encyclopedia of the North American Colonies,* ed. by Jacob Cooke (1993). An analysis of how and why slaves resisted, ran away, or rebelled is Gerald W. Mullin's *Flight and Rebellion: Slave Resistance in Eighteenth-Century Virginia* (1972). Mullin establishes the relationship between level of acculturation and methods of resistance that seemed to apply throughout the colonial period. In a subsequent book, *Africa in America: Slave Acculturation and Resistance in the American South and the British Caribbean, 1736–1831* (1992), he uses a comparative perspective to answer questions relating to why, in his analysis, rebellions in British North American colonies tended to be African-led through the 1760s and then creole-led thereafter. Several studies treat particular topics related to resistance or rebellion. John Thornton's "African Dimensions of the Stono Rebellion," *American Historical Review,* 96 (1991), brings up the possibility that soldiers from the Kingdom of Kongo formed the core of the Stono uprising and used their knowledge of firearms and military tactics to their temporary advantage. Walter C. Rucker's *The River Flows On: Black Resistance, Culture, and Identity Formation in Early America* (2006) shows that the mix of African cultures was not an impediment to collective rebellion.

Thomas J. Davis in *A Rumor of Revolt: The "Great Negro Plot" in Colonial New York* (1985) argues the plot was more than rumor and that "slaves in New York City during 1741 clearly talked of doing damage to the society enslaving them"; legal historian Peter Charles Hoffer writes that it was only a small number of those deemed guilty who actually did "conspire to violate the laws of the colony" in *The Great New York Conspiracy of 1741: Slavery, Crime, and Colonial*

Law (2003); Jill Lepore writes eloquently of the larger context of the plot and its aftermath in *New York Burning: Liberty, Slavery, and Conspiracy in Eighteenth-Century Manhattan* (2005), providing a nuanced study that leaves one less sure than Davis is that a plot existed, let alone a great one. Peter Linebaugh and Marcus Rediker's *The Many-Headed Hydra: Sailors, Slaves, Commoners, and the Hidden History of the Revolutionary Atlantic* (2002) includes the plot in their Marxist interpretation of the actions of a trans-Atlantic, multi-ethnic, multi-racial working class. For these authors, the plotters were "a motley proletariat" involved in efforts "Atlantic in scope . . . to incite an urban insurrection." Alex Bontemps examines the effects of slavery on the outlook of individuals in *The Punished Self: Surviving Slavery in the Old South* (2001), arguing that "slavery's true brutality was the psychic condition it imposed on survivors" and showing the effects of that condition on slave actions, including defiance.

Historians of African Americans increasingly are relying on the work of archaeologists for study of the material culture of pre-Revolutionary slaves. Summarizing relevant archaeological work since the 1960s are *"I, Too, Am America": Archaeological Study of African-American Life,* ed. by Theresa A. Singleton (1999), and Leland Ferguson's *Uncommon Ground: Archaeology and Early African America, 1650–1800* (1992). Willie Graham, et al., discuss more recent analysis of archaeological evidence for the Chesapeake in "Adaptation and Innovation: Archaeological and Architectural Perspectives on the Seventeenth-Century Chesapeake," *William and Mary Quarterly,* 3rd series, 64 (2007). The most interesting archaeological discovery in the North in recent years is a black burial ground in New York City, described in Joyce Hansen and Gary McGowan's *Breaking Ground, Breaking Silence: The Story of New York's African Burial Ground* (1998). Studies of archaeological work from the Chesapeake region include William M. Kelso's *Kingsmill Plantations, 1619–1800: Archaeology of Country Life in Colonial Virginia* (1984), which provides details of slave quarters, gardens, wells, pots, root cellars, and garbage pits, from which the author draws inferences about slave living conditions, and Anne E. Yentsch's *A Chesapeake Family and Their Slaves: A*

Study in Historical Archaeology (1994). Two additional works by Singleton are useful to colonial historians: *Archaeology of Slavery and Plantation Life* (1985) and "Breaking New Ground," *Southern Exposure,* 15 (1988). Kathleen Deagan and Darcie McMahon's *Fort Mose: Colonial America's Black Fortress of Freedom* (1995) is an award-winning catalogue that accompanied the touring Fort Mose exhibit. Elizabeth J. Reitz analyzed the diet of blacks at Fort Mose and determined they ate as much as the neighboring Indians—and Spaniards—in "Zooarchaeological Analysis of a Free African American Community: Gracia Real de Santa Teresa de Mose," *Historical Archaeology,* 28 (1994).

A solid body of work considers health, nutrition, disease, and medical practice in the slave community. Kenneth F. Kiple and Virginia Himmelsteih King's *Another Dimension of the Black Diaspora: Diet, Disease, and Racism* (1981) is the most valuable for the colonial period. The authors discuss African immunities, New World epidemics related to the Atlantic trade, blacks' susceptibility to disease because of nutritional deficiencies, and problems unique to transplanted tropical Africans. A handful of pages on "The Slave Trade and the Atlantic Exchange" in Mark Harrison, *Disease in the Modern World: 1500 to the Present Day* (2004) provide necessary background; Richard H. Steckel uses statistical data, among other kinds, to show that young Africans and African Americans experienced "A Dreadful Childhood: The Excess Mortality of American Slaves" in *The African Exchange: Toward a Biological History of Black People,* ed. by Kenneth F. Kiple (1987); and Wilma King pulls together material relating to children's experience in the Atlantic slave trade in a chapter of *African American Childhoods: Historical Perspectives from Slavery to Civil Rights* (2005). Tom W. Shick's "Healing and Race in the Carolina Low Country" in *Africans in Bondage: Studies in Slavery and the Slave Trade,* ed. by Paul E. Lovejoy (1986), describes black "root doctors" and their holistic approach to healing. Gary Puckrein's "Climate, Health, and Black Labor in English America," *Journal of American Studies,* 13 (1979) argues that the white notion that African Americans could live longer under conditions of hard labor in tropical climes—in spite of there being no clear evidence to support the supposition—was a factor in landowners' decisions to turn to Africa for slave labor.

There is not a deep literature on the more personal aspects of the folk culture of slaves and free blacks during the colonial period. Shane White and Graham White crack open the world of black expression in *Stylin': African American Expressive Culture from Its Beginnings to the Zoot Suit* (1998), writing elegantly about such matters as "the ways in which African Americans have clothed themselves, styled their hair, and communicated meaning through gesture, dance, and other forms of bodily display," some of it from colonial times. Philip D. Morgan addresses song, dance, and play in the last chapter of *Slave Counterpoint*. One can supplement this with the second chapter of Eileen Southern's *The Music of Black Americans: A History,* 2nd ed. (1983); portions of John Lovell, Jr.'s *Black Song: The Forge and the Flame* (1972); and Michael J. Morgan's improbably titled "Rock and Roll Unplugged: African-American Music in Eighteenth-Century America, *Eighteenth-Century Studies,* 27 (1994).

African Americans in the Revolutionary Era

For more than a quarter century following its 1961 publication, Benjamin Quarles's *The Negro in the American Revolution* (2nd ed., 1996) was the standard work not only on African-American participation in the revolutionary struggle but on its effect on black lives. Written at a time of hope for progress in American race relations, the book rests on Quarles's view that "the colored people of America benefited from the irreversible commitment of the new nation to the principles of liberty and equality." The bicentennial of the Revolution brought renewed interest in the subject; Ira Berlin's "The Revolution in Black Life" in *The American Revolution: Explorations in the History of American Radicalism* (1976), ed. by Alfred F. Young, and essays by various authorities in *Slavery and Freedom in the Age of the American Revolution* (1983), ed. by Berlin and Ronald Hoffman, pointed toward new directions in scholarship relating to the topic. More recently, a number of studies have questioned Quarles's optimistic view of the Revolution's effect on black lives. Douglas R. Egerton reviews the literature in "Black Independence Struggles and the Tale of Two Revolutions: A Review Essay," *Journal of Southern History,* 64 (1998).

More recently, Gary B. Nash picked up the theme, first treating African Americans with other overlooked groups of the period— white workingmen, backcountry farmers, white women, and Native Americans—in *The Unknown American Revolution: The Unruly Birth of Democracy and the Struggle to Create America* (2005), and then focusing on blacks alone in *The Forgotten Fifth: African Americans in the Age of Revolution* (2006), a small book that argues, among many points, that America's founders could have abolished slavery had they had the moral courage to do so. Now, Egerton has added the elegantly written *Death or Liberty: African Americans and Revolutionary America* (2009), which, in showing the extent of the revolution's ill effects on African Americans and, with Nash, arguing a betrayal of blacks by the nation's founders, will be the place to start on the subject for some time to come.

It is not a simple matter to separate African Americans' fighting on one side or the other in the American Revolution from their resistance to slavery during the period. Sylvia R. Frey's *Water from the Rock: Black Resistance in a Revolutionary Age* (1991) sees blacks during the Revolution as persons struggling with two warring groups of determined slaveholders to gain greater freedom. Peter H. Wood's "'Liberty is Sweet': African-American Freedom Struggles in the Years before White Independence" in *Beyond the American Revolution: Explorations in the History of American Radicalism,* ed. by Alfred F. Young (1993), examines the wave of hope and discontent that welled up among African Americans between 1765 and 1776, resulting in efforts of resistance and struggles to free themselves from slavery, nearly all of which ended in death and disappointment. Graham Russell Hodges touches on related themes in chapters on "Violence and Religion in the Black American Revolution" and "Black Revolt in New York City and the Neutral Zone, 1775–1783" in his *Slavery, Freedom, and Culture among Early American Workers* (1998).

Works dealing with use of black troops in the fighting forces include Philip D. Morgan and Andrew Jackson O'Shaughnessy,

"Arming Slaves in the American Revolution," in *Arming Slaves: From Classical Times to the Modern Age*, ed. by Christopher Leslie Brown and Philip D. Morgan (2006); Pete Maslowski's "National Policy Toward Use of Black Troops in the Revolution," *South Carolina Historical Magazine*, 73 (1972); and Luther P. Jackson's "Virginia Negro Soldiers and Seamen in the American Revolution," *Journal of Negro History*, 27 (1942). Sylvia R. Frey's "Between Slavery and Freedom: Virginia Blacks in the American Revolution," *Journal of Southern History*, 49 (1983) covers British attempts to lure away Virginia slaves, showing the strength of the British appeal and the unhealthy living conditions for those who escaped to British armies. For the fate of blacks who cast their lot with the British and left the country at the war's end, see Simon Schama's *Rough Crossings: The Slaves, the British, and the American Revolution* (2006); Mary L. Clifford's *From Slavery to Freedom: Black Loyalists After the American Revolution* (1999); James W. Walker's *The Black Loyalists: The Search for a Promised Land in Nova Scotia and Sierra Leone, 1783–1870* (1992); Ellen Gibson Wilson's *The Loyal Blacks* (1976); or Cassandra Pybus's *Epic Journeys of Freedom: Runaway Slaves of the American Revolution and Their Global Quest for Liberty* (2006). Pybus's book contains "biographies of flight" of thirty persons who left with the British pullout, one of whom was Harry, one of George Washington's slaves.

Two books by David B. Davis, *The Problem of Slavery in Western Culture* (1966) and *The Problem of Slavery in the Age of Revolution, 1770–1823* (1975) are standard treatments of the broad range of issues connecting slavery with Western and libertarian ideology. Peter H. Wood's "'Taking Care of Business' in Revolutionary South Carolina: Republicanism in a Slave Society" in *The Southern Experience in the American Revolution*, ed. by Jeffrey J. Crow and Larry E. Tise (1978) takes a narrower focus on the topic. Jean R. Soderlund's *Quakers and Slavery: A Divided Spirit* (1985) is a good survey and *The Journal of John Woolman* (1775) is good for getting a sense of the strength of Quaker sentiment against slavery. Paul Finkelman's *Slavery and the Founders: Race and Liberty in the Age of Jefferson*, 2nd ed. (2001) brings the focus to the first generation of leaders of the United States, examining critically how they dealt with slavery in such documents as the Declaration of Independence, the Northwest Ordinance, and the Constitution. Patricia Bradley in *Slavery, Propaganda, and the American Revolution* (1998) argues that Patriots used the slavery metaphor to argue their debased state under British control while failing generally to support abolition. By such action, they fueled white Americans' prejudices against blacks.

Where slavery fit into Thomas Jefferson's thinking is the subject of two good, if now dated, books: John C. Miller's *The Wolf by the Ears: Thomas Jefferson and Slavery* (1977) and Robert McColley's *Slavery and Jeffersonian Virginia,* 2nd ed. (1973). More recent thinking on the matter, reflecting greater knowledge of Jefferson's relationship with his slave, Sally Hemings, and other of his relatives whom he kept in bondage, is reflected in Finkelman's *Slavery and the Founders.* A 1999 update of Annette Gordon-Reed's analytical *Thomas Jefferson and Sally Hemings: An American Controversy* (1997, 1999) has a new preface, written with the recent DNA findings in mind, and further argument on the issue is in *Sally Hemings and Thomas Jefferson: History, Memory, and Civic Culture,* ed. by Jan Ellen Lewis and Peter S. Onuf (1999). It is interesting to compare these findings with those of Joseph J. Ellis in *American Sphinx: The Character of Thomas Jefferson* (1997), who concedes in a 1998 edition of the book that he was wrong about the matter a year earlier, or Kevin J. Hayes in *The Road to Monticello: The Life and Mind of Thomas Jefferson* (2008), who largely ignores it. Douglas R. Egerton's "Thomas Jefferson and the Hemings Family: A Matter of Blood," *The Historian,* 60 (1997), reviews some of the literature from a critical perspective. Gordon-Reed does justice to the African-American side of Jefferson's family in *The Hemingses of Monticello: An American Family* (2008); Andrew Burstein imagines Jefferson near the end of his life, looking back on his duplicitous ways in *Jefferson's Secrets: Death and Desire at Monticello* (2005).

Criticism of other of the founders in terms of their dealings with slavery and race is justifiably more muted. George Washington as slave owner comes under the microscope in Fritz Hirschfeld's

George Washington and Slavery: A Documentary History (1997) and Henry Wiencek's *An Imperfect God: George Washington, His Slaves, and the Creation of America* (2003). Dorothy Twohig in "'That Species of Property': Washington's Role in the Controversy over Slavery" in *George Washington Reconsidered,* ed. by Donald Higginbotham (2001) shows that Washington's thinking on slavery evolved until, late in life, he was opposed to the institution. Philip D. Morgan and Michael L. Nicholls argue, in "Slave Flight: Mount Vernon, Virginia, and the Wider Atlantic World," in *George Washington's South,* ed. by Tamara Harvey and Greg O'Brien (2004), that his experience with runaway slaves "helped convince him that slavery had no future." Those who judge Benjamin Franklin in part for his later-in-life antislavery activities should read David Waldstreicher's *Runaway America: Benjamin Franklin, Slavery, and the American Revolution* (2004). Waldstreicher sees Franklin's hand in some of the constitutional compromises involving slavery and believes Franklin's life "serves as a central connecting thread tying the social history of unfree labor to the political history of nation-making."

Arthur Zilversmit's *The First Emancipation: The Abolition of Slavery in the North* (1967) argues that idealism prevailed over economic interest to end slavery north of Maryland. Gary B. Nash in *Race and Revolution* (1990) tends to agree, noting how close the Revolutionary generation came to abolishing slavery, yet how quickly abolitionist sentiment waned in the new country. Joanne Pope Melish's *Disowning Slavery: Gradual Emancipation and "Race" in New England, 1780–1860* (1998) agrees with Nash on the speed of the decline of any Revolutionary idealism. She brings to light how frequently and in what ways New England slave owners ignored or abused the gradual abolition laws. One can supplement these with Robin Blackburn's more broadly focused *The Overthrow of Colonial Slavery, 1776–1848* (1988). T. H. Breen's "Making History: The Force of Public Opinion and the Last Years of Slavery in Revolutionary Massachusetts" in *Through a Glass Darkly: Reflections on Personal Identity in Early America,* ed. by Ronald Hoffman, Mechal Sobel, and Fredrika J. Teute (1997), places Quock Walker's suit to gain his freedom in the context of two previous slave executions and their effect on public opinion in Massachusetts. David Gellman's *Emancipating New York: The Politics of Slavery and Freedom, 1777–1827* (2006) plays down the role of revolutionary ideology and plays up a variety of factors that affected public debate and slowly altered people's thinking. Robert W. Fogel and Stanley L. Engerman's "Philanthropy at Bargain Prices: Notes on the Economics of Gradual Emancipation," *Journal of Legal Studies,* 13 (1974) shows how arrival of white immigrants provided northern states an adequate labor supply and made adherence to ideals about slavery, and gradual emancipation, possible. T. Stephen Whitman's *The Price of Freedom: Slavery and Manumission in Baltimore and Early National Maryland* (1997) explains how Baltimore could have such a high rate of manumission and yet still have so many slaves, arguing that slave owners used the promise of freedom as an incentive to gain work from their slaves, eventually did indeed free them, and then purchased more slaves with profits derived from the recently emancipated men and women.

Books that focus more on the effects of freedom on the free black population, as opposed to how its constituents became free, include James Oliver Horton and Lois E. Horton's *In Hope of Liberty: Culture, Community and Protest Among Northern Free Blacks, 1700–1860* (1997), for the North, and Ira Berlin's *Slaves Without Masters: The Free Negro in the Antebellum South* (1974), for the Upper South. A number of good works deal with free African Americans in particular places in colonial America. Articles by Jane G. Landers, Daniel Schafer, Paul Lachance, Kimberly Hanger, and Robert Olwell in *Against the Odds: Free Blacks in the Slave Societies of the Americas,* ed. by Landers (1996), examine free black communities in Spanish Florida, Spanish Louisiana, and South Carolina. John Hope Franklin's *The Free Negro in North Carolina, 1790–1860* (1943) is a detailed study of the "unwanted people" in that state. Shane White's *Somewhat More Independent* and Nash and Soderlund's *Freedom by Degrees,* both noted above, show how long it took freedom to come in those states and how marginal remained the existence of former slaves.

Articles by Gary B. Nash, Richard S. Dunn, Philip D. Morgan, and Allan Kulikoff in *Slavery and Freedom in the Age of the American Revolution,* which trace changes in black society in various regions through the period, spawned debate and further study. Betty Wood's *Women's Work, Men's Work: The Informal Slave Economies of Lowcountry Georgia* (1995) stresses that disruption caused by the Revolution helped bring about increased slave autonomy and black participation in the region's informal economy, and her subsequent *Gender, Race, and Rank in a Revolutionary Age: The Georgia Lowcountry, 1750–1820* (2000) focuses on the general absence of bonds among African-American women across the period, not only between black and white women, but between enslaved and free black. Gary B. Nash and Peter Coclanis in review essays in the *Georgia Historical Quarterly*—Nash's in Volume 77, 1993 ("Review Essay: Slavery, Black Resistance, and the American Revolution") and Coclanis's in Volume 79, 1995 ("Review Essay: Slavery, African-American Agency, and the World We Have Lost")—and Michael Mullin in *Africa in America,* disagree with Wood, arguing that no thriving informal economy could have existed given the master's overwhelming control and the work regime of Low Country slaves. Jacqueline Jones picks up Wood's theme in "Race, Sex, and Self-Evident Truths: The Status of Slave Women during the Era of the American Revolution" in *Women in the Age of the American Revolution,* ed. by Ronald Hoffman and Peter J. Albert (1989).

Robert Olwell's "Revolutions Achieved and Denied: Charles Town and the Low Country, 1775–1782," in his *Masters, Slaves, and Subjects,* shows how some slaves gained temporary autonomy during the Revolutionary fighting, but in the end had to come to terms with the "culture of power" in which they existed. Studies in David Colin Crass, Steven D. Smith, and Martha Zierden, eds., *The Southern Colonial Backcountry: Interdisciplinary Perspectives on Frontier Communities* (1998) include enslaved men and women in the treatment of movement into the interiors of South Carolina, North Carolina, Virginia, and Tennessee following the Revolution. For the lot of African Americans during British occupation of New York City see the chapter on "Crossing Freedom's

Line" in Judith L. Van Buskirk's *Generous Enemies: Patriots and Loyalists in Revolutionary New York* (2002).

Duncan J. MacLeod's *Slavery, Race and the American Revolution* (1974) stresses the importance of the Revolutionary era for the establishment of racism in America, a subject John Wood Sweet amplifies in *Bodies Politic: Negotiating Race in the American North, 1730–1830* (2003). Michael A. McDonnell's *The Politics of War: Race, Class, and Conflict in Revolutionary Virginia* (2007) argues that blacks' desire for the same freedom whites were fighting for caused resentment among slaveholders and fear among poor whites. This fits with Woody Holton's *Forced Founders: Indians, Debtors, Slaves, and the Making of the American Revolution in Virginia* (1999), which shows the threat slaves, Indians, and poor whites posed to Virginia's gentry as these powerful white men planned for war. William R. Ryan's "'Under the Color of Law': The Ordeal of Thomas Jeremiah, a Free Black Man, and the Struggle for Power in Revolutionary South Carolina," in Harvey and O'Brien, eds., *George Washington's South*, shows that the Revolution heightened whites suspicions of all blacks. The early chapters of Douglas R. Egerton's *They Shall Go Out Free: The Lives of Denmark Vesey*, rev. ed. (2004) offer evidence that these suspicions were valid, showing how people of African descent in North America were tied into an Atlantic world of revolutionary ideas. Mark M. Smith in *How Race is Made: Slavery, Segregation, and the Senses* (2006) shows how, beginning in the eighteenth century, southern whites manufactured sensory stereotypes about blacks to help justify slavery.

Staughton Lynd's *Class Conflict, Slavery, and the United States Constitution* (1967); Edmund S. Morgan's "Conflict and Consensus in the American Revolution" in *Essays on the American Revolution* (1973), ed. by Stephen G. Katz and James H. Hutson; and Richard R. Beeman's *The Evolution of the Southern Backcountry: A Case Study of Lunenburg County, Virginia, 1746–1832* (1984) are provocative studies that relate the revolution to heightened racism.

Books that deal with the issue of slavery in the writing of the Constitution are Lawrence Goldstone's *Dark Bargain: Slavery,*

Profits, and the Struggle for the Constitution (2005) and Mark E. Brandon's *Free in the World: American Slavery and Constitutional Failure* (1998). The former is a popular account emphasizing how slavery lay at the crux of many issues at the Constitutional Convention and, reminiscent of Charles Beard, how the framers argued out of self-interest; the latter is a book of constitutional theory, using the slavery issue to show how the United States Constitution failed the nation. In his recent, balanced account, *Plain, Honest Men: The Making of the American Constitution* (2009), Richard Beeman saves his strongest criticism for the founders' dealings over slavery, writing, "we cannot avert our eyes from the magnitude of the evil." Alfred W. Blumrosen and Ruth G. Blumrosen in *Slave Nation: How Slavery United the Colonies and Sparked the Revolution* (2005) make a broader case for the role of slavery in the revolution and the subsequent creation of a united group of states. Larry E. Tise's *The American Counterrevolution: A Retreat from Liberty, 1783–1800* (1998) is a widereaching argument about how the major figures in American public life, at the Revolution's end, began rejecting the ideas on which they had based it.

INDEX

African Americans in the Colonial Era:
From African Origins through the American Revolution
Developmental editor and copy editor: Andrew J. Davidson
Production editor: Linda Gaio
Proofreader: Claudia Siler
Typesetter: Bruce Leckie
Printer: McNaughton & Gunn, Inc.